T0334196

"This book is for our times and has my wholehearted recommendation. It channels our collective yearning for a better world into evidence-based actions. In weaving together the latest well-being science with accessible stories of hope, it offers a blueprint of what works to create flourishing lives and communities. Let it inspire us all to create a better, fairer, and more sustainable world."

Barbara Fredrickson, Author of Positivity *and* Love 2.0, *Kenan Distinguished Professor, Department of Psychology and Neuroscience, University of North Carolina, Chapel Hill*

"This beautiful book informs us of the science and inspires us to apply it. It is based on the best of positive psychology, which has shown how the goal of wellbeing can be as relevant to those who are flourishing as to those who are languishing – and as relevant to education, work and public policy as to our inner private world."

Professor Lord Richard Layard, Co-Director, Well-Being Programme, Centre for Economic Performance, London School of Economics

"This is one of the best books I have read in a long time. It offers a superb developmental and contextual approach to integrative well-being. Moreover, it is a wonderful contribution to our holistic understanding of personal, interpersonal, occupational, communal, and environmental wellness. An amazing group of authors tackle contemporary issues that go beyond individual pursuits of happiness. By combining evidence with values and pragmatism, this book offers hope and actionable steps. This volume is destined to become a classic in the emerging field of integrative well-being. With great clarity and beautiful writing, the authors encourage us to align our values with our actions. I highly recommend this book to anyone interested in the well-being of present and future generations. This is a much needed corrective to efforts to define and increase well-being in individualistic ways. The value-based nature of the treatise reminds us that there cannot be wellness without fairness."

Isaac Prilleltensky, Ph.D., Professor, Vice Provost for Institutional Culture, Dean Emeritus, School of Education and Human Development, Erwin and Barbara Mautner Chair in Community Well-Being, University of Miami

"What kind of world do we want to live in? In shifting from the narrow perspective of individual well-being to a global systems-informed one, this question and its potential answers point towards an important new wave in positive psychology. How do we create a positive eco-system to ensure sustainable well-being for generations to come? What can a truly multi-disciplinary approach offer us over and above the existing scope of positive psychology? This book offers intriguing answers to these complex questions, based on extensive research and practical know-how of its stellar author cast. A beautiful read!"

Professor Ilona Boniwell, Executive Directeur, Positran/Strategic Programme Leader, IMAPP- Anglia Ruskin University/ Visiting and Associate Professor CentraleSupelec, HEC and University of East London

"I was truly impressed by this volume. Integrating the best knowledge and theories within the social and behavioural sciences and neuroscience, the authors masterfully chart the possibilities for, and pathways to, greater flourishing as individuals and as societies. Will be of interest to parents, practitioners, politicians and people of all generations and cultures."

Richard M. Ryan, Professor Emeritus of Psychology, University of Rochester, NY, Professor, Institute for Positive Psychology and Education, Australian Catholic University, Sydney

"This is a timely and important book that truly rises to the challenges of our difficult age. It beautifully exemplifies the compassionate, clear-eyed, multidimensional thinking and strategizing that humankind is going to need over the years ahead. Moreover, not only is its message vital, it is very-well articulated, written in accessible language that helps ensure its meaning is not lost or diluted. A must-read for everyone helping to make the world a better place."

Dr Tim Lomas, School of Psychology, University of East London

"A useful and timely guide to a positive psychology that focuses on 'our' wellbeing rather than on 'my' wellbeing."

Howard Gardner, Hobbs Research Professor of Cognition and Education, Harvard Graduate School of Education, Author of A Synthesizing Mind

"*Creating the World We Want to Live In* is a book that aims high, and quite rightly so. The authors are all highly acclaimed experts in positive psychology who work, write, and live with passion and purpose. Each brings years of wisdom to this shared undertaking, to envisage a better more equitable world for us all. There are an enormous number of books that aim to help individual wellbeing; this book takes a broader, more collective perspective. As such it presents a clear call to improve the wellbeing of the world."

Dr Helen Street, The Positive Schools Initiative, Honorary Fellow, The University of Western Australia

"A great book that brings together key insights from positive psychology, and related scientific fields studying what makes life worth living. It could not come at a better time than this, in which the mere amount of accessible information is enough to overwhelm many of us – and where it is often difficult to reach common understandings of even simple facts, let alone agreement on common strategies for moving forward. The authors succeed wonderfully in both: They provide a clear overview of current knowledge and they illuminate compelling, common pathways to a better future informed by this knowledge. Highly recommended!"

Hans Henrik Knoop, Associate Professor with Distinction, Aarhus University, Denmark, Extraordinary Professor, Optentia, North-West University, South Africa, Past President, European Network for Positive Psychology

CREATING THE WORLD WE WANT TO LIVE IN

This book is about hope and a call to action to make the world the kind of place we want to live in. Our hope is to provoke conversation, and gently challenge possibly long-held views, beliefs, and ideologies about the way the world works and the people in that world.

Written by eminent researchers and experienced practitioners, the book explores the principles that underpin living well, and gives examples of how this can be achieved not just in our own lives, but across communities and the planet we share. Chapters cover the stages of life from childhood to ageing, the foundations of everyday flourishing, including health and relationships, and finally wellbeing in the wider world, addressing issues such as economics, politics and the environment. Based in the scientific evidence of what works and supported by illustrations of good practice, this book is both ambitious and aspirational.

The book is designed for a wide audience – anyone seeking to create positive change in the world, their institutions or communities.

Authors: Bridget Grenville-Cleave, Dóra Guðmundsdóttir, Felicia Huppert, Vanessa King, David Roffey, Sue Roffey and Marten de Vries.

This unique collective of seven authors from the United Kingdom, Australia, Iceland, and the Netherlands are a mix of distinguished academics, positive psychology researchers and practitioners, authors and authorities in their respective fields.

CREATING THE WORLD WE WANT TO LIVE IN

HOW POSITIVE PSYCHOLOGY CAN BUILD A BRIGHTER FUTURE

Bridget Grenville-Cleave,
Dóra Guðmundsdóttir,
Felicia Huppert, Vanessa King,
David Roffey, Sue Roffey and
Marten de Vries

Routledge
Taylor & Francis Group

LONDON AND NEW YORK

First published 2021
by Routledge
2 Park Square, Milton Park, Abingdon, Oxon OX14 4RN

and by Routledge
605 Third Avenue, New York, NY 10158

Routledge is an imprint of the Taylor & Francis Group, an informa business

British Library Cataloguing-in-Publication Data

A catalogue record for this book is available from the British Library

Library of Congress Cataloging-in-Publication Data
Names: Grenville-Cleave, Bridget, author.
Title: Creating the world we want to live in: how positive psychology can build a brighter future/Bridget Grenville-Cleave [and six others].
Description: Abingdon, Oxon; New York, NY: Routledge, 2021. | Includes bibliographical references and index. | Identifiers: LCCN 2020044452 (print) | LCCN 2020044453 (ebook) | ISBN 9780367468880 (hardback) | ISBN 9780367468859 (paperback) | ISBN 9781003031789 (ebook)
Subjects: LCSH: Positive psychology. | Well-being. | Quality of life. | Social change–Psychological aspects.
Classification: LCC BF204.6. C74 2021 (print) | LCC BF204.6 (ebook) | DDC 150.19/88–dc23
LC record available at https://lccn.loc.gov/2020044452
LC ebook record available at https://lccn.loc.gov/2020044453

ISBN: 978-0-367-46888-0 (hbk)
ISBN: 978-0-367-46885-9 (pbk)
ISBN: 978-1-003-03178-9 (ebk)

Typeset in Palatino
by KnowledgeWorks Global Ltd.

Contents

Contents

The authors

Bridget Grenville-Cleave is a positive psychology consultant and trainer for both public and private sectors in the United Kingdom and abroad. She designs and delivers evidence-based training such as the 'Happiness and Wellbeing at Work Program' for the UAE Ministry of State for Happiness, as well as school and university happiness curricula for staff and students, and runs online positive psychology courses. Bridget lectures on the International Masters in Applied Positive Psychology at Anglia Ruskin University, Cambridge, specialising in positive psychology practice, and is an accredited trainer for the award-winning resilience program 'Bounce Back'. She is the author of five positive psychology books. More information at www.workmad.co.uk

Dóra Guðmundsdóttir is Director of Public Health at the Directorate of Health in Iceland where she leads work on health promoting schools, workplaces and communities. Dora is a clinical and organisational psychologist with a special interest in evidence-based knowledge in policy making and interventions. She is director of Graduate Diploma programme on Positive Psychology at the University of Iceland, and current president of the European Network for Positive Psychology (ENPP) www.enpp.eu

Felicia Huppert is Founding Director of the Well-being Institute, University of Cambridge, and Emeritus Professor of Psychology. She is Visiting Professorial Fellow at the University of New South Wales, and Honorary Professor with the Body Heart and Mind in Business Research Group, University of Sydney Business School. Felicia is a member of the Global Mindfulness Initiative and Director of the Australian Compassion Council Scholars Program. Specialising in the science of well-being and the promotion of human flourishing, her current research focuses on mindfulness and compassion training in education and healthcare, and high-quality measures of subjective well-being. feliciahuppert.com

Vanessa King is a leading expert in the practical application of positive psychology in the workplace and in the community, a writer and public speaker. She gained her Masters in Applied Positive Psychology from University of Pennsylvania (UPenn) studying with Dr. Martin Seligman and trained as a facilitator on UPenn's Master Resilience Training program. An experienced consultant, Vanessa advises organisations, and designs and delivers development programs in workplaces around the world. She is a Board Member, Head of Psychology and Workplaces at Action for Happiness (AfH), the leading UK-based not-for-profit that focuses on proactively building skills for psychological wellbeing and resilience. Vanessa is the architect of AfH's 10 Keys for Happier Living and author of the book of the same name. She has two TEDx talks, is regularly quoted in the print and broadcast media. Early in her career Vanessa qualified as a chartered accountant with PWC and worked in HR in investment banking. www.thechangespace.com

David Roffey was a partner in an international management consultancy, where he advised many post-communist and developing country governments on how to balance competition with public interests and needs. He has been a magistrate, a trade union official, a local councillor in a London borough, a board member of the Child Poverty Action Group in the United Kingdom and New South Wales state chair of Oxfam Australia. He now manages Growing Great Schools Worldwide www.growinggreatschoolsworldwide.com

Sue Roffey FRSA FBPsS is a psychologist, academic, author, activist, and speaker. She is an honorary associate professor at University College London and Western Sydney University, Associate Fellow at Exeter University, and an affiliate of the Wellbeing Institute at Cambridge. Sue was the founder of Wellbeing Australia and is now director of Growing Great Schools Worldwide. Sue is a prolific author on issues related to school and student wellbeing, behaviour, belonging, relationships, and social-emotional learning. Now based in London, she continues to work internationally – though currently remotely – and is a member of several advisory boards. www.growinggreatschoolsworldwide.com

Marten de Vries, emeritus Professor of Social Psychiatry at Maastricht University and anthropologist, responded to the global mental health challenge with studies in human development and the experience of mental illness under diverse socio-cultural, and traumatic circumstances. Following on international academic, medical and NGO leadership positions, he has focused on producing mixed-media products with the Mind Venture International (MVI) group to reach diverse global communities for improving human resilience and providing social benefit. He was recently knighted for this work in the Order of the Dutch Lion.

Acknowledgements

We would like to thank the following people who were instrumental in helping us shape this book by contributing ideas or by reading and commenting on draft chapters. Many are academics and specialists in other fields, and others represented non-specialists. The inclusion of non-specialists was critical in ensuring that we produced a text that would reach out to a general readership. We are immensely grateful for your time and thoughts.

Dominic Boddington, Mieneke Bakker, Jeannie Cohen, Ella Coleman, Miranda Crowhurst, Willem de Vries, Andy Detheridge, John Dowling, Peter Downs, Rhiannon Dwyer, Mark Fox, Tessa Fluence, Jane Gaukroger, Elizabeth Gillies, Euan Gillies, Julian Huppert, Rowan Huppert, Klasien Horstman, Nick Jaspers, Gabrielle Kelly, Sarah Lewis, Tara McLeod, Alexi Marmot, Sir Michael Marmot, Emma Marshall, Alma Montoya, Nancy Nicolson, Grant Rhodes, Jamie Q Roberts, Evie Rosset, Jose Feliciano Perez Sanchez, Pim Schippers, Nicky Sloss, Andrea Stern, Audrey Stern, Jaap Swart, Mark Valentine, Rianne Wesenbeek, Guido Wevers.

We would also like to thank Joanne Forshaw and Daradi Patar at Routledge for their enduring support.

This book was not a small undertaking. Everyone involved in writing these chapters has worked hard on them around the demands of other work and life. However, two of our group need to be especially highlighted. Sue and David Roffey kindly and bravely volunteered to take on the mammoth task of copy editing, co-ordination, publisher liaison and production management. This took up much of their time, headspace and energy over many months. We know it wasn't easy. The rest of the group are deeply appreciative, this book wouldn't have been completed without them.

Preface: A new beginning

The idea for this book came out of frustration and concern with how our world seemed to be developing.

We saw widening gaps in wealth, health, education and employment; climate change; growing movements towards individualism and nationalism, fuelled by a 'post-fact', divisive media – all contributing to fragmented communities and divided societies.

For many individuals, the speed of life, overload at work and financial pressures were leaving little time for all that makes life more joyful, meaningful, and worth living. Loneliness was growing and many young people were experiencing a lack of purpose. All this exacerbated by social media fuelling 'fear of missing out' and negative self-comparison.

As a group immersed in positive psychology, we saw that the science of wellbeing might provide a new paradigm to help shape a different future. Drawing on our different individual fields of expertise we each had ideas for how this emerging body of knowledge could provide the basis for innovation and change.

Our aim was to write a book that might help create a world that enabled a more flourishing future for us all. Our first draft was all but completed when the COVID-19 pandemic struck.

As if someone had pressed a huge pause button, much of the world went into some form of lockdown, and it drove rapid change. The long-anticipated transition to a more online world arrived in an instant, and formerly slow, bureaucratic systems suddenly mobilised at top speed as we all faced the unknown. Old ways of relating, learning, and working had to transform overnight. Countries and communities sought to find a way through the trauma of personal illness, the grievous loss of loved ones, huge financial difficulty, and an upsurge of anxiety about both the present and the future.

Shortly afterwards the Black Lives Matter movement rose up on a global scale, galvanising awareness that many in black, Asian and ethnic minority (BAME) communities are undervalued, unheard, and underrepresented in positions of power.

There is now the opportunity to press another huge 'button', a reset one. The pandemic revealed the many flaws in our systems and how we have been living. It has also given rise to wonderful examples of humans at their best, and how life can be when we slow down, or can step off the treadmill and focus on what really matters.

Both the pandemic and the Black Lives Matter movement provide a 'burning platform' for the change clearly needed for people and our planet. A catalyst for creativity and innovation to create a better, more physically and psychologically sustainable world, one where we work to build mutual understanding, recognising we have more in common than divides us.

For the last two decades there has been growing evidence on what human beings need to both feel good and function well. As we emerge now, into a new world and navigate through uncertainty, we have the potential to move forward informed by this science. As the spread of the virus, and the response to it has shown this is not just about individuals, we exist in wider interconnected systems. So we have explored what the science of wellbeing means for our communities, education systems, workplaces, the media, health systems, the economy, and beyond. There is evidence too that when we truly flourish so will the planet.

To bring the science to life and engage hearts as well as minds, we have included in every chapter stories of good practice, incidents where ordinary lives have been changed, examples of what has made the difference and some ideas for moving forward. Our hope is to provoke conversation, and gently challenge possibly long-held views, beliefs, and ideologies about the way the world works and the people in that world.

About this book

This book is about hope and a call to action to make the world the kind of place we want to live in.

Our aim is to inspire readers to see why we urgently need a different approach to how we live our lives and to begin to make changes individually and with others.

We give a flavour of the main issues and offer a set of evidence-based principles that underlie human wellbeing. We also offer practical ideas based on these principles that can be applied to create positive change in different areas of life.

We invite readers to reflect on how the ideas presented relate to their own experiences and how they can generate further strategies for action.

This book is not intended to be a comprehensive review of the scientific literature. We are, however, proud to be adding our voices to those of other authors, academics, and practitioners arguing for wellbeing-driven societal change.

In each chapter we provide selected key sources that support the evidence provided. More comprehensive references, along with further reading and resources, can be found on the website https://www.creatingtheworldwewanttolivein.org/

Science is a dynamic process and is never perfect and complete. While there have been important advances in the science of wellbeing, much remains to be discovered. Where possible we include examples from diverse contexts, but we recognise that most of the current research on wellbeing has been undertaken in a Western context, among high-income and middle-income countries. There is some emerging evidence from other contexts and we strongly support the need for more.

PART A
Introduction

Foundations for a brighter future

Vanessa King & Felicia Huppert

This book is about choice and hope. At its core are caring, compassion, and courage to discover and be our better selves. We hope it will inspire and be a catalyst for action, so that together we can create a flourishing future for humanity, and the planet we share.

Our world is experiencing an accelerating level of change unprecedented in modern times. New and emerging technologies; the multiple impacts of globalisation, demographic shifts; increasing polarisation; the challenge of discrimination and racism, pandemics and the ramifications of climate change all impact on our well-being, our societal structures, peace among nations, and the viability of our planet. How we respond to these changes will determine our own wellbeing and importantly, that of future generations.

Based on a growing body of research we can together create a flourishing future for humanity, and the planet we share. We have a choice. We can passively watch change happen, or we can individually and collectively, take action to create a world that's better for everyone, and all living things.

The potential that positive psychology offers

A little over 20 years ago, the advent of positive psychology expanded the traditional emphasis of psychological science on identifying and treating problems, by exploring what enables human beings to flourish – to feel good and function well, even when times are tough. Rather than only focusing on how and why things go wrong, psychology began to investigate how and why things go right, what makes people feel happy and lead fulfilling lives. According to one of the founders of the field, Christopher Peterson, *"Positive psychology is the scientific study of what makes life most worth living"*.[1] Research in positive psychology and related fields such as mindfulness has increased exponentially, and has been integrated into other domains including neuroscience and health. This has created a multi-disciplinary science of wellbeing – a science of optimal human functioning. The findings from this new science give both fresh insight, and often support wisdom from ancient traditions.

Positive psychology was founded to *"understand and build the factors that allow individuals, communities, and societies to flourish"*.[2] Yet despite the early recognition that the field should extend beyond individual wellbeing, these broader aspects have to-date received less attention. Humans do not exist in isolation. The contexts in which we live, love, work, and play subtly and profoundly impact who we are and how we act. We in turn shape our environment. There is now an increasing recognition that positive psychology has the potential to make a much broader contribution, and it is this we explore across major domains of life.

Wellbeing matters

What do we mean by wellbeing or flourishing? People often equate wellbeing with experiencing pleasure, but pleasure is a transient state, and can be attained through means that are not always helpful over the longer term (such as partying before an important interview). In contrast, real wellbeing or 'flourishing' is a sustainable state that combines feeling good and functioning well. This includes having positive relationships, feeling valued, regarding ourselves as competent, developing our potential, and having a sense of meaning and autonomy. Wellbeing doesn't mean feeling good all the time. Life has ups and downs. Difficult or painful emotions are an appropriate response to experiences such as sadness following loss or misfortune, and distress or even anger following injustice. Understanding and dealing well with such emotions is a key component of wellbeing, helping us to cope when times are tough.

Research shows that higher wellbeing is linked to many desirable outcomes, such as healthier relationships, more pro-social behaviour (collaboration, kind actions), better health and life expectancy, stronger learning outcomes, greater productivity at work, and increased creativity.[3]

It has sometimes been suggested that happy people tend to be complacent, but a recent study found that happy people are more likely to take action about social, political, and environmental issues.[4] The effect of higher wellbeing on how we think, and what we choose to do can help us face and deal with the many challenges that collectively confront us, so that we can build a better world together.

Developing wellbeing is particularly important in young people as this underpins a positive future[5] for both individuals and the society they will create, developing cognitive, emotional, and social capabilities, interests and creative potential. We explore this in more detail in the chapters on Childhood and Education.

What kind of world do we want to live in?

We may answer this question differently depending on our culture, values, and whether we regard ourselves as being among the less or more fortunate in society. But what if we were responding without knowing where in the social hierarchy we or our descendants would be? Philosopher John Rawls proposed a thought experiment for working out, as objectively as possible, what a just and fair society would look like. He concluded that a rational, self-interested person would try to ensure everyone has an equal opportunity to prosper, and the maximum liberty possible (without infringing the freedom of others), since this would maximise the likelihood of beneficial outcomes for any individual. His resulting theory of 'justice as fairness' recommends equality of basic rights and opportunities, and promoting the interests of the least advantaged members of society.

Rawls' conclusions are not mere speculation. In an uncertain, fast changing world, none of us can be sure how our lives will unfold. During times of extreme financial crisis, destitution may be suffered by the poor and wealthy alike, as happened in the Great Depression. In the COVID-19 pandemic even royalty and heads of government were not immune, though they did not suffer as much as minority groups, or those who were already struggling financially. Any one of us could be involved in a serious accident or health crisis, violent conflict, or natural disaster, and become dependent on the support of others, institutions, or even the kindness of strangers.

Rawls' conclusion is supported by a generation of wellbeing research. Countries that provide good opportunities for all their citizens, as typified by Nordic countries, report the highest levels of wellbeing. These countries have the lowest levels of inequality, access to good healthcare, education, and employment, and a system of social welfare that supports people when they need it. Across 150 countries, freedom to make life choices (a key measure of liberty) is the largest determinant of positive emotions, followed by social support, generosity, and the perception of low corruption.[6]

Rawls challenges us to think more widely about our choices. Not just what is beneficial individually in the short-term, but balancing this with the wellbeing of others in the longer-term, as depicted in Figure 1.

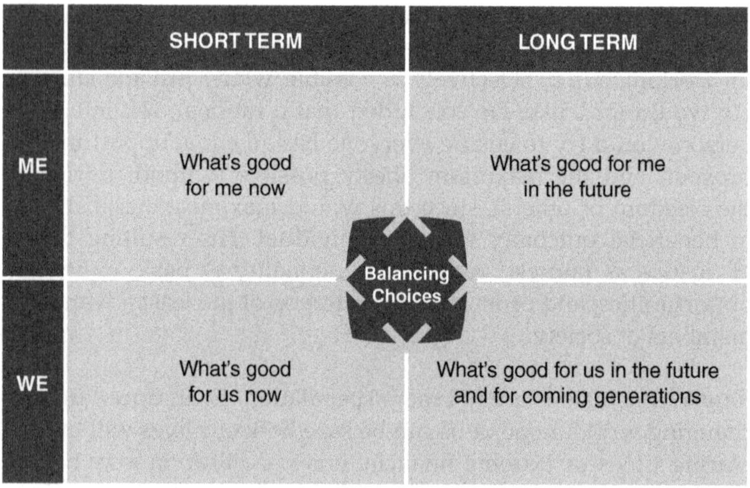

	SHORT TERM	LONG TERM
ME	What's good for me now	What's good for me in the future
WE	What's good for us now	What's good for us in the future and for coming generations

Balancing Choices

Figure 1: The choices we face

The psychological foundations of wellbeing

Many factors influence our wellbeing. We all need somewhere safe to live, and sufficient food, and clean water, but these alone are not enough. Emerging from the growing evidence base of positive psychology and the broader science of wellbeing are a set of key psychological principles that are essential for human flourishing. Whilst these principles have been primarily derived from individual psychology, they have implications at a collective and systemic level, and can be applied to shape our institutions, economic and political systems, and our natural environments. The principles are underpinned by three core capabilities that apply both individually and collectively. Below we provide an overview of these principles and core capabilities, and throughout the rest of this book explore how they apply in different domains of life.

Principles for psychological wellbeing

The five principles below were selected on the basis of evidence demonstrating them to be essential for psychological wellbeing. When these principles are absent the impact is not neutral, it's actively detrimental. Taking account of each is therefore critical.

1. Feeling connected to others

Wellbeing begins with 'we'. Humans evolved in social groups and feeling connected to other people – having a sense of belonging, feeling considered and cared for, and considering and caring about others is a vital psychological need.[7]

Feeling excluded elicits brain activation in the same regions as physical pain.[8] Loneliness, which makes us more likely to experience depression, has effects on our physiology, including our immune function. This makes lonely people more vulnerable to viral infection,[9] and has effects on physical health and mortality that are comparable to smoking or obesity.[10]

Our close relationships have the greatest impact on our wellbeing, but the myriad of moments when we come into contact with others in our communities also add up. It is often easiest to form connections to people with whom we have most in common – family, workmates, those with similar interests or views, people of the same race, ethnic identity, or social class. It can be harder to build relationships when it appears we have less in common, as we can be fearful of people from different backgrounds, or whom we perceive as 'not like us'. It can take greater conscious effort to build these connections, yet this investment is worthwhile – good not only for us individually, but for collective wellbeing. Within our communities, even brief interactions, such as smiling at a local shop keeper or greeting a neighbour, can have a ripple effect and contribute to a sense of trust which boosts wellbeing and resilience locally.

Relationships thrive when we recognise our common humanity, and 'see no strangers' – when we use our natural curiosity to find out more about people. When we act with contempt, superiority, or blame, this cuts us off from others to our own detriment as well that of our community.

In Chapter 5 we look at relationships and wellbeing in greater depth.

2. Having a sense of autonomy

A sense of autonomy in our lives – perceiving that we have some choice, rather than feeling coerced or overly controlled by external factors, makes a major contribution to wellbeing. Autonomy has been shown to be important across the life span and cross-culturally, in both individualistic and collectivist cultures. Wellbeing is supported when people not only have agency (the power to act) but are able to act in ways that they have chosen and are aligned with their values and intrinsic interests.[6]

The psychological need for autonomy applies in the daily lives of individuals, and also at a community and societal level. For individuals, examples might range from some choice over what we eat and wear, or how we manage our time, to where and how we live and work. Complete autonomy however is neither possible nor desirable, since to exist in social groups entails balancing our own choices with the needs of others.

At a community and societal level, it is empowering when we are involved in the decisions that impact our lives, homes, workplaces, and communities. Such engagement fosters a collective sense of choice, confirms that our voice matters and that our actions can make a difference. Having the right and the opportunity to vote is fundamental. When institutions and organisations provide opportunities for people to participate and co-design the policies and programs that affect them, these policies and programs are generally better accepted and often more effective.

There are areas of life where many people feel overwhelmed and helpless to change anything, such as reducing global warming or strengthening democracy. Finding ways of invigorating people's sense of agency and autonomy, so they feel empowered to take action, however small, can positively impact their wellbeing. We discuss these challenging situations in the chapters on Politics and Environment.

3. Feeling competent

Feeling competent in what we do, able to function effectively in the contexts in which we live and operate, is another important psychological need. We get a psychological boost from being able to do things well and experiencing progress, whereas persistent feelings of incompetence are detrimental to our wellbeing.[6]

As we encounter new situations or try out new ideas, it is likely we will initially lack competence. How we perceive this experience impacts our ability to learn. If we see difficulties and failure as part of the learning process we are more likely to grow in our capabilities, whereas if we see them as a sign of incompetence or lack of ability, we avoid seeking challenges and our learning is limited. We can enhance wellbeing for children by providing appropriate challenges and helping them treat failure as a learning opportunity.

As adults, cultivating a growth rather than fixed mindset[11] can help us continuously learn throughout our life, seeking opportunities to try new things and developing new skills. All adults can benefit from opportunities for lifelong learning. We explore the value of this, in the chapter on Ageing.

In a world that is increasingly complex and unpredictable, cultivating the ability to rapidly learn, adapt and develop new ways of doing things will be ever more crucial both individually and collectively. We also need systems, products, and processes to be designed in a way that makes them easy to navigate – so that people feel effective rather than incompetent.

4. Paying attention to what's going well

In our evolutionary past, being constantly alert to potential threats helped our ancestors survive life-threatening dangers. Although most people no longer routinely face life or death situations this 'negativity bias' persists today, causing us to often overlook what's going well,[12] yet research shows that when we also pay attention to what's going well, extensive wellbeing benefits result.

Positive emotions such as joy, gratitude, serenity, interest, and amusement don't just feel good, they have beneficial physiological, psychological, and behavioural effects. Researcher Barbara Fredrickson and colleagues have demonstrated that the experience of positive emotions broaden our perceptual fields, so we notice more, are more open to others, more flexible in our thinking, see more options, and are better at creative problem solving.[13, 14] Her work has shown positive emotions can also make us less susceptible to a form of racial bias.[15]

Gratitude is a particularly powerful emotion. Developing a regular practice of appreciating what we are grateful for or what has gone well has been shown to reduce stress, lower blood pressure, boost immunity, and help us sleep better.[16] More generally, shifting the balance of our focus towards what is going well has been shown to have distinct benefits; for example, psychologist John Gottman showed that in stable and happy marriages there are at least five positive interactions for every negative one.[17]

Positive attitudes such as an optimistic outlook are associated with both improved wellbeing, and better physical health. Optimists' health benefits derive from a faster recovery from stressful experiences and higher motivation to undertake health-promoting behaviours. Optimism has also been linked to achievement in education, sport, business, and politics.[18, 19]

Paying attention to what's going well doesn't mean ignoring what's wrong. But it does give us a more constructive and energising place from which to tackle problems and put things right. When we focus on identifying strengths in ourselves and others, we become more confident, and more likely to achieve our goals. A strengths-based approach can be applied at a systemic level too. For example, constructive journalism identifies what is working, and explores solutions to issues, rather than just purveying problems. An approach to organisational and community change called Appreciative Inquiry starts with an examination of existing strengths and what's already working, building on this to develop a positive vision and strategy for the future. It tackles problems in the process rather than making these the focus.[20] Justice systems that build strengths through rehabilitation have been shown to produce greater societal benefits than those that are primarily punitive, described in more detail in the Society chapter.

5. Having a sense of meaning

When we have meaning in our lives, we see ourselves as both part of something bigger and making a positive difference to something, or someone, other than ourselves. Sources of meaning may include: relationships, faith, connection to nature; having a sense of purpose through fulfilling work, creative expression, engaging leisure pursuits, or contributing to community, or to a cause we care about. A sense of meaning offers direction, helping us prioritise what matters most, and guiding life goals and decisions. Having a clear sense of meaning is associated with higher life satisfaction, greater resilience, healthier ageing, and a lower likelihood of depression, anxiety and suicide.[21] In the workplace context, even in high stress occupations, employees who find their work meaningful are far less likely to experience burnout. This is explored more in Chapter 3 on Work.

At a community level, meaning can also arise from people feeling they belong, are valued, and have opportunities to make a contribution. From a societal perspective, wellbeing is enhanced when we create conditions, and develop systems that support all citizens living fulfilling, and meaningful lives.

Reflection:

Think of a time you were flourishing in your life – feeling good and doing well. How did the principles above contribute to this and in what ways?

Core capabilities

The psychological principles essential for wellbeing are underpinned by three core capabilities. These capabilities are both characteristics and skills that can be learned.

1. Open mind – mindful awareness

Many of us function on autopilot, rushing headlong through our busy lives or with our minds lost in thought, so we are not consciously present. In this state we react automatically to what is happening in the moment, rather than making deliberate choices about how best to respond. The first step to being less reactive and more in control of our choices is increased awareness of our ongoing experience as it unfolds in the moment. Once we start to really notice what we are experiencing, we can decide if that is where we want to place our attention, and whether this is beneficial or harmful for our own and others' wellbeing. This includes noticing what evokes pleasant emotions such as joy, interest, or contentment, and what triggers difficult feelings such as anger, sadness, or fear.

The next step is learning how to focus attention. This has become increasingly challenging since digital, media, and marketing companies, political organisations, and the like have become skilled at capturing and holding our attention for their own purposes. This may not, in the long term, support our individual wellbeing and how we interact with the world. By developing the skills to choose where to direct our attention, and learning to pause before responding, we take back control.

Mindfulness practice is an evidence-based form of awareness and attention training that is increasingly popular.[22] Mindfulness trains the mind just as exercise trains the body. It is a way of paying attention to what is going on in the present moment in the mind, the body, and the external environment, observing our experience with gentle curiosity, rather than supressing or over identifying with it. Learning to observe our thoughts and emotions in this open and friendly way builds self-acceptance, self-regulation, and mental clarity. The increasing scientific evidence for the benefits of mindfulness practice on physiology, the brain, and on emotions, thoughts and behaviours, is explored in the Health chapter.

Practising mindfulness can create a peaceful space in busy or stressed lives. Even more importantly, it is a route to self-knowledge, a basis for self-regulation and enhances our sensitivity to our impact on others. It is also a foundation for constructive interactions with others and helps build positive relationships. For instance, pausing before we speak, listening deeply to someone, and giving them our full attention, benefits both parties. Being more aware of our thoughts and motivations may help to counter any false judgements we are making that may impact our interactions. Mindful awareness also allows us to recognise our biases, values, and motivations, freeing us to make better decisions.

Although sometimes criticised as a self-indulgent pursuit, mindfulness has been shown to increase prosocial behaviour,[23] and its role in leadership and social action is growing in importance. It has the potential to lead to less self-serving, more collective, and systemic responses to social injustice, and the ecological challenges we face. If we want to change the world for the better, we may first need to change ourselves. Transformation towards a just society needs to happen at intrapersonal, interpersonal, and collective levels.

2. Open heart – kindness and compassion
Cultivating the capabilities of kindness and compassion is the foundation of positive and enduring relationships, collaboration, and making choices that benefit the wellbeing of all. Although humans can undoubtedly be selfish and cruel, the overwhelming evidence is that our success as a species stems from being innately helpful, caring, and collaborative. Studies show that even very small children will go to the aid of a stranger who has dropped something. Neuroscience suggests this tendency is hard-wired in our brains. Small acts of kindness, such as sharing, comforting, helping, and

co-operating, typically abound in our daily lives – although we are not always conscious of them.

Feeling empathy, sharing the feelings of another, can lead us to act with kindness and compassion. While kindness can be shown any time, compassion is a specific response to suffering or distress. Compassion opens our hearts to the experiences of others and involves a feeling of concern and the motivation to take action to alleviate suffering. This is often illustrated following disasters, when people provide meals, shelter or comfort to neighbours or strangers who have lost homes or loved ones. It was also evident in the recent COVID-19 pandemic when people spontaneously looked out for their neighbours, while medical staff and key workers risked their own lives to help save others. Too much empathy, without the action component of compassion, can lead to feelings of hopelessness, personal distress, and burnout that make us turn away from those in need.

Doing things such as spending money on ourselves bolsters our happiness, but evidence shows that doing things for others creates an even greater boost. When we show kindness or compassion to others there is activation in the reward centres of our brain, so both parties benefit. Such positive behaviours are also associated with increases in the hormone oxytocin, sometimes known as the 'love hormone', and with activity in the parasympathetic nervous system, which mediates calming responses and enhances our immune system.[24] Importantly, kindness and compassion can be rekindled if these natural tendencies have been supressed.

Kindness has also been shown to have benefits in the workplace. Employees of a corporation in Spain were randomly assigned to give or receive kindness, or neither (the control group). Over a four-week period, the givers were asked to carry out five acts of kindness per day such as bringing someone a beverage, cheering up a co-worker, or e-mailing a thank you note. Compared with controls, autonomy, competence, and overall wellbeing were boosted in both givers and receivers. Kindness was also contagious. Receivers 'paid kindness forward', showing almost three times as many helpful behaviours as those in the control group.[25]

There is mounting evidence that our physical and mental health are better when we show compassion towards ourselves.[26] Many of us have a harsh inner critic which judges us as being not good or attractive enough, a fraud, or failure. Accepting that personal struggles, flaws, and failure are just part of being human helps us to accept ourselves, and feel greater contentment in our life. This in turn increases our ability to connect with and care for others.

Helping and caring behaviours can be enacted towards other people, but also for the benefit of social organisations, and the natural world. Examples include supporting our local hospitals, schools, theatres, sports clubs, or charities. And there are innumerable examples of caring for the natural world, including protecting and nurturing animals, plants, and physical environments.

Although compassion is generally associated with warmth and nurturing, psychologists Chris Germer and Kristin Neff use the term "fierce compassion" to refer to its qualities of strength, courage, and empowerment. Fierce compassion may be called upon if we are to confront injustice and change it. It can give us the courage to speak truth to power or take on leadership positions required to rectify unjust conditions.

3. Clear thinking – informed appraisal

A third capability fundamental to sustainable wellbeing is how we evaluate information. The unprecedented volume of information we receive every day challenges our ability to process what we're exposed to. We are also confronted with information that we generate in our own minds: worries, plans, memories, fantasies, and feelings. How can we evaluate this information to identify what is true, what is important, what we should act on, and what we should disregard? Whether the information is coming from internal sources (our mind or body), or from external sources (e.g. other people or media), we need to be able to think clearly so that we can make an informed judgement. This process is sometimes referred to as 'critical thinking', not because we are being critical, but because we are making a critique of the available evidence. In other words holding it up to scrutiny. In this way we can critique our own thoughts such as *"she doesn't like me"*, or *"I'm not good enough"*, to establish whether such thoughts reflect reality, or are related more to low self-esteem or negative stories we tell ourselves.

Being able to scrutinise the claims made by others, such as advertisers, journalists, politicians, bloggers, or in posts on social media, is increasingly essential. How can we know that what we are being told is true? The growing pervasiveness of fake news and micro-targeted marketing, which uses algorithms to identify and intensify our beliefs, makes this capability even more vital. At a time when young people in particular are under increasing pressure to consume and conform, teaching children to evaluate what they are being told, and think for themselves has never been more important. More in the Media and Education chapters.

Clear thinking – informed appraisal – is not just an intellectual pursuit and is more than being rational. It is influenced by how open our minds are to the information we are evaluating and how open our hearts are to the human condition.

Institutions such as schools, workplaces, and community groups can all play a role in teaching these capabilities. Developing all three skills across populations, would provide a solid foundation for living good lives and creating a flourishing world. Together, as Figure 2 illustrates, these three capabilities promote wise action.

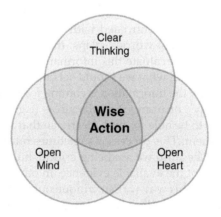

Figure 2: The core capabilities for wise action

Wise action

Wise action can be defined as understanding the complexity of a situation, and choosing to do what yields the greatest long-term benefit for us and others. Mindful awareness, kindness, and compassion together with informed appraisal, are powerful ways to gain insight into complex situations. By developing these capabilities, we will be better equipped to make wise choices for ourselves and others. This is not about depriving ourselves, but about feeling good about doing good, helping to create wellbeing for all, now and for generations to come.

Reflection:
In what ways could having an open mind, open heart, and clear thinking enhance your ability to take wise action for wellbeing?

In summary

The psychological principles for wellbeing and the core capabilities can help us as individuals and societies to flourish, especially in increasingly complex times. Integrating these into our homes, relationships, educational institutions, communities, workplaces, and politics can give us the critical tools to develop our full humanity, solve the challenges that confront us, and shift our relationship to ourselves, to each other, and the world around us.

They have the potential to create a world where the wellbeing of people and the planet is optimised for current and future generations.

Key sources

Full references and resources are available at our website https://www.creatingtheworldwewanttolivein.org/references/introduction/

1 Peterson *et al.* (2008). Group well-being: morale from a positive psychology perspective. *Applied Psychology*, 57, 19–36.
2 Seligman & Csikszentmihalyi (2000). Positive psychology: An introduction. *American Psychologist*, 55(1), 5–14.

3 Kansky & Diener (2017). Benefits of well-being: Health, social relationships, work, and resilience. *Journal of Positive Psychology and Wellbeing, 1*(2), 129–169.

4 Kushlev *et al.* (2019). Do happy people care about society's problems? *The Journal of Positive Psychology*, 1–11.

5 Richards & Huppert (2011). Do positive children become positive adults? Evidence from a longitudinal birth cohort study. *The Journal of Positive Psychology, 6*(1), 75–87.

6 Helliwell, Layard & Sachs (2017). *World Happiness Report.* Sustainable Development Solutions Network.: Helliwell, Layard, Sachs & De Neve (2020). *World Happiness Report 2020.* Sustainable Development Solutions Network.

7 Ryan & Deci (2017) *Self-Determination Theory: Basic Psychological Needs in Motivation, Development and Wellness.* Guilford Press.

8 Eisenberger & Lieberman (2004). Why rejection hurts: a common neural alarm system for physical and social pain. *Trends in cognitive sciences, 8*(7), 294–300.

9 Cole *et al.* (2015). Myeloid differentiation architecture of leukocyte transcriptome dynamics in perceived social isolation. *PNAS, 112*(49), 15142–15147.

10 Holt-Lunstad (2017). The potential public health relevance of social isolation and loneliness: Prevalence, epidemiology, and risk factors. *Public Policy & Aging Report, 27*(4), 127–130.

11 Dweck (2008). *Mindset: the new psychology of success.* Ballantine Books

12 Baumeister *et al.* (2001). Bad is stronger than good. *Review of General Psychology, 5*(4), 323–370.

13 Fredrickson & Cohn (2008). Positive emotions. In Lewis, Haviland & Barrett (Eds.), *Handbook of Emotions* (3rd ed., pp. 777–796). Guilford Press.

14 Fredrickson (2009) *Positivity.* Crown.

15 Johnson & Fredrickson (2005). "We All Look the Same to Me": Positive Emotions Eliminate the Own-Race Bias in Face Recognition. *Psychological Science, 16*(11), 875–881

16 Lomas *et al.* (2014). Gratitude Interventions: A Review and Future Agenda. *The Wiley Blackwell Handbook of Positive Psychological Interventions*, 1–19.

17 Gottman (2014). *What predicts divorce? The relationship between marital processes and marital outcomes.* Psychology Press.

18 Forgeard & Seligman (2012). Seeing the glass half full: A review of the causes and consequences of optimism. *Pratiques psychologiques, 18*(2), 107–120.

19 Puig-Perez *et al.* (2015). Optimism and pessimism are related to different components of the stress response in healthy older people. *International Journal of Psychophysiology, 98*(2), 213–221.

20 Whitney & Cooperrider (2011). *Appreciative inquiry: A positive revolution in change.* ReadHowYouWant.com.

21 Shin & Stegar (2014). Promoting Meaning and Purpose in Life. *The Wiley Blackwell Handbook of Positive Psychological Interventions*, 90–110.

22 Huppert (2018). Living life well: The role of mindfulness and compassion. In *The social psychology of living well*. Routledge.
23 Donald *et al.* (2019). Does your mindfulness benefit others? A systematic review and meta-analysis of the link between mindfulness and prosocial behaviour. *British Journal of Psychology*.
24 Hamilton (2010). *Why kindness is good for you*. Hay House.
25 Chancellor *et al.* (2018). Everyday prosociality in the workplace: The reinforcing benefits of giving, getting, and glimpsing. *Emotion, 18*(4), 507–517.
26 Neff (2003). Self-compassion: An alternative conceptualization of a healthy attitude toward oneself. *Self and Identity, 2*(2), 85–101.

What makes for a good life?

CHAPTER 1
Childhood

Sue Roffey

"There can be no keener revelation of a society's soul than the way in which it treats its children" – Nelson Mandela, speech at the launch of the Nelson Mandela Children's Foundation, 1995.[1]

How we raise children matters for universal wellbeing

Most parenting handbooks give advice on what children need to become healthy and happy. Although such things matter, we need to think beyond this to create a world we all want to live in. This requires a different emphasis on what is important in raising the next generation. Mandela urges us to treat all our children well, but it is not only care that matters but the messages children receive about themselves, other people, and the world around them.

A Harvard Survey of 10,000 young people in 33 schools in the United States across a wide spectrum of race, class, and culture was published in 2014.[2] This showed that almost 80% valued personal success and happiness over concern for others. They also ranked fairness low in comparison to other values. Some made it clear that their self-interest is paramount: *"If you are not happy, life is nothing. After that, you want to do well. And after that, expend any excess energy on others"*. This is largely attributed to the messages that children receive at home about what is important. The report goes on to say that when young people do not prioritise caring and fairness over aspects of personal success, and see their peers as even less likely to do so, they are more likely to engage in behaviour that is cruel, disrespectful and dishonest, and take risks with their own wellbeing. Youths were three times more likely to agree than disagree with this statement: *"My parents are prouder if I get good grades in my classes than if I'm a caring community member in class and school"*. It would seem that what children and young people hear at home in the United States about the importance of achievement and happiness are drowning out messages about concern for others.

In other cultures, such as in Japan, Korea, and Aboriginal Australia, community and family needs are traditionally paramount and values such as cooperation and generosity highly regarded.

A healthy civil society depends on adults who are committed to their communities and who, at pivotal times, will put the common good before their own. This is most evident when crises strike, such as the volunteer fire-fighters whose primary concern is to save the lives and homes of others, and the doctors, nurses, and care-workers who risked their own safety in treating patients with COVID-19. In the United Kingdom many people checked in on their neighbours and others in need as the country shut down for weeks. Children's pictures of rainbows supporting front-line workers were evident everywhere. This is likely to reflect conversation in households. When self-advancement is so dominant that we lose this community spirit, we are in trouble.

The quality of experiences in a child's formative years impact on how well they develop, the person they become, and the society they create and inhabit. Most families want their children to do well and be happy, but how can we also raise children to become caring, community-minded, open to discovering what gives them meaning in life, and motivated to take responsibility for positive change?

When young people have experiences that undermine their own well-being this may affect their ability to become responsible and caring adults. Many live with poverty that impacts their development,[3] and others experience neglect, abuse, poor mental health, family breakdown, and domestic violence. Despite the work of many agencies, there are still children in both developed and developing countries who are subject to forced marriage, female genital mutilation, unpaid work, sexual services, and are without schooling. On the other hand, there are also parents who give their children everything they ask for without any expectation of responsibility towards others. These individuals may grow to have a sense of entitlement. Ultimately, this may damage their future relationships and wellbeing.

How can we ensure the next generation is not only physically and psychologically healthy but also attuned to others? Urie Bronfenbrenner's ecological model of child development[4] shows how everything is connected just as it is in the natural world. For example, the level of social support a pregnant woman or young mother receives from her friends and family has far-reaching consequences not just for her, but on the future wellbeing and development of her infant.[5] We need to notice and pay attention to what is happening in families, communities, workplaces, and in government policies, to ensure good practice is initiated, supported, and developed.

This chapter addresses these issues across the stages of childhood, from the first months of life through to adolescence. We explore different ways of parenting and ask how young people can become the best version of themselves: how can they develop the positive qualities and values that will contribute to building a fairer, more humane, and compassionate world.

From birth to adolescence

First experiences of life

Whether an infant is born into challenging or privileged circumstances, all need similar responses from the adults around them. Overwhelmingly, the quality of the relationship between the child and their primary carer(s) matters for their emotional, social, and cognitive development, especially in the first months of life. A strong and secure attachment is where a carer tunes into the baby's needs, so that they spend as little time as possible feeling cold, hungry, uncomfortable, fearful, or in pain. When a baby cries and someone familiar responds, they begin to develop a sense of trust, security, and competence. Holding, making eye contact, and smiling begins a dance of social interaction that does much more than promote good feelings, it is fundamental to optimal learning and healthy development.[6] Positive and predictable interaction is also linked to children's later ability to regulate their emotions and stay calm in times of challenge.[7] Other people than parents can look after an infant, but they need to be equally responsive.

A new mother who is isolated, mentally unwell, had a child against her will, or is living in stressful circumstances may not have the inner resources to connect with her child. Some parents may need to return to work soon after the birth and are exhausted when they come home. Their baby may become a nuisance rather than a welcome responsibility. Some infants are not easy to settle or resist social interaction. Parents who experience such issues with their infants need even more support.

If we want to start creating a better world for everyone, then children in such circumstances need 'a village' to raise them, where they not only have their basic needs for food and shelter met but also experience kindness, acceptance, support, and encouragement – as do their families. Sometimes it is clear who comprises that 'village', but in modern cities, where people are less likely to know each other, it could include not only grandparents and other members of the extended family but also neighbours, teachers, parents of children's friends, people who run clubs, or organisations attached to places of worship. Although practical hands-on support is optimal, we have learnt from the lockdown that emotional support and advice can be accessed on-line to reduce feelings of isolation.

Reflections:

What national policies would help ensure every newborn has an optimal start to life?

Do workplaces have a responsibility towards the infants of their employees? Do you know examples of good practice?

Some parents need a kind or encouraging word from time to time. What opportunities are there to do this in your community?

The early years

From birth to three, a child's brain has been estimated to produce more than a million new neural connections a second. This development is influenced by many factors, including a child's relationships, experiences, environment, and genetic predispositions. An important aspect of this is the communication that others have with the growing child. Infants can understand language long before they can form words, so talking with them from their very first days is vital – sharing experiences, expressing feelings, asking questions, reading stories, and simply wondering with them fosters language, thinking, and social skills.

As children begin to develop spoken language, the role of every adult matters, especially those who spend most time with the child. There are thousands of opportunities every day to engage in interactive communication. This could include talking together about shopping trips to what is fair in playing games to showing pride in emerging skills and strengths. What people say to a child helps form their understanding of who they are becoming and the world around them. Small children spending hours every day sitting in front of a screen may be missing out on this vitally important face-to-face interaction.[8] Betty Hart and Todd Risley[9] found that these early experiences had far-reaching implications for future language and intellectual development. Parents and carers need to feel valued as a child's first teacher, and to know what this means.

Middle childhood: becoming part of a social world

Young children are ego-centric – everything is centred around them – but as they grow they need to begin to take account of other people. How this happens will powerfully influence how they see others and the relationships they have with them, first in their immediate world, and then outside in neighbourhoods, schools, and communities.

Children first look to significant figures in their lives as role models; usually these people are members of their family. Children listen, watch, and copy. If a parent is fair and even-handed, children learn to share; if a sibling belittles and bullies without restraint, children learn to put others down; if an uncle derides those of a different race or religion, then children learn that some people are worth less than those like them; if a grandmother shows kindness and interest, a child will understand how to be empathic and kind towards others. If children's behaviours and attitudes meet with approval from those around them, this embeds them as a preferred way of being.

Feeling you belong is a basic psychological need. There are many places a child might feel they belong, including their family, school, place of worship, sports club, or drama group. When they identify with a group, they are likely to take on the values espoused there. If they are in a competitive culture, winning may become all-important; if they are in a team then cooperation may matter more. Belonging can be either inclusive or exclusive.[10] Exclusive belonging can enhance wellbeing for those inside the group but might maintain a sense of superiority by rejecting others who are different. This can victimise outsiders by dehumanising them. Examples of this range from bullying in schools, to homophobia in communities, to blaming migrants for social ills, and at its worst to genocide that emanates from political or military authorities. Inclusive belonging welcomes all as part of our shared humanity.

Reflection:

Who do children look up to and how might we generate more positive role models for them?

Learning values

Aspirations are linked to the values children develop, and this is reflected in their attitudes and behaviours as they grow. Geoffrey Williams and his colleagues found that children whose parents encourage both autonomy and responsibility tend to have intrinsic goals linked to a sense of meaning and making a difference.[11] Where parents are more controlling and less supportive of agency, adolescent children are more likely to place stronger value on extrinsic aspirations for wealth, fame, and image. Extrinsic values are also associated with lower wellbeing.

Creating a world we want to live in requires a strong focus on values that enhance wellbeing for everyone. Rather than children worrying about being richer, cleverer, or better looking than other people, perhaps families could stress what we have in common, and show compassion for those who fall on hard times. Kindness boosts a positive self-concept and having a sense of meaning beyond the self can lead to a life well lived. Caring and fairness does matter to young people, but this needs support from others to embed as a way of being.

> **Reflection:**
>
> *How might we pay attention to the values we are promoting by our comments, conversations, and everyday actions?*

Adolescence

During adolescence young people explore what matters and who they want to be. As they become increasingly independent, especially in Western societies, they often challenge the values and way of life of the older generation and look to create new ways of being. Sometimes that is challenging for both young people and their parents, especially as in a teenager's brain the limbic system, responsible for emotions, is more active than the neo-cortex, which deals with rational thinking, organisation, and planning. Teenagers are therefore often driven more by how they feel than how they think. Adolescents, more than people at any other age, are vulnerable to a wide range of influences and open to trying out new experiences, not all of them positive. This includes the ever present and dominant influence of social media (see the Media chapter). In order for adolescents to move through this period of development safely, with an intact sense of self, they need to have already learnt to understand how to regulate their emotions, know where their support lies, be able to think critically and get things into perspective. These factors support resilience, so that something like a low mark or an unfavourable comparison does not lead to depression.

Although often disparaged for being impulsive or self-centred, many adolescents are also idealistic. This has been brought to the fore by young women who are taking leadership on big issues, notably Greta Thunberg on climate action, Emma Gonzalez on gun control, and Malala Yousafzai on the education of girls. They have taken the lead, but other young people are following, taking risks to make a difference to the world of their future.

Growing 'good' men

Toxic masculinity is at the root of many social ills, including family and community violence, 'winning at all costs', and suicide, which is the highest cause of death of men under 45 in many countries.[12] Despite decades of female emancipation, employment and enfranchisement in the West, there are still boys who grow up believing in the superiority of men, and what this means about being 'strong'. Despite good intentions, men may not have learnt to manage relationships or stressful situations well. They may feel it is 'unmanly' to talk about their feelings, or consider it beneath them to take on roles traditionally seen as 'female'. This inevitably presents problems in modern households and workplaces. Unemployment can leave such men without a sense of purpose and they may resort to alcohol and other drugs – often in the guise of sociability. Family breakdown can also be devastating for fathers who may lose contact with their children.

We need pay attention to how we bring up boys, so they have broader perspectives of how to be in the world, especially encouraging them to talk about issues that really matter and have relational skills that foster positive, open, and respectful communication (see the Education chapter for more on social and emotional learning). Girls also need to have a positive sense of self that is not simply aligned to being attractive or popular. Children come to understand how to 'be' male or female from all the images, conversations, and messages that surround them. This can be overt or subtle but has a profound impact on gender identity and all that this means, including for those who later identify as transgender. Raising awareness can lead to better outcomes for everyone. This needs to begin early in life, but by middle childhood at the latest.

Neurodiversity

Not all children develop in the same way. Positive psychology moves away from the deficit language of 'abnormality' and 'disorders' to embrace the value of neurodiversity. This term usually applies to those on the autistic spectrum who often struggle with the social world but also increasingly to others who do not fit the 'norm'. Such individuals do not need to be 'cured' or treated for a 'disability', but rather provided with an environment that both accepts their differences and facilitates their alternative abilities.[13]

Reflections:

What might encourage young people to reflect on what gives them meaning in life?

What gives them courage to try new things and be resilient when such things don't work out?

Families that enable children – and the future – to flourish

Parenting is a process – you do not have the same conversations with a 2 year old as with a 12 year old. But there are fundamentally different ways of being a parent, from letting children get away with unacceptable behaviour to being highly controlling. There is one parenting style, however, that research says has the best outcomes, at least in Western societies.[14] Children in such families are more likely to become not only confident and independent but also thoughtful, kind, and conscientious. This parenting style has the following features:

- Parents are warm and affectionate, ensuring their child feels loved and wanted. Children who feel secure are better able to form positive relationships with others and are more open to learning.
- They accept their child for who he or she is, fitting their expectations to the child, not the other way around.
- They do not give their child everything they ask for and explain why. This avoids the development of a sense of entitlement. Children who are able to 'delay gratification' and encouraged to wait in order to have something better later have been shown to have better self-control, leading to higher physical and mental wellbeing.[15]
- They have clear expectations about social behaviour, letting them know that being unfair or unkind is not acceptable, and encouraging them to be considerate and inclusive.
- They talk with their children about important issues such as illness or loss – a child imagines the worst unless they hear the truth. The language used needs to be at the child's level of development.
- They have high expectations about their child's potential and give encouragement to become the best of themselves, not better than others.

- They do not, however, expect their child to be perfect. Children who develop extremely high aspirations are more at risk of mental health problems.
- When their child is struggling, parents listen to their concerns, do not make quick judgements, and show they can be flexible. This models empathy for others.
- They communicate positively, talking about the strengths their child is developing, such as gentleness, responsibility, creativity, or thoughtfulness, and do not label them negatively as lazy, naughty, or selfish. Children need positives to reach up to, not negatives to live down to.
- They value all their children equally and do not favour one over another.
- They also encourage agency: supporting children to make their own decisions and think through what this means.

Reflections:

What might encourage and support parents to have this style of interaction with their children?

What might get in the way?

All over the world, families were thrust together as a result of the COVID-19 pandemic. For some this was a welcome opportunity to have time to play, learn, and talk together. The internet is now full of ideas for shared activities. Some children, however, have been in households where the lockdown exacerbated what was already a toxic environment. To prevent this leading to increased inequality and inter-generational disadvantage we need to actively address the issues in this chapter, putting the principles of kindness and compassion into practice and all taking responsibility for the wellbeing of every child.

Examples of positive action

It is the children of today who become the parents and citizens of tomorrow. Their ability to positively connect with others, have empathy, find meaning, and purpose in their lives and believe they can make a positive difference is rooted in their childhood experiences. Everything that happens in families, schools, and communities matters. Below are just a few of the initiatives happening across the world. More on the website.

Roots of empathy

This program is designed to raise empathy in young children. A parent and baby visit a primary classroom every three weeks over a school year. A trained instructor focuses the children's attention on the infant's development, and the feelings they express. Students also watch how the parent tunes into the infant and respond to their feelings and needs.

This helps the children to identify their own feelings as well as those of others. The experience is used as a hook for discussion about emotions and relationships. As a result, there is more kindness and pro-social behaviour in the classroom, less bullying, and more awareness of the need for social justice.[16]

Respectful relationships

NAPCAN stands for the National Association for the Prevention of Child Abuse and Neglect in Australia. Its main aim is to develop child-friendly communities where everyone is responsible for the wellbeing of children and where young people themselves learn how to be responsible towards others. This has included several local initiatives. The Respectful Relationships one-year program in the Northern Territory sought to develop a trauma-informed approach to Respectful Relationships Education (RRE). Adults became aware of the impact of negative life experiences on young people, including their thinking, feelings, and behaviour. A major outcome was the development, in consultation with practitioners, of individualised, trauma-informed RRE modules for youth with complex difficulties. The pilot showed very promising application for this vulnerable, high-risk group.[17]

Kindness matters for the SDG

Run by UNESCO MGDIEP,[18] this global youth campaign aims to mobilise youth aged 15–35 to achieve the 17 Sustainable Development Goals (SDG) through transformative acts of kindness. 7,300 young people from 120 countries have so far submitted their stories to the UNESCO. They are worth reading and sharing. *"An act of kindness is not a trivial task"*.

Hope and optimism

In some ways, children have never had it so good – especially in the West. Many more children survive into adulthood, medical advances have enabled more to stay healthy and smaller families in many cultures mean individual children often have more of everything.

The United Nations Convention on the Rights of the Child (UNCRC)[19] has been ratified by 194 countries across the world with the United States and South Somalia being the exceptions. Despite this significant achievement there is still a long way to go to make UNCRC a reality rather than aspirational. But things are moving in the right direction.

There is increasing recognition that children are not the property of their families. Embedded in this is entitlement to protection from all forms of violence including forced marriage, female genital mutilation, and corporal punishment. Since its adoption as Article 19 in the UNCRC around 55 countries have prohibited corporal punishment in all settings and another 50 are committed to doing so – compared to only one prior to the UNCRC.

There is recognition in principle, if not always in practice, of Article 12 of the UNCRC, which acknowledges that children are entitled to be heard and taken seriously. This represents acknowledgement of human dignity, as important for children as it is for adults.

Visibility and legal protections of children with disabilities are still a major challenge, but frameworks for protection now exist. Many countries have been shifting resources to community rather than institutional care, and many are exploring inclusive education.

As this chapter briefly summarises, we have learnt much about factors that promote healthy child development. There is increasing awareness that when children are raised with love and also encouragement to see beyond the self then not only does this maximise their own wellbeing but also that of others – and ultimately the world we will live in. This is not just up to families but to workplaces, communities, the media, corporations, and government.

Finally, young people themselves are becoming more active in the conversation – if not on the streets! They care about the future of our planet and the people in it and are showing the rest of the world what matters to them. We need to grow children who will become adults who will create the world we all want to live in. Many are already doing it.

Ideas for action

What might governments do?

Put the 42 articles on the United Nations Convention of the Rights of the Child into practice.

Ensure families are supported in the early years of a child's life with paid parental leave and services to help promote secure attachment.

Ensure no child lives in poverty.

What might communities do?

Give children agency and respect their voice

Promote the message of responsibility for the safety and wellbeing of every child.

Show that every child, from whatever background, has the right to be treated with fairness and dignity.

What might schools do?

Be inclusive and put wellbeing at the heart of school endeavours.

Include social and emotional learning on the curriculum to develop positive relationships, resilience, and responsibility.

What might families do?

Talk with children. Ask good questions and listen to the answers.

Model and talk about positive values and focus on strengths.

Help children understand and regulate their emotions.

Expect children to do things for others.

Ask for help when needed.

What might individuals do?

Be there with sympathy, tea, baby-sitting, and random acts of kindness for families who need support.

Not jump to judgement about children's behaviour – you do not know their story.

Key sources

Full references and resources are available at our website https://www.creatingtheworldwewanttolivein.org/references/childhood/

1 https://www.mandela.gov.za/mandela_speeches/1995/950508_nmcf.htm
2 Harvard Making Caring Common Project (2014). *The Children we Mean to Raise: The Real Messages Adults are Sending about Values.* Harvard Graduate School of Education.
3 Young (2019). The Psychological Impacts of Poverty. *BPS Research Digest*, December 2019.
4 Bronfenbrenner (1979). *Ecology of human development.* Harvard University Press: Bronfenbrenner (2005). The developing ecology of human development: Paradigm lost or paradigm regained. In Bronfenbrenner (Ed.), *Making human beings human: Bioecological perspectives on human development.* Sage.
5 Upshur (1990). Early intervention as preventive intervention. In Meisels & Shonkoff (Eds.), *Handbook of early childhood intervention* (pp. 633–650). Cambridge University Press.
6 Gerhardt (2003). *Why Love Matters: How Affection Shapes a Baby's Brain.* Routledge.
7 University of Turku. (2019). Predictability of parent interaction positively influences child's development. *ScienceDaily*, 15 August 2019.

8 Zimmerman, Christakis, & Meltzoff (2007). Associations between media viewing and language development in children under age two years. *The Journal of Paediatrics, 151*(4), 364–368.

9 Hart & Risley (1995). *Meaningful Differences in the Everyday Experiences of Young American Children.* Paul H Brookes Publishing.

10 Roffey (2013) Inclusive and Exclusive Belonging: The impact on individual and community wellbeing. *Educational and Child Psychology, 30*(1), 38–49.

11 Williams *et al.* (2006). Extrinsic life goals and health-risk behaviours in adolescents. *Journal of Applied Social Psychology, 30*(8), 1756–1771.

12 Canetto & Cleary (Eds.) (2012) Men, masculinities, and suicidal behaviour. *Social Science and Medicine Special Issue, 74*(4), 461–636.

13 Silberman (2015). *Neurotribes: The Legacy of Autism and How to Think Smarter about People Who Think Differently:* Allen and Unwin.

14 Morris, Cui & Steinberg (2013). Parenting research and themes: What we have learned and where to go next. In Larzelere, Morris & Harrist (Eds.), *Authoritative parenting: Synthesizing nurturance and discipline for optimal child development* (35–58). American Psychological Association.

15 Hughes, Roman & Ensor (2014). Parenting and Executive Function: positive and negative influences. In Cooper (Ed.) *Wellbeing: A complete reference guide Volume 1 Children and Families, Part 2 Parenting and Children's Development.* Wiley On-line library.

16 Schonert-Reichl *et al.* (2012). Promoting children's prosocial behaviours in school: Impact of the "Roots of Empathy" program on the social and emotional competence of school-aged children. *School Mental Health, 4*(1), 1–12.

17 Dobia (2019). *"Every client has a trauma history". Teaching Respectful Relationships to Marginalised Youth. An evaluation of NAPCAN's Respectful Relationships Program in the Northern Territory 2017–2018.* Western Sydney University.

18 mgiep.unesco.org/kindness

19 en.wikisource.org/wiki/United_Nations_Convention_on_the_Rights_of_the_Child

CHAPTER 2
Education

Sue Roffey

"*Education is the most effective means that society possesses for confronting the challenges of the future. Indeed, education will shape the world of tomorrow*". – *UNESCO, 1996*[1]

Why and how is education important for wellbeing?

We begin to learn from the moment we are born, possibly even before. We learn from watching, listening, copying, and trying things out. Then we begin to ask questions. We learn what things are for, how things work, how to communicate, and what matters. We learn not only about the world around us, but about ourselves, and others who share that world. Although most of a child's brain is developed by the time they are five, learning continues throughout life.[2]

The experiences young people have determine who they become, and the future they will create. Schooling is a significant part of this, from pre-school through to higher and adult education. 'School' therefore applies here to all institutions whose primary purpose is learning.

Education is UN Sustainable Development Goal 4, with ten targets to aim for by 2030. In the past decade, major progress has been made towards increasing access to education with more people achieving basic literacy; 265 million children are however, still not receiving any schooling at all, many of them in conflict zones.

If the purpose of education is to create a world where individuals, families, communities, and society thrive, then some education systems may need to change. What is the point of academic 'excellence' for young people who are anxious, depressed, or feel life has no meaning.[3] There are schools across the world where diversity is actively valued and the wellbeing of the whole student (and teacher) are centre stage so there is much good practice on which to build. However, while we still have schools who marginalise, or even exclude students who do not fit the 'norm' of compliance or academic excellence, the system is not working for all. The same applies for those beset by fear of not achieving the 'success' defined by high academic grades. Broad, relevant, and engaging educational programs need to replace a narrow curriculum and reflect the diversity of students, and the needs of both the world we live in now and that of the future.

One of the most powerful impacts of the COVID-19 pandemic has been on education. It has offered new perspectives on how children might learn, what they need to learn, and the critical relevance of both the social dynamics of schools, and the mental health and wellbeing of students. Parents attempting to home educate have perhaps developed a new respect for the multi-faceted skills of teachers. School lockdown in some countries, however, has exacerbated inequality and highlighted how the availability or lack of resources and support at home can either hinder, or help learning. There is a groundswell of hope from commentators that policymakers will now move from an education system rooted in competition and control to one that enables all students to flourish and become the best of themselves. Here we offer alternatives that will help build a better world for everyone. Some may seem radical, but the evidence suggests that such changes are necessary for the wellbeing of future generations. As we have seen from actions in crisis, nothing is impossible.

Reflections:

What are the most important things young people need to learn for their own future?

What are the most important things young people need to learn for the future of the world they will live in?

What do we need to learn?

UNESCO's report *Learning, the Treasure Within*[4] quoted at the beginning of this chapter, provides a conceptual framework for on-going, life-long learning. This model organises learning into the following five pillars:

- Learning to Know – the development of skills and knowledge needed to function in this world, e.g. formal acquisition of literacy, numeracy, science, and general knowledge.
- Learning to Do – the acquisition of a wide range of applied skills.
- Learning to Live Together – the development of social skills and values such as respect and concern for others, and the appreciation of cultural diversity.
- Learning to Be – the learning that contributes to a person's mind, body, and spirit. This can be fostered in sport, the arts, literature, and social and emotional learning.
- Learning to Transform Oneself and Society – the knowledge, skills, critical thinking, and values for creating lasting positive change in organisations, communities, and societies.

A criticism of current education is that the first two pillars have been overly dominant in the name of academic 'excellence', and that the other three have been sidelined. Nevertheless, social and emotional/relationship education has been introduced in many countries and ethics is sometimes offered as an alternative to religious education. Any social and emotional learning, however, needs a clear pedagogy for implementation, so it is a safe and supportive experience for both teachers and students. It needs to be delivered by educators who see students regularly, so that the learning can be reinforced in everyday interactions. This is an area that can address not only skills development, but challenge attitudes and perceptions. The Black Lives Matter movement shows how much this is needed for a safe and inclusive society.

A more recent document on education is from the Organisation for Economic Cooperation and Development, entitled *OECD: Future of Education and Skills 2030.*[5] This reflects many of the issues raised in this chapter, including student voice, values, curriculum design and implementation, and the wellbeing of the whole child.

The fundamental elements of education

In school it matters:

- What children and young people are taught – the formal curriculum.
- How they are taught – pedagogy.
- The context in which they are taught – the learning environment.

Although addressed separately below, all interact with each other.

The formal curriculum
There is much talk about 'quality education' and 'raising standards' but, despite the UNESCO guidelines and documents such as the Australian Alice Springs (*Mparntwe*) Declaration, governments have rarely been clear about what education needs to be *for* or *about*. Who determines what is taught, and importantly, what is left out? A history curriculum for instance, can gloss over the impact of colonial invasions if those who write this do not give due weight to the past destruction of established cultures whose descendants are still affected. No curriculum is value free.

Policymakers have an agenda about what they want from the citizens of the future. The UN sustainable goals of *"skills for decent work"*, *"youth and adult literacy"*, and education for *"sustainable development and global citizenship"* are laudable, but do not mention the equally important education needed for day to day living: how to relate to each other in healthy ways, child development and parenting, mental health and wellbeing, political awareness, and subjects that honour imagination and the creative arts. In many countries academic subjects are valued above all else and school success is only available to those with a good memory who can pass exams in those subjects. As can be seen from those who do well in their lives despite having few formal qualifications, and those who pass exams but have little competence in other ways, a good education goes well beyond this. Making the same demands on all students, regardless of their interests, background, or ability means a significant proportion of young people grow up to believe they are failures. The COVID-19 pandemic has raised awareness of the value of those who do significant work to keep things going – from care-workers, to van drivers to garbage collectors, many of whom do not have high academic qualifications, and are often regarded as low-status. A well-functioning society, however, does not only need doctors, lawyers, and bankers, it also needs these keyworkers. There is also a reinforced acknowledgement that the arts industry is valuable, not only in giving enjoyment, but also in income generation.

There is an underlying assumption that the world will remain the same for the next generation. The reality is that things are changing fast, and we need flexibility, and innovation to respond to the challenges we face. A rigidly prescribed set of learning targets might under-estimate the potential of many to both develop their strengths and work towards solutions.

Pedagogy & teaching approaches

There are two basic forms of school learning: being told and finding out. The first is known as didactic, where the teacher imparts knowledge and the student is a passive recipient. Students are tested on how well this knowledge is remembered rather than applied or critiqued. Although useful for basic skills such as literacy, numeracy, science, and technology, this approach is limited. It leads to a controlled teaching style, where motivation is extrinsic – students may not so much be inspired by learning but by the rewards of a high grade. Richard Ryan and Edward Deci[6] cite a raft of research that supports greater autonomy for students, not only for their motivation, but also their self-worth and wellbeing. Despite advances in technology where information is often presented in vibrant visual ways, some schools still focus on didactic learning, where the teacher is the authority and channel of knowledge. Early years teachers, however, often engage and motivate children with play-based learning, and even older students value those who can instil some fun in the classroom.

Socratic learning, on the other hand, is active, shared, guided discovery, where the student is the primary agent and encouraged to explore and question. The role of teachers is to structure the learning environment, so that students work on targeted areas, do research, ask questions, and are provided with support. Student learning is evaluated on how well concepts have been understood, and can be generalised and applied.

Teachers are essential facilitators of learning. According to John Hattie's synthesis of over 800 meta-analyses of effective education,[7] it is the specifics of the teacher-student relationship that make the most difference to outcomes. Good teachers make learning objectives clear, engage student agency, and respect student ideas. Feedback is critical – not so much from the teacher about what a student can or cannot do, but from the learner to the educator in order for the educator to understand how the student is making sense of the learning. One of the things Hattie highlights is the necessity of a class climate where *"errors are welcomed as key levers for enhancing learning"* (p. 4). Educators who are considering leaving the profession are more likely to stay if they are valued and respected for the important work they do.

The value of on-line learning has been headline news, as students being educated at home have few other options. This, however, has potential risks in discriminating against those who either do not have the necessary technology, or the space to use it effectively. It requires targeted investment to balance these disadvantages.

The learning environment
Children learn about themselves and others, what is valued, and what is not, in the 'informal curriculum'. School culture determines the learning environment, how people feel about being there, the relationships they experience, and the values that underpin everything that happens.[8] Practices that demonstrate culture include how decisions are made, the levels of inclusion, participation by stakeholders, the language used, the behaviour expected, and how expectations are communicated and reinforced. Where accountability and micro-management prevail, relational quality is unlikely to be top of the agenda. This can lead to a toxic culture where bullying, exclusion, and cliques thrive.

In such undesirable environments, behaviour policies are more likely to be based in rewards for compliance, and sanctions for what is deemed unacceptable. When the range of sanctions available are ineffective the default position is to move the young person on or out. In the United Kingdom, the figures for both formal exclusions and suspensions, and informal 'off-rolling' are now a serious problem, as schools compete to be 'the best' in terms of test results. Teacher retention is also an issue, as exhausted and undervalued individuals leave for less stressful occupations.

School climate is increasingly recognised as critical for the mental health of both students and educators. Positive education defines this as ensuring everyone feels valued and included, and relational values such as kindness, respect, empathy, and trust are promoted at all levels. Such a school climate is strengths and solution focused – building on what works.

Case-study: The Thinking School

In his school, headteacher Dr Kulvarn Atwal[9] has focused on teacher learning in order to progress pupil learning. Rather than sending staff on one-day courses, professional development is integral to everyday activity and conversation. Situated, informal, collaborative learning is seen in constructive dialogue, joint activities, reflective practices and creative risk-taking in a trusting, safe, and supportive environment. Teachers are encouraged to participate in both peer learning and action research to evaluate their practice. In this dynamic learning culture everyone has a voice, but the focus is firmly on what works for the pupils and their learning. Outcomes after three years indicate that this approach is highly effective.

If we believe that a world where everyone thrives is both worth aiming for and achievable, then we perhaps might begin by challenging the 'givens' of education. Many approaches developed in the past and supported by evidence such as the WHO 'healthy schools' approach may now need to be revisited to promote both social mobility and wellbeing. How can positive psychology inform a 'good education' for all?[10]

Change begins with questions. These reflections are just a start.

> **Reflections:**
>
> *What does it mean to be 'educated'?*
>
> *Who should determine what is taught in school?*
>
> *How can schooling mirror healthy child development?*
>
> *How can we ensure all learners feel safe, valued, and included?*
>
> *How can we give a voice to all students and teachers?*
>
> *How can we ensure that a student's natural curiosity is stimulated so they continue to seek out new knowledge and skills?*
>
> *What else is valuable beside academic skills, and why?*

An alternative education to build a thriving future

Here we outline how we might address the issues raised, and develop education aligned with the challenges of the 21st century. We need to foster innovative solutions and promote values that go beyond wealth promotion and consumption to those that involve care for the planet and each other. We also need schooling that motivates all young people to learn together with an approach that mirrors the healthy child development outlined in the previous chapter.

Most information is now on-line, accessible by a quick search. Those with access to technology have the world's library at the touch of a button. The scenario of a class of students all sitting quietly at desks with their books open to the same page is rapidly becoming outdated.

Young people need to learn about themselves and the world around them. As well as understanding the science of the natural and physical world, this also includes developing a positive identity and understanding what keeps themselves, their communities, and the environment functioning well.

Here we suggest how to make education relevant, engaging, and empowering for all students in a way that addresses both basic and higher-level knowledge and skills. It takes education out of the realm of homogenous tests and reliance on memory, to a level of deep learning, and hopefully a joy in discovery and development.

> **Reflection:**
>
> *What elements of your own education have been valuable to you in your life on a daily basis, and what has not?*

What students need to learn

In *'learning to know'*, students need to acquire the basic skills of language, literacy, numeracy, and science and technology as they do now. There is no sign this will be less so in the future. Curriculum focus beyond basic skills would be varied, and dependent on student age, interests, strengths, and specific needs.

In *'learning to do'*, students also require skills to navigate the vast worlds of knowledge, explore, investigate, ask searching questions, ascertain risk, and check the validity of what they discover, sometimes known as 'digital literacy'. Many schools have now embraced a 'growth mindset' approach to learning.[11] This means that instead of seeing themselves as having fixed abilities, pupils become aware that every effort empowers them to develop their knowledge base, understanding, and strengths. Rather than not knowing, or making mistakes, being interpreted as failure, this becomes the launchpad for growth.

Students also need to develop the understanding and skills in *learning to be*, and *learning to live together*. The personal, interpersonal, and intercultural aspects of education are higher on the agenda as policymakers realise that emotional and social competencies have many positive outcomes, from working in teams to family relationships to community safety and mental health. This impacts on how well societies function. The human and economic cost of dysfunction affects everyone.

Optimal social and emotional learning (SEL) combines specific lessons alongside a school culture that integrates this learning in both everyday interactions and the curriculum. In NSW for instance, all teachers are now required to consider the SEL implicit in all lessons. Research indicates that SEL extends beyond developing personal understanding and skills to changing attitudes, and enhancing academic learning.[12,13] Issues that impact strongly on young people's lives need be addressed in a safe and supportive place with an appropriate pedagogy.[14] Interventions for bullying behaviours, for instance, are often reactive and teacher led. Giving young people the opportunity to create a safe and happy class and take responsibility for the wellbeing of everyone can be far more effective. A pro-kindness program in a primary school, for example, was shown to improve relationships, academic performance, emotional regulation, and the ability to delay gratification.[15] The recent worldwide protests about continuing race discrimination show that much more needs to be done within education to help young people learn both the value of difference, and our shared humanity – how much we have in common. Teaching black history to every student will also help address the myths that are maintained by ignorance and prejudice.

Mindfulness has been introduced into many schools with the aim of increasing self and emotional awareness, developing empathy, and reducing negative emotion. Kimberly Schonert-Reichl and Molly Stewart Lawlor found that students who engaged in mindfulness three times a day become more optimistic as well as developing social and emotional competencies.[16] Mindfulness education also had positive effects on how young people thought about themselves.[17] This is also linked to teacher wellbeing.

Aboriginal Girl's circle

Australian Aboriginal secondary girls involved with a multi-year program that incorporated fun, agency, creativity, and collaborative activities felt more connected to their community, more resilient, and more confident. Some changed their educational aspirations and entered higher education.[18]

Many of the positive psychology principles listed in the introduction are at the heart of the fifth pillar, "*learning to transform oneself and society*". This includes developing skills to evaluate the application of knowledge, taking into account ethical considerations and impact – what does this mean for people and the planet? The curriculum needs to encompass an understanding of democracy and citizenship so that individuals can make informed choices.

How students might learn

Active and collaborative learning comes naturally to children. Many prominent educationalists note that much cognitive development emanates from social interaction. Not only is this more enjoyable and aligned with healthy child development, but collaborative effort can often achieve more than individual endeavour. Although some have taken the lead, few great developments in science, technology, or the arts have depended on one person alone but on teams working together.

Project-based cooperative work is a way to make learning come alive. This requires pre-requisite skills alongside interdependence so everyone contributes.[19] Students, who do not necessarily have to be of the same age, have a given area of investigation and work together over a specific amount of time. The teacher is the director of learning, and facilitator of progress, providing a structure that determines expectations for learning. Each group reports to others, so learning is shared. Project-based work entails a good deal of planning to cover curriculum targets. For instance, a project on earthquakes and volcanoes could include geology, history, physical, and human geography, mathematics, and possibly journalism, politics, crisis management, and various aspects of science. It may also address human survival, issues around sharing, or fighting for scarce resources and relate this to climate emergencies. This combines information, application, and higher thinking skills. Such a project can also engage creative arts – especially in relation to disseminating findings to others.

In Csikszentmihalyi's model of 'flow', people are at their most engaged in a task when this builds on their knowledge and skills but also presents a challenge. If a challenge is too hard, students will become anxious and give up; if it's too easy, they'll become bored. Students may require tasks to be scaffolded into manageable steps, or be given activities to extend their learning. Project based learning has the potential to facilitate both.

All pupils need to see that learning is achievable, they are making progress, and this is acknowledged. You only have to spend a few hours with pupils with severe learning difficulties to realise that even the smallest of steps can be celebrated.

Another aspect of future learning is paying attention to the burgeoning literature in neuropsychology; how the brain works, how we learn, and the links between experience, emotion, and behaviour. Positive psychology in schools promotes positive actions and positive feelings. Nowhere is this more important than with students in distress, whose behaviour can be challenging.[20]

All educators need both pre-service and in-service input to understand trauma, and how this may manifest in the classroom, guidance in how to establish and maintain positive relationships with students who are potentially challenging, the use of strengths-based rather than deficit language, strategies to respond effectively to confrontation, and ways in which to maintain their own resilience and wellbeing. There are resources on the website that may help.

One way of thinking about young people who are presenting with difficulties is called the *Power: Threat: Meaning Framework (PTMF)* published by the British Psychological Society.

For education systems to flourish, teachers need to be positioned as significant and valued professionals. In a re-structured system, their role would be multidimensional, including detailing options available, clarifying expectations, and resources, co-evaluating with students what has been learnt, and offering support where needed.

An optimal environment in which to learn

A positive school environment puts wellbeing at the heart of everything that happens. This includes:

- Leaders with a clear vision for the wellbeing of the whole child and every child.
- Communicating this vision clearly and regularly to all stakeholders, especially families, and building a team of like minds.
- Maximising agency, giving all stakeholders both a say and a responsibility for crafting an environment that fosters wellbeing for all.
- Using the language of strengths and inclusion where everyone is accepted for who they are, and the aim is for each to be the best they can be.

- Being flexible to enable those who have a range of needs, capabilities, and challenges to thrive and learn at their own pace.
- Behaviour policies that acknowledge the reality of student lives and support young people to understand their emotions, and choose better behaviour.
- Promoting positive behaviour, reducing teacher control while responding effectively to challenges, requires teacher learning and support
- Building relationships that promote social capital across the school that entails trust, acknowledgment, gratitude, and support.
- Having intercultural awareness and developing positive links with local communities.

Reflections:

What would you see, hear, and experience on a visit to a school that would tell you how people feel about being there?

What questions might you ask to find out more?

The statements above are supported by an increasingly extensive positive education literature. More information and examples of good practice at https://www.creatingtheworldwewanttolivein.org.

Hope and optimism

There are signs that positive change is happening all over the world. Finnish education actively aligns curriculum and teaching with natural child development, and has a reputation of being one of the best systems in the world:

> *"The nature of a child is to want to know new things, to be inquisitive, curious about the world around them, and to experiment with what they learn. Finland's education system builds on this, taking advantage of the natural curiosity, and placing it at the heart of education planning and curricula".*[21]

In Australia the eight 'general capabilities' are seen as a key element of the national curriculum, and are addressed and threaded through the content of learning areas. These general capabilities are: literacy, numeracy, information, and communication technology (ICT), critical and creative thinking, personal and social capability, ethical understanding, and intercultural understanding. The aim is for every student to become a successful learner, a confident and creative individual, and an active and informed citizen.

Case-study: Glasgow's nurturing approach

A nurturing approach includes having high aspirations for all young people, and a belief that all have potential. Nurture groups were originally established to provide extra support to children entering school who needed extra care. The Boxall principles for nurture groups are: that a child's learning is understood developmentally; that the classroom is a safe place; that the importance of nurture for the development of wellbeing is recognised; that language is seen as a vital means of communication but also, that all behaviour is recognised as communication; and that the importance of transition in children's lives is acknowledged. Scotland, and particularly Glasgow, have taken these principles and extended them to become the basis of whole school wellbeing. For the Glasgow initiative three more principles have been added: all young people feel they belong, young people's lives and experiences are respected, permission for disagreements ensures that staff and children are both heard. According to Maureen McKenna, Director of Education, Glasgow is a different place now than it was in 2007, with no permanent exclusions since 2017, evidence of a 50% reduction in youth crime for children aged 10–16, and a doubling of young people getting 'highers' – the qualifications taken at 18 – with over two thirds going onto higher education.

A new paradigm for education is overdue but aspects of this are already happening in schools all over the world. We need to build on this good practice.

Perhaps we begin by questioning the criteria for 'success'. Rather than getting high scores, perhaps the aim might be for every student to become the best they can be, be mentally healthy, and able to connect well and empathically with others. This may mean valuing education beyond academic skills to all other areas of knowledge and human development.

Ideas for action

What might governments do?

Invest resources so everyone has access to an education that reflects the changing needs of the world we live in.

Honour and respect teachers as vital facilitators of learning.

Ensure all educators have training in child development and the impact of adverse childhood experiences on learning and behaviour, and ways to redress this.

Pay attention to all five Pillars of Education as set out by UNESCO.

Reduce high-stakes testing to a minimum, and offer a range of assessment strategies.

What might schools do?

Ensure that wellbeing is at the heart of all policies and practices, giving everyone a voice.

Have strengths and solution focused approaches.

Have cultural awareness and make positive links with local communities.

Engage constructively with families, sending regular, positive messages home.

Develop behaviour policies that promote positive relationships, and a sense of belonging.

Develop a school culture that is inclusive, safe, and respectful.

Acknowledge the importance of play for resilience and wellbeing.

Focus on identifying 'personal bests' rather than a competitive culture.

Have protected time for social and emotional learning, and embed this learning throughout the school day.

Accept mistakes as part of learning, fostering a growth mindset.

What might teachers do?

Find something to like about every student and let them know!

Not take difficult behaviour personally.

Look after their own wellbeing and be kind to themselves – no-one can do everything perfectly.

What might families do?

Know they are their child's first teacher.

Encourage schools to focus on bringing out the best in each student, and do not expect their child to be 'top' in a competitive culture.

Show pride in all children's achievements and efforts.

Before enrolling a child, check out the school's wellbeing and inclusion approach.

Key sources

Full references and resources are available at our website https://www.creatingtheworldwewanttolivein.org/references/education/

1 Delors *et al.* (1996). *Learning: The Treasure Within.* UNESCO.
2 Center on the Developing Child (2007). *InBrief: The Science of Early Childhood Development.* https://developingchild.harvard.edu/resources/inbrief-science-of-ecd/
3 PISA (2018) *Results (Volume III): What School Life Means for Students' Lives.*
4 Delors *et al.* (1996). *Learning: The Treasure Within.* UNESCO.
5 https://www.oecd.org/education/2030-project/
6 Ryan & Deci (2017). *Self-Determination Theory – Basic Psychological Needs in Motivation, Development, and Wellness* (Ch.14). Guildford Press.
7 Hattie (2009). *Visible learning: A synthesis of over800 meta-analyses relating to achievement.* Routledge.
8 Street (2018). *Contextual Wellbeing: Creating Positive Schools from the Inside Out.* Wise Solutions.
9 Atwal (2019). *The Thinking School: Developing a dynamic learning community.* John Katt Educational.
10 See our website for a reading list on Positive Education.
11 Andersen & Nielsen (2016). Reading intervention with a growth mindset approach improves children's skills. *PNAS, 113*(43), 12 111–12.

12 Zins *et al.* (2004). *Building Academic Success on Social and Emotional Learning: What Does the Research Say?* Teachers College Press.

13 Durlak *et al.* (2011). The impact of enhancing students' social and emotional learning: a meta-analysis of school-based universal interventions. *Child Development, 82*(1), 405–432.

14 Roffey (2017). The ASPIRE Principles and Pedagogy for the Implementation of Social and Emotional Learning, and the Development of Whole School Well-Being. *International Journal of Emotional Education, 9*(2), 59–71.

15 Flook *et al.* (2015). Promoting pro-social behaviour and self-regulatory skills in pre-school children through a mindfulness-based kindness curriculum. *Developmental Psychology, 51*(1), 44–51.

16 Schonert-Reichl & Lawlor (2010). The Effects of a Mindfulness-Based Education Program on Pre-and Early Adolescents' Well-Being and Social and Emotional Competence. *Mindfulness, 1*(3) 137–151.

17 For an authoritative review see Weare & Huppert (2019). *Mindfulness and Education.* The Oxford Bibliography, bit.ly/2XMVJnt.

18 Dobia *et al.* (2013). *Aboriginal Girls Circle: enhancing connectedness and promoting resilience for Aboriginal girls: Final Pilot Report.* Western Sydney University.

19 Gillies (2016). Cooperative Learning: Review of Research and Practice. *Australian Journal of Teacher Education, 41*(3).

20 Roffey (2011). *Changing Behaviour in Schools: Promoting Positive Relationships and Wellbeing.* Sage Education.

21 https://www.educationfinland.fi/why-finland

CHAPTER 3
Work

Vanessa King

> *"The richest and fullest lives attempt to achieve an inner balance between three realms: work, love, and play". – Attributed to Erik H. Erikson*[1]

Why work matters for wellbeing

As Erikson is reputed to have said, work is vitally important for wellbeing – individually, in our communities, and for society as a whole. But our experiences at work are crucial. What happens in the workplace makes a difference to whether someone thrives or languishes.

Plentiful employment opportunities and a productive workforce are central to prospering economies, and this has been brought into sharp focus by the COVID-19 pandemic, which also served to highlight how crucial many previously under-appreciated and under-valued roles are to the effective functioning and health of our societies. Supermarket workers, delivery people, carers, hospital cleaners, alongside teachers, doctors and nurses were all seen to be key.

Work and workplaces impact on the communities they serve. For individuals, work provides income, but often so much more. Work can shape our identity, provide social connection, opportunities for growth, and can be a source of meaning and purpose, all important ingredients for wellbeing. Our day-to-day experience at work impacts on how happy we are, and this has a ripple effect out into other areas of our lives.[2] If generally we enjoy what we do, and where we do it, this effect is positive. Yet, too often, work environments are toxic, and seriously undermine our wellbeing.

The OECD's Better Life Index of 40 countries, indicates that adults spend on average a third of their days engaging in paid work (with 11% of people reporting working more than 50 hours per week).[3] Yet people often say they do not find their work enjoyable or engaging, and at its worst it can be a source of mental and physical harm. Time and again, studies show that only a small proportion of employees are engaged or motivated at work.[4] A recent study[5] buzzed its 60,000 participants at random times of the day, asking where that person was, and how they were feeling. Paid work ranked at the bottom in terms of wellbeing, higher only than being sick in bed!

Long working hours negatively impact health, personal safety, and stress. They leave people less time to engage in social and leisure activities, rest, or take care of themselves and others.[3] The 'always on' culture driven by technology means employees feel less able to switch off outside of normal working hours.[6] In the United Kingdom, 2 in 5 employees report experiencing work-related mental health difficulties, with 52% saying this is due to pressures such as too many priorities and targets.[7] The UK Chartered Institute of Personnel and Development report that work-related stress is in the top three causes of sickness absence. According to the American Psychological Association, 65 percent of US employees cite work as a significant source of stress, with more than one-third reporting this as chronic. This impacts not just on employees themselves but on their colleagues. When a worker is absent, others have to pick up the slack. In the United States, an estimate in 2013 suggested that stress-related absenteeism and presenteeism (being in work while unwell) cost more than $600 billion[8] a year, likely to be higher today, and does not include the knock-on impact on families and communities.

Despite all this evidence on the potential negative consequences, work remains an important net contributor to wellbeing. People in work rate their lives as more satisfactory than those who are unemployed but want to be working. They also have more positive emotional experiences and fewer negative ones than people without work, regardless of whether the latter are wanting to work or not.[4]

For individuals, being unemployed is damaging to wellbeing, with greater decreases in life satisfaction the longer this goes on, even after controlling for reduced finances. The experience of unemployment may have permanent 'scarring' effects.[9] This has significant community and public health implications, and is one of the most worrying fallouts from the pandemic, where millions are losing their jobs. Individual negative effects tend to be lower at times of mass unemployment, the scale is wider. The impact of unemployment on mental health and wellbeing is an important consideration, as Governments focus on recovery from the pandemic and building resilience for the future.

Wellbeing is good for work

A growing body of research gives clear evidence that employee wellbeing matters for sustained organisational success.[10] Beyond simply reducing absenteeism, wellbeing is related to higher: individual and organisational performance, productivity, collaboration, cognitive flexibility, and creativity. Doctors with higher wellbeing, for example, have been shown to make faster and more accurate diagnoses. Individuals who have higher wellbeing are more likely to be rated highly by their supervisors, and have higher future earnings.[10]

An analysis of studies covering data from 1.9 million employees across 49 industries and 73 countries showed a clear relationship between how positively people feel about their job, and business performance indicators such as greater customer loyalty, employee productivity, and lower staff turnover.[11] London Business School professor Alex Edmans tracked the earnings per share of organisations that prioritise employee engagement and wellbeing. Over a 26-year period, he found that those organisations out-performed their stock market peers by an average of 3.2% a year, suggesting that investors might do well by looking at wellbeing indicators, alongside more traditional performance measures, when making investment decisions.[12]

> **Reflections:**
>
> *How does work impact your wellbeing – positively and negatively?*
>
> *What factors at work do you think are most important for wellbeing?*

What makes work good for wellbeing?

In 1994 The GoodWork™ project set out to identify what exemplified 'good' work – work that is excellent in quality, is socially responsible, and meaningful to those engaged in it. This research identified three features of good work: the opportunity for excellence; that it is engaging and is ethical. In work that enables excellence, the worker 'knows their stuff', and is able to keep their knowledge and competencies up to date. Engaging work is personally interesting, absorbing, and a good fit for the worker. Ethical work can be carried out in a way that is responsible, and serves the wider good, even (perhaps especially) when it goes against the immediate interests of the worker.

More recently, organisational psychologist Wilmar Schaufeli argued that increasingly work will require innovation, creativity, continuous learning, and adaptation, so nurturing the 'psychological capital' of workers has never been more important. It's no longer enough to minimise the risks of burnout or boredom, work must be enriching, exciting, and energising. Balancing the demands of the role with adequate 'job resources' is central to this. Whilst excessive demands or workload are often seen as the prime source of stress at work, Schaufeli's research shows that it is missing, ineffective, or misaligned resources that have a greater negative impact. Job resources encompass much more than the right tools and equipment. They include: social factors; the design of the work and how it gets done; the organisational climate and culture; and opportunities for learning and growth.[13]

Improving the alignment and nature of resources both enhances employee wellbeing and enables sustained performance. It is perhaps unsurprising that leadership, management capability, and a person's own inner psychological resources mediate the balance necessary for good work and wellbeing.

Schaufeli argues we are in a psychological era of work where people need to be treated as human beings and valued as individuals rather than as 'resources' or 'assets', and that this benefits everyone.

The science of wellbeing can help guide the design of good work and good job resources, better meeting the psychological needs of workers and enabling sustained performance and innovation for the future. We explore this in more detail later in this chapter.

Reflection:

Think of a time you felt good and functioned at your best at work: what most enabled this?

Wellbeing is a corporate social responsibility

Wellbeing is a corporate social responsibility (CSR). Beyond raising performance, economic value, and physical health and safety requirements, there is a social responsibility to invest in the conditions that support and sustain employee psychological wellbeing. Beyond the impact on workers, this impacts families and communities. Many organisations have CSR programs that contribute to charity or offer volunteer opportunities, but at the same time may have overly stressful work environments without thinking of the ripple effect this has.

Beyond building the resilience skills of employees to help them cope with increasing pressure, constant change, poor management, or toxic organisational environments. The science of wellbeing offers a basis to better shape organisation culture; design meaningful work; and the development of capabilities, policies, and practices to create psychologically sustainable workplaces.

This science can also benefit the wider eco-system of work. Outsourcing has been leading cause of a rise in the number of self-employed and gig workers. Whilst self-employment can offer greater flexibility and autonomy, valued by some, it comes with inherent perils. Gig-workers, especially on low wages or zero-hours contracts, may need to work long hours or have several types of work simply to make ends meet. The self-employed don't receive holiday or sick pay. They risk isolation through lack of connection with others, and may lack time or money to keep their skills current. Many provide services to organisations that might once have employed them. The social and economic cost of the savings those organisations achieve from re-structuring to reduce headcount, manage the bottom line, and so enhance executive bonuses, are being effectively borne by some of the lowest paid in our societies.

If organisations are to be truly responsible, strategic decisions should not only be based on increasing annual shareholder returns but take into account the wider and longer-term consequences for communities and society as a whole. For example, redundancies can lead to mental and physical illness, sometimes across whole communities, and it is then up to individuals, families, communities or the government to pick up the pieces as health and social care costs are increased and tax revenues decline.

As we explore in the chapter on Economics, there are growing calls for wellbeing to be included alongside traditional economic metrics. A drive to broader corporate accounting for wellbeing should also become a reality.

The psychological principles at work

The psychological principles in the Introduction provide a firm basis to shape good work, good workplaces, and develop individual, manager and leadership capabilities for the future. They are factors that make a difference to people both feeling good and functioning well, and help sustain and improve organisation performance, but they are often not regarded as high priority. Often they translate into simple behaviours that require awareness and conscious intent, yet cost very little to implement.

These principles not only apply to employees, but also to people within the wider eco-systems of organisations such as contractors, suppliers, and customers, and could even positively influence products and services. They are important too for the self-employed, to ensure they are able to sustain both their performance and wellbeing.

1. Feeling connected to others
Feeling connected and cared about applies at work as well as at home. It is often said that employees join because of the organisation but leave because of the people. The thousands of momentary daily interactions we have at work, not just in formal meetings, can convey respect, care, belonging, and give people a voice – or not. These seemingly inconsequential moments may be regarded

as soft or secondary, yet if positive can contribute to sustained performance and higher employee engagement.

Organisational psychologist Jane Dutton studied these 'brief high quality connections' in workplaces, and found that such no-cost moments over time boosted psychological and physical wellbeing. They also benefitted individual, team, and organisation performance, through enhanced trust, greater co-operation, more creativity, and higher loyalty of employees, customers and suppliers.[14]

Our observable micro-behaviours are the demonstration of how respectful, inclusive, and supportive we are. For example, respect is signalled by giving another person our full attention rather than having our eyes and mind also on our devices. It means being aware of our tone of voice and body posture; and whether the language we use shows due regard or is perfunctory – not just face-to-face but in emails and messaging too. Taking an interest in a colleague's life outside work, celebrating personal events as well as successes, noticing what others have done, and expressing gratitude all matter. Support might include lending a hand, sharing potentially useful information, speaking positively about others, offering emotional care, or cutting someone some slack when they are having difficulty.[14]

Mindfulness practice can underpin more positive interactions at work. US research with 57 senior business leaders found that mindfulness training helped develop greater collaboration and the ability to lead in complex situations. Those who practised at least 10 minutes a day showed greater improvement than others.[15]

Reflection:

As a colleague, leader, or manager, what actions might you take to make interactions at work more positive, engaging and energising?

---

2. Autonomy and the importance of managers

The extent to which what we do in work and how we do it is freely chosen, aligned with our own values, and what we are interested in and good at, influences how likely we are to be motivated and our wellbeing.[16] In a now classic study of UK civil servants, Michael Marmot found that whilst more senior roles might be perceived as more stressful and challenging, people in lower ranking roles were significantly more likely to experience ill-health. Across a range of workplace and lifestyle factors, perceived lack of control was the factor most impacting health. Numerous studies since have found perceived autonomy as a critical factor for both performance and wellbeing.

Vital in creating a sense of autonomy at work is the behaviour of managers and supervisors. Poor management style is one of the top contributors to stress-related sickness absence.[3,7] For example, one of the reasons for teachers leaving the profession is being micro-managed by senior leaders in schools where trust is low and accountability high.[17]

Traditional 'carrot and stick' approaches may achieve short-term performance goals, but are ultimately dis-engaging and detrimental to long-term positive outcomes for both workers, and the organisation. Managers who are 'autonomy supportive', however, enable teams to both flourish and perform well.[18] Developing these capabilities in managers is essential for sustained performance, and a key component of corporate social responsibility.

Supportive management behaviours include:

- Finding ways to involve the team in decisions, problem solving, and idea generation.
- Offering people choice in what they do, or how they do it (or both), and when choice isn't possible provide meaningful explanations why.
- Facilitating feelings of effectiveness and helping team members see how what they do matters (see below).
- Positioning negative feedback as a 'problem to be solved' together.[19]

Reflection:

Think about a manager or leader who has motivated you at work – what did they do, or say that was energising and engaging for you?

---

3. Feeling competent

People naturally want to feel competent at work and experience a sense of progress. Feeling ineffective undermines our sense of self, agency, and wellbeing. This helps explain why ensuring appropriate resources and conditions in place for employees to perform their work is more effective than simply reducing demands. Work can also be a source of continued learning, which can be both personally satisfying, and enabling us to adapt to changing needs.

A range of approaches are emerging from positive psychology that support a sense of competence and facilitate learning, as well as enhancing positive emotional experiences (see below). These include identifying and nurturing strengths and cultivating growth mindsets.

Strengths are our individual *"pre-existing capacities for particular ways of behaving, thinking, or feeling that are authentic, and energising"*.[20] Studies have shown that we are most likely to perform well and learn readily when using our strengths. We can, of course, learn to perform well in many ways but if these aren't energising to us, performance is hard to sustain. Evidence suggests that a strengths focus in the workplace can lead to reduced employee turnover, higher productivity and sales, and higher profitability.[21]

Giving and receiving regular strengths-based feedback to colleagues builds a sense of competence. Rather than ignoring weaknesses, this recognises that everyone has both strengths and weaknesses, and provides a way of addressing these constructively. Indeed, under-performance can be due to a job/task/project not utilising what we do best, or the reverse, using our strengths inappropriately. Some organisations or teams re-distribute tasks or roles based on identified strengths. Reviewing the distribution of strengths within a team also helps identify individual and collective gaps and strategies to mitigate these, such as recruitment and training.

As organisations need to innovate and adapt, the ability to try new approaches and learn from mistakes is crucial. The concept of growth mindsets originated from research in education by Carol Dweck. She found that, whilst individuals vary in their natural capabilities, how we think about our struggles and failures impacts how much we are willing to try, and consequently how much we learn. If we have a 'growth mindset' we see failure as an inevitable part of the process and are more likely to experiment, persist, and learn. Whereas if we feel we struggle because we lack sufficient capability in a particular area (i.e. a 'fixed mindset'), we either don't try in the first place, or give up sooner.

This is now being applied in organisations. For example, it was introduced to Microsoft by CEO Satya Nadella, and is credited with helping to triple the value of the organisation. Nadella is quoted as saying *"It's not about how much we know, but how much we learn"* and role-modelled this to employees across the global corporation by putting out monthly videos sharing his own learning.

Reflections:

What are your strengths? How do you use these in your work and everyday activities? Are there any you could use more?

What's something you struggled with at work, but persevered and learned from?

As a leader or manager:

- *What are the strengths of your team and its individual members?*
- *How might you structure opportunities for people to use their strengths more?*
- *How do you support your team to learn from failures.*

---

4. Emotionally positive work environments

A growing body of research shows that regular experience of pleasant emotions at work facilitates wellbeing and stress resilience for workers, and leads to better organisational outcomes, including enhanced creativity, teamwork, customer satisfaction, and job performance.

Studies by Nicholas Christakis and James Fowler, amongst others, show that mood states ripple out across social groups, suggesting that everyone has a role to play in cultivating a positive climate.[2]

This doesn't mean putting on a smile when we are feeling the opposite, but being aware of our moods and their potential to affect those around us, and building skills to manage our emotions well. It also means noticing and acknowledging how others are feeling.

Some workplaces now put much thought and effort into creating upbeat physical environments and providing benefits such as free food, yoga, and mindfulness sessions at lunchtimes, together with a calendar of optional social events. But investing in a positive emotional culture needs to go beyond these more tangible benefits. Positive psychology research has shown that ways to enhance our experience of positive emotions can be learned. For example, spending time at the end of each working day reflecting on what has gone well has been shown to help employees detach from work, and report fewer physical and mental symptoms.[22]

As well as cultivating positive emotions in the workplace, creating environments where people feel safe to share more difficult feelings, ideas, and concerns is also a key to team performance and innovation.[23] Google's research into effective teams found a sense of 'psychological safety' to be the number one factor in high performance. In such environments, employees can take some risks; flag issues and failures early; and 'out there' ideas aren't ridiculed or suppressed (indeed these may lead to the next big thing!).[23]

Being able to effectively express and manage uncomfortable emotions such as anger, worry, shame, or fear is conducive to higher performance and wellbeing. Being aware of our feelings, and the thoughts and beliefs that underpin them, enables us to respond constructively rather than reacting impulsively. We also need awareness of how others are feeling. All employees can benefit from developing such skills in emotional intelligence and these are essential for managers and leaders to foster psychologically safe and healthy working environments.

5. Meaning at work

Definitions of meaning at work vary, but there are two common themes. The first is that the individual worker sees their effort making some form of meaningful contribution, whether inside the organisation, or for the greater good, or both. The second is the subjective sense that what they do has personal significance or purpose, and is broadly aligned with what is meaningful for them more widely in their life.[24]

The type of work does not necessarily dictate whether we see our work as meaningful. Some senior leaders of global firms, having achieved career success, find that what they do lacks meaning, whereas cleaners in schools or hospitals can see their work as making a vital contribution to healthy and healing environments. The COVID-19 crisis brought greater recognition of the important contribution that these more humble roles make.

The importance of having meaningful work has long been recognised, deriving from studies of the relationship between unemployment and suicide following the industrial revolution. More recently, meaningful work has been associated with a wide range of benefits, including: higher individual wellbeing, more positive emotions, less anxiety and depression, and seems to also contribute to quality of life outside of work. It is also associated with higher engagement, greater commitment to the organisation, higher perseverance, lower hostility, better teamwork, and more frequent organisational citizenship behaviours (helpful behaviours beyond role requirements).[24]

Finding meaning in work is by definition personal, but organisations can make a difference. For example, they can enable people to apply their strengths and do work that is intrinsically engaging; they can support volunteering (whether those opportunities are provided by the organisation or not); and promote a sense of autonomy and trust. Leaders and managers are central to this. If they are seen as authentic, ethical, have energy and passion, articulate a clear vision, help people see how their work matters and is appreciated, they are likely to facilitate their team members experiencing meaning.

The way leaders respond in difficult or crisis situations can have a significant impact on the sense of meaning that employees experience. For example, in the United Kingdom, when a large outsource provider collapsed overnight, making the workforce instantly redundant, the CEO of a UK financial organisation to whom 100s of contractors were supplied took the instant decision to make them all in-house employees, demonstrating the importance of doing the right thing in the wider world. This gave the wider organisation an immense shared pride that their organisation cared for its wider community of workers, and put this before pure financial considerations.

Meaningful work is so important to workers that surveys suggest that a significant number of employees would take a pay cut to have it. Another study found that workers in the United States said they'd be willing to forego 23% of their entire future lifetime earnings in order to have a job that was always meaningful.[25] The younger generation of workers especially seem to look for work to provide meaning as well as money. They want the organisations to which they give their time, efforts, and energy to make a difference in the world, such as commitments to taking action on climate change, or improving people's lives. Michael Steger, an expert on the psychology of meaning, suggests that as the physical and virtual mobility of the workforce increases, competitive financial rewards will not be enough, and organisations will need to provide more profound reasons for its employees to stay.[25]

Increasingly, organisations are recognising the need to have purpose in the world beyond, or alongside profit. One of the best examples is the global giant, Unilever, which is actively demonstrating the role corporates can play in creating a sustainable world – both for the planet and for people, and in driving a new form of capitalism. CEO Alan Jope says that *"Purpose is the bridge between the responsibilities of a business and the trust of its stakeholders (including employees)"*. He believes that *"companies with purpose last, brands with purpose grow and people with purpose thrive"*. As part of this initiative, they've invested in programs to help employees find their purpose and many brand divisions have established ground-breaking, global social responsibility programs.

People management processes

The principles outlined above have important implications for the many people management processes in organisations, such as: job design; performance management; recognition and benefits; communication; selection; career progression; and training and development. There isn't space here to examine all of these, so we highlight below, one of the most central – pay and performance.

A growing body of research has explored the role of pay, bonuses, and other forms of recognition on motivation and performance. The more pay is contingent on individual performance, the greater the likelihood of it negatively impacting engagement, wellbeing, collaboration, and organisation performance in the longer-term. There is an oft-quoted saying in organisations that 'what gets measured gets done'. Performance-contingent rewards focus workers' attention on key performance indicators, often to the detriment of behaviours and actions that build a positive work culture. This increases the likelihood of employees 'gaming the system' to achieve personal targets rather than acting in the best interests of the organisation and those it serves. For example, an airport wanted to reduce customer waiting time at the baggage carousel, so introduced an incentive scheme based on the shortest times between the plane landing and the first bags arriving in the baggage hall. It wasn't long before the baggage handlers figured out who was the fastest runner and had them run with two bags to the carousel, without the overall passenger wait time being improved. Instead of focusing on how they could contribute to great customer experience and organisation performance, their attention had been diverted to maximising their pay.

Misguided performance targets impact 'helping' professions too. For example, in teaching, focusing on standard test scores can encourage 'teaching to the test' and exclusion of the less able, at the cost of a more rounded educational goals and individual student progress (see the Education chapter).

Richard Ryan and Edward Deci[18] advise strong caution at the top of organisations too, where senior executive reward is commonly linked to external indicators such as increases in company stock price. This can fuel motivation to *"take the shortest route to the end, often with considerable collateral damage"*, citing Enron as a notable example.

Pay needs to be perceived as liveable, fair, and equitable. Perceptions of unfairness risk undermining job satisfaction, commitment, and loyalty to the organisation,[18] and have the potential to undermine collaborative relationships. Whilst performance-based pay and bonus systems usually purport to be fair, this does not always play out in practice. Not surprisingly, it is employees who do well under such schemes who are more likely to perceive these as fair. Gender and other pay gaps, and large differentials between the pay of the most senior executives and the lowest paid workers, are also important sources of actual and perceived unfairness.

As jobs become more complex, and their context ambiguous or rapidly changing, ensuring that performance and reward systems support autonomy, innovation, and collaboration, rather than be directed towards narrow, individual targets is likely to become essential. Employees will need to be trusted to make good judgements about how outcomes are achieved, and be supported to work together. This might include replacing individual performance bonuses with collective ones, or eliminating them completely, and focusing on longer-term outcomes rather than short-term measures.

The science of wellbeing and the future of work

Work and workplaces have continuously evolved, but perhaps never as fast or with such uncertainty as now. New technology and globalisation have been transforming where and how work gets done, and who does it, and will continue to shape its future, creating new opportunities and roles, rendering others obsolete. This has important short and long-term consequences for individual and societal wellbeing. Integrating the science of wellbeing in shaping these changes will ensure psychological and societal sustainability.

Technology has enabled more channels of communication across the world, greater access to information, lowered market barriers for start-ups, and created the possibility of more flexible ways of working. The switch to a technology-driven workplace was accelerated by the COVID-19 pandemic. Businesses and services rapidly switched online, and those that couldn't suffered. Workers had to work remotely from home or not work at all, unless they were a key worker. All of a sudden flexible working was here and seems unlikely to go away, and the future of big, expensive central offices called into question.

This shift to remote working has been a benefit to many of those whose roles meant they are able to take advantage of working from home and had adequate space and tools to do so. For them it has reduced unpleasant, time-wasting commutes, enhanced autonomy, and enabled more time with family. All conducive to higher well-being. For others the isolation has been difficult and the intangible benefits from being physically present with others sorely missed. We have yet to see the lasting impact on wellbeing, corporate cohesiveness, and processes such as innovation and communication. The COVID-19 pandemic also highlighted the millions of jobs and workers for which this choice is not possible, potentially increasing wellbeing inequities.

Human beings are naturally driven to evolve, learn, and adapt. As the recent pandemic showed, they can do so rapidly when needed. But fast-paced and accelerating change has implications for psychological health, and the loss of work as we know it may also compromise identity, sense of meaning and of community. The boundaries between home, leisure, and work were already blurred, and the pandemic has blurred them much further. Long hours spent in virtual meetings, without built-in breaks, can be even more exhausting than days packed with in-person meetings. We need to evolve sustainable working practices for remote work, not just transfer over the old ones.

If artificial intelligence (AI) delivers what is promised, the shifts in work will be even greater, with many traditional jobs disappearing as new ones emerge. This, coupled with demographic shifts and working longer across our lifespan, means developing new skills, and re-inventing our career several times over. Governments, tech companies, and organisations more generally, will need to play an increasingly active role in helping people of all ages build the competence needed to work and thrive, not just for their employees but more expansively in their wider communities. The skills and capabilities at the core of what make us human and most enable flourishing are the likely to be the hardest to replace by technology, such as the capacity to care for and build genuine connections with others, to feel empathy and compassion, to think creatively, and make ethical decisions.

The new and growing science of wellbeing has emerged just in time. It can guide us in creating meaningful work, even when it is technology-based, and support us in developing the capabilities we'll increasingly need. If integrated in how the future of work is shaped, it can help ensure the wellbeing of the many, not only a few, for now and into the future, which ultimately serves us all.

Ideas for action

What might governments do?

Require wellbeing metrics in corporate accounts.

Ensure businesses are held to account for the societal and health impact of redundancies and re-structuring.

Implement legislation that protects gig-workers and those on zero-hours contracts.

Provide programs for the self-employed and those in small and medium enterprises (SMEs) to develop wellbeing skills, and the skills and capabilities needed for the future.

What might leaders do?

Implement measures of psychological wellbeing (not only ill health or absence) or ensure these are incorporated in existing engagement surveys.

Ask for 360 feedback on their own micro-behaviours and how these positively motivate and impact the psychological wellbeing of those you work with.

Use the psychological principles as a basis for reviewing and re-designing people management processes to ensure these positively and healthily support wellbeing and motivation.

Build the capabilities of managers and supervisors based on the principles of positive psychology and wellbeing.

What might you do?

Identify the aspects of your work that are most engaging, energising, and meaningful for you.

Know and find ways to use your strengths. Find ways to craft what you do, or how you do it. Even small changes can help.

Develop your emotional intelligence and collaboration skills.

Identify future skills in your field and seek to develop these.

Key sources

With special thanks to Bridget Grenville-Cleave, who provided helpful suggestions and feedback on this chapter.

Full references and resources are available at our website https://www.creatingtheworldwewanttolivein.org/references/work/

1 Goodwin (2008). *Lessons from past presidents.* http://www.ted.com/talks/doris_kearns_goodwin_on_learning_from_past_presidents.html.
2 Christakis & Fowler (2009). *Connected: The surprising power of our social networks and how they shape our lives.* Little, Brown Spark
3 OECD. (2018). Better Life Index – Work-Life Balance http://www.oecd-betterlifeindex.org/topics/work-life-balance/; WHR 2018 p77
4 De Neve (2018). Work and Wellbeing: A Global Perspective. In Global Happiness Council. (2018). *The Global Happiness Policy Report 2018.* Sustainable Development Solutions Network.
5 Bryson & MacKerron (2016). Are You Happy While You Work? *The Economic Journal, 127*(599), 106–125.
6 Chartered Institute of Personnel and Development. (2018). *Health & Wellbeing at Work Survey Report 2018.* CIPD.
7 *Mental Health at Work 2019 Report: Time To Take Ownership.* BITC
8 Hassard *et al.* (2014) *Calculating the cost of work-related stress and psychosocial risks. European Risk Observatory Literature Review.* Report for The European Agency for Safety and Health at Work
9 De Neve & Ward (2017) Happiness at Work. In Helliwell, Layard & Sachs (2017). *World Happiness Report 2017.* Sustainable Development Solutions Network.
10 De Neve *et al.* (2013). The Objective Benefits of Subjective Wellbeing. In Helliwell, Layard & Sachs (2013). *World Happiness Report 2013.* Sustainable Development Solutions Network.
11 Krekel, Ward & De Neve (2017). Employee Wellbeing, Productivity and Firm Performance: Evidence and Case Studies. In Global Happiness Council (2019), *Global Happiness Policy Report 2019.* Sustainable Development Solutions Network.
12 Edmans (2011). Does the stock market fully value intangibles? Employee satisfaction and equity prices. *Journal of Financial Economics, 101*(2011), 621–640.
13 Schaufeli & Taris (2014). A critical review of the job demands-resources model: Implications for improving work and health. In Bauer & Hämmig (Eds). *Bridging occupational, organizational and public health: A transdisciplinary approach* (43–68). Springer.
14 Stephens, Heaphy & Dutton (2012). High Quality Connections. In Cameron & Spreitzer (Eds.), *The Oxford Handbook of Positive Organizational Scholarship* (385–399). Oxford University Press.

15 Reitz & Chaskalson (2016). How to bring mindfulness to your company's leadership. *Harvard Business Review*, Dec 2016.

16 Slemp *et al.* (2018) Leader autonomy support in the workplace: A meta-analytic review. *Motivation and Emotion in the Workplace, 42*, 706–724.

17 Troman (2000). Teacher Stress in the Low Trust Society. *British Journal of Sociology of Education, 21*(3), 331-353

18 Ryan & Deci (2017). *Self-Determination Theory – Basic Psychological Needs in Motivation, Development and Wellness.* Guildford Press

19 Deci, Olafsen & Ryan (2017). Self-Determination Theory in Work Organizations: The State of the Science. *Annual Review of Organizational Behaviour 2017, 4,* 19–43.

20 Linley (2008). *Average to A. Realising strengths in yourself and others.* CAPP Press.

21 Asplund & Blacksmith (2012). Productivity through Strengths. In Cameron & Spreitzer (Eds.), *The Oxford Handbook of Positive Organizational Scholarship*, (353–365). Oxford University Press.

22 Bono *et al.* (2013). Building positive resources: Effects of positive events and positive reflection on work-stress and health. *Academy of Management Journal, 56*(6).

23 Edmondson (2019). *The Fearless Organisation: Creating Psychological Safety in the Workplace for Learning, Innovation and Growth.* Wiley.

24 Steger (2017). Creating Meaning and Purpose at Work. In Oades, Steger, Delle Fave & Passmore (Eds.), *The Wiley Blackwell Handbook of the Psychology of Positivity and Strengths-Based Approaches at Work.* John Wiley & Sons.

25 Achor *et al.* (2018). 9 Out of 10 People Are Willing to Earn Less Money to Do More-Meaningful Work. *Harvard Business Review,* November 06, 2018

CHAPTER 4

Ageing

Bridget Grenville-Cleave

> *"You are never too old to set a new goal, or to dream a new dream".*
> *– Les Brown*[1]

Why think about ageing?

Ageing affects everyone but not necessarily in the same way: some of us feel concerned, some give it no thought, whilst others embrace it. There are differences at a societal level too. In some countries, elderly people may be viewed as a burden whereas elsewhere they are respected, if not revered, for their wisdom and experience. We may be more aware of ageing now, due to the disproportionate risk of the COVID-19 virus to older people. In normal circumstances we're encouraged to plan financially for retirement and old age, but how do we prepare for the emotional and psychological changes that accompany getting older?

As Les Brown suggests in the opening quotation, later life can become a time of further opportunity with a renewed sense of meaning and purpose. In this chapter we explore the idea of positive ageing and the research, which supports it as well as consider how social systems can facilitate it.

Across the world, people are generally living longer. In 1950, someone aged 65 could expect to live on average another 11 years. Today it is 17 years, and the United Nations forecasts that this will increase by another 5 years by the end of the century. According to the World Health Organization[2] there will soon be more people aged over 60 than children younger than 5. Although the trend towards ever-increasing life expectancy is slowing down, especially in the United States, United Kingdom, and several European countries, it seems that we're still more likely than ever before to live to a very old age – especially if we are living in more privileged circumstances. As a result, the shape of our lives is changing. Lynda Gratton and Andrew Scott[3] argue that the traditional 'three-stage life' (education/career/retirement), common in the industrialised world, is being replaced by the 'multi-stage life' in which we move in and out of the stages multiple times. Although this gives us greater flexibility about who we are, what we do, and how we do it, making the most of our later years requires us to be better prepared both financially, and psychologically. The positive psychology research on ageing, some of which is explored in this chapter, gives us different ways of thinking about capability, happiness, health, and wealth in later life.

> Examples of the multi-stage life include artist and broadcaster Sue Kreitzman, who was originally a successful food writer before becoming an artist about 30 years ago. Now approaching her 80s, Sue continues to make waves with her art and jewellery, which she uses to promote female empowerment.
>
> Aged 96 and 200 days, Shigemi Hirata became the oldest person in the world to graduate. In 2016, he received his Bachelor of Arts degree in Art and Design, specialising in ceramics, from Kyoto University. His first career was in the navy.

Capability and ageing

Ageing well can be challenging. Our reactions get slower, we're more forgetful, and we can't move around as quickly and easily. Our physical sensations lose their edge as our sight, hearing, and sense of smell diminish. We can make adjustments but often the changes creep up, so we tend not to notice them until a problem occurs. Even then, negative stereotypes about ageing might convince us that there is nothing we can do. Philosopher Susan Neiman argues that the West is fixated on youth. We may fear that the best years of our lives are behind us, but if growing older were celebrated, the best years might be ahead. We can't turn the clock back on our chronological age, but our physiological age is not set in stone. And if we work at it, we can even continue to build physical strength, muscle, and stamina into our 90s.

After a career in sales, 85 year old track and field athlete Flo Meiler has accumulated over 700 medals, and broken numerous world records for pole vaulting. She only started competing in athletic events at the age of 60.

Some researchers argue that age-related decline in functioning is not as severe as we might think, nor do losses necessarily outweigh the gains.[4] Our ability to process information starts to decline in our early 20s, but continues at roughly the same rate throughout our lives. We compensate by increasingly turning to our stores of knowledge and experience. As long as we don't have a condition like dementia, getting older should not stop us learning new things, nor significantly affect our ability to think. Some types of memory tend to stay stable, such as remembering how to ride a bicycle, or use a keyboard. Importantly, physical activity has a beneficial effect on thinking skills. According to Chandra Mehrotra and Lisa Wagner, *"Exercise the body, and the mind benefits"*.[5] Continuing to keep the mind active also helps – you either 'use it or lose it'.

There may even be some gains. Studies suggest that many older people have better vocabulary and communication skills, enhanced cultural awareness, and better emotion regulation than the young. They also tend to be better at finding solutions in situations which are emotionally charged.[6] Long life experience may enhance the ability to put things in perspective, and this, coupled with emotional balance, is what we often refer to as 'wisdom'.

Participating in valued leisure activities is linked to successful ageing.[7] These include putting time and effort into maintaining good social relationships, engaging in hobbies and crafts, and continuing to learn new things. Doing activities that we see as meaningful in our spare time prior to retirement can help us have a higher level of wellbeing as we get older.

Happiness and ageing
Whilst for the average person happiness dips from childhood until we reach midlife, it then rises again, and only starts to tail off in very old age.[8] As we pass midlife, we begin to reprioritise what is important, putting more emphasis on relationships and meaning.[9]

As well as exploring the experience of happiness across the lifespan, researchers have also studied whether happier people live longer, concluding that the link works both ways. Not only are older people happier than we might expect but people who are happier tend to live longer. In a study of nearly 10,000 older men and women, who were followed up for ten years, higher wellbeing was associated with longer life expectancy as well as a greater proportion of these later years spent in good health, free from chronic disease or disability.[10]

Population health is usually measured using 'Healthy Life Years'. Bearing in mind the experience of happiness changes as we age, how would our lives and society generally be further improved if, as has been suggested by the New Economics Foundation, we routinely measured 'Happy Life Years' as well?

Health, wealth and longevity

The opportunities that ageing brings depend on health and income as well as individual and social attitudes. Ill-health and poverty make it more difficult to realise the benefits from living longer, and unsurprisingly there are vast differences across the world. Across and even within countries there is considerable variation in life expectancy. For instance, the life expectancy of the most deprived males in Glasgow (2008–2010) was 67.5 years, yet the least deprived males in the same city lived almost 14 years longer, with a life expectancy of 81.2 years.[11] Across the world financial inequality affects older people as much as the rest of the population – a small proportion are incredibly wealthy, and a much larger number relatively poor (see chapters on Society and Economics).

Social challenges in ageing well

Retirement

Typically, we retire somewhere between our mid 50s and late 60s. Many countries, however, are in the process of raising their state pension age to combat the financial pressure of having fewer younger workers to support the health, social care, and pension needs of their ageing populations. In 2019 the Centre for Social Justice recommended that the UK accelerates increasing the state pension age to 70 by 2028, and to 75 by 2035. But this is not a straightforward solution. Organisations may not welcome employing older workers, as their additional expertise makes them more expensive. Health and social factors, such as caring responsibilities, also mean that people may not have the same ability, or capacity to continue working. Simple lack of stamina and reduced energy can also affect whether people want to, or are able to, continue working. Recent research suggests that minimising physically demanding work, and offering greater autonomy through more flexible working hours could help.[12] Although many derive great satisfaction and meaning from working, being prevented from retiring takes away choice and agency, and can therefore reduce wellbeing. Raising the state pension age may not be the silver bullet that policymakers anticipate.

Although we may look forward to life without the demands of paid work, it may be difficult to adjust to a lower income and having less structure to our lives. We need to be well prepared. Financial planning, whilst important, isn't enough. Thinking about ageing as a lifelong process, rather than something which only occurs post-retirement, might help us plan pro-actively rather than reactively.

Loneliness

It is generally believed that older people suffer most from loneliness and are getting more lonely. Declining physical health can make it difficult to get out, and relationships are lost through bereavement. Studies suggest that loneliness in older people has not increased over the past two decades.[13] But loneliness is a problem we cannot ignore; the social distancing measures implemented in many countries during the COVID-19 pandemic brought loneliness to the top of the mental health agenda. Even so, it seemed to affect younger people more than older people.

Researchers suggest that the risk to health from a lack of social relationships is greater than the risk from obesity and smoking, and lonely people are more likely to die prematurely.[14] To flourish both physically and mentally in older age we need to see and interact with other people. In the UK, the Campaign to End Loneliness is encouraging people of all ages to put down their phones and take the initiative to talk briefly to others, even strangers. It takes a matter of seconds to make a connection with another person that makes both people feel good. These micro-moments of connection can make all the difference to our wellbeing.

> **Reflections:**
>
> *Knowing that even small connections help boost wellbeing, and combat loneliness:*
>
> - *How can you make a friendly connection with older people in your community by perhaps starting a simple conversation at a bus stop, in a queue, or in a waiting room? The weather, the wait, or the state of the service are usually safe options.*
> - *How might you respond if an older person began such a conversation with you? Would you welcome the connection?*

Social attitudes

Ageing is frequently perceived as a process of decline rather than a stage of life that can have benefits. Anthropologist Neil Thin points out that even saying *"I don't feel old"* implies that 'feeling old' is a bad thing.

Negative stereotypes can lead to discrimination, which impacts on health and wellbeing, especially in high income countries where we find the lowest levels of respect. A study of over 7700 people aged over 50 suggested that those who believe they had been discriminated against because of their age had a higher incidence of illness including coronary heart disease, stroke, diabetes, and depressive symptoms.[15]

Stereotypes about the elderly are not uniformly negative. In some societies, older people attain leadership positions where their wisdom and emotional stability are valued by others in the community who seek their advice, especially in resolving conflict. In Native American society the term 'elder' refers to a leadership position acquired through experience and contribution to the community, rather than age. In 2007, recognising the potential of this idea, businessman Richard Branson and musician Peter Gabriel persuaded Nelson Mandela to found 'The Elders', a group of independent global leaders working together to promote world peace.

There are many examples of elderly people in our communities making a positive difference in the world.

Zimbabwean psychiatrist Dixon Chibanda and colleagues realised that the elderly were an untapped community resource that could be used to support people struggling with mental health difficulties such as depression. They set up 'The Friendship Bench' where grandmothers, who have been given training, deliver free basic talking therapy to those in need. In 2017, the Friendship Bench helped over 30,000 people. The approach has been shown to be more effective in some instances than standard treatment.[16]

Reflection:

What difference would it make if there were a group of Elders in your community available for advice and support?

Positive ageing

Having explored some of the research on ageing and the common challenges associated with getting older, how might we do things differently? How might we make our later life as good as it can possibly be?

Preparing for new priorities

We all know, or know of, people who are ageing well, in that they are still active, engaged, and continue to have a positive approach to life. What has made a difference for them?

Sarah Raposo and Laura Carstensen[17] found that when people vividly envision their distant future, they are more motivated to adopt healthy behaviours, and thus age better. As outlined in the Introduction, when we identify and focus on what's working, other benefits often follow. Figure 3 shows how a positive approach towards ageing might influence what actually happens.

Inevitably things change as we age, and this includes our priorities. Getting qualifications and a good job is often a major focus for young adults, but as we pass midlife we may be more interested in

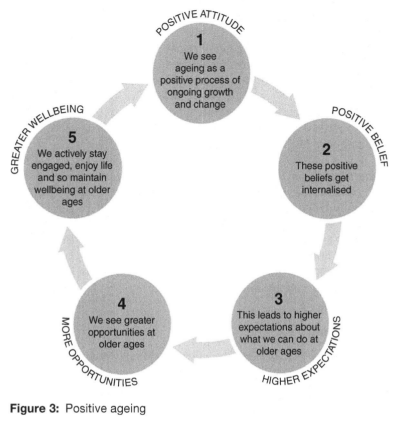

Figure 3: Positive ageing

whether what we do every day has meaning and purpose. Caring for our relationships may become more important than putting in long hours at work, and we may begin to be more appreciative of the everyday things in life.

Reflection:

Who do you look up to as a role model for ageing well? What is it about them that you admire?

The older worker

Employment rates for older people vary significantly from country to country. The management consultancy PwC's 2018 Golden Age Index, which measures workforce participation in the OECD, shows that Iceland employs 84% of 55–64 year olds, followed by New Zealand (78%) and Sweden (76%). The United States is in 9th place and United Kingdom well below, in 21st place. The lowest ranked countries are Turkey (34%), Greece (38%), and Luxembourg (40%).

Occupational psychologist Nancy Doyle suggests replacing the traditional career ladder with a career 'pyramid', so that the skills and knowledge gained throughout our working lives can still be accessed as we age, but in different, less demanding ways. For instance, teachers might become exam-markers and A&E nurses might become community nurses. This also prevents the sudden, potentially stressful jolt from working full-time to not working at all, with all the adaptation this demands.

Reflections:

However old you are now, how might you plan for your later years to maximise your wellbeing?

How might you help others to age well?

Intergenerational care

Intergenerational care, such as combining care for the elderly with nursery schools, has been around for decades in Japan and the United States, yet is relatively new elsewhere. Studies across the world[18] suggest that older and younger people doing activities together such as reading, crafting, and gardening, positively changes the way children see and talk about their elders, and increases self-reported health and wellbeing for the elderly. The 'Grandfriends' program involves elderly people and children working in pairs for 45 minutes per week for 12 weeks, in activities such as discussions, crafts, and games. In an Australian evaluation, a group of forty people with an average age of 91, 80% of whom were suffering from cognitive impairment, were randomly assigned to Grandfriends or a control group. Those involved in Grandfriends reported increased engagement and enjoyment.

Reflections:

How many of your friends are much older or younger than you?

How much interest do you take in the stories, and life experience of those outside your age group?

What clubs or projects help connect people across the generations where you live?

With design in mind

Good design can facilitate a full and engaged life while bad or thoughtless design can inhibit it. This is as true for computer apps as it is for kitchen appliances, or buildings. In the past few decades, designers have been considering how to create products and services that empathically address wellbeing, including the needs and lived experiences of the elderly, and those with disability, but there is still a long way to go. This includes providing free or cheap public transport; having elevators and escalators as an alternative to steps; installing hazard-free surfaces; enlarging the font size on newspapers and documents, signs and packaging; ensuring user-friendly controls on all sorts of technology from TV remotes to iPads; making sure that packages can be opened easily, and installing good lighting everywhere. Innovations with the elderly in mind can also meet the needs of many other groups – inclusive design is good design.

Some innovative designs are aimed at specific populations. For example, the baby seal therapeutic robot PARO can support dementia care by providing some of the benefits of animal therapy. The robot responds as if it is alive, interacting with movement and sound. Similarly, based on the research of Johan Hoorn and his team at the Vrije University, Amsterdam, the emotionally-intelligent humanoid 'care-bot', Alice, was designed to help support vulnerable and lonely elders. Given the importance of connecting as an enabler of wellbeing, however, this raises questions about how we tackle social isolation, and whether new technologies are an ethical answer.

The bigger picture

Ageing well requires more than individual attitudes and capabilities. It requires action from governments, institutions, and organisations. From 1985 to 1996, the Research Network on an Aging Society studied the factors which contribute to continued good physical and mental functioning. They found that a successfully ageing society is one which maintains social connectedness within and between generations (cohesion); facilitates engagement through work and volunteering (productivity); and is healthy, equitable and secure, both financially and physically. This early work led to the creation of the Hartford Aging Index which uses these five factors to measure how successfully different countries are adapting to societal ageing.

Norway, Sweden, and the United States are most successful on all five factors overall, with Ireland being top for cohesion, United States top for productivity, Japan for health, Norway for equity, and Spain for security. Only Denmark, Sweden, Spain, Japan, and the Netherlands appear in the top 3 more than once. No single country appears in the top 3 for all five measures. Using the best performers as a role model, other countries could identify potential actions to address the gaps in their own policies. For example, what could we learn about the strong cohesion in Ireland which could be applied or adapted in other countries?

In the UK, the Centre for Ageing Better makes five overall recommendations to government to improve the lives of older people: change building regulations to make housing more accessible; promote health in later life; create flexible workplaces; create age-friendly communities and cities, for example by improving transport, and promote an age-friendly culture, for example by using more positive language about later life.

The World Health Organization's project to make cities and communities more age-friendly is congruent with the positive psychology principles covered in Chapter 1. The project commits to support older people so that they can:

- Build and maintain relationships (Connecting to others).
- Meet basic needs themselves (Feeling competent).
- Keep learning and make their own decisions (Autonomy).

- Be mobile (Autonomy).
- Keep contributing to society (Meaning).

Reflections:

Every government, city, and community can become more age-friendly: what is happening where you live?

What changes would you like to see for yourself, and older members of the community and how might you lobby for these?

People who are able to make their own decisions tend to be happier and this is just one example of supporting successful ageing.

The New Brighton Co-Housing in Santa Cruz, California, is designed, owned, and managed by residents themselves. Here people of all ages live independently in their own homes, but share and run a common house and courtyard, used for meeting, eating together, playing, and housing guests. It's described as a more caring, active, and fun way to live, as well as being more efficient, as resources such as washing machines, and tools, meals, and even stories and problems, are shared.

This initiative differs significantly from public and private residential homes for the elderly found in many developed countries, which are generally owned and managed by non-residents. In these, residents rarely make decisions themselves: the management of the home and grounds, including activities, cleaning, and meals are all organised for them.

Going forward

Although many of us are living much longer in good health, we still need an all-encompassing approach to promote wellbeing in later life.

Both governments and individuals need to plan long-term solutions with creativity and empathy alongside financial considerations. As we can see from the few examples in this chapter, there are many ways to maximise the chance of fulfilment and flourishing as we grow older though much depends on individual and societal perceptions, and political will.

Ideas for action

What might governments do?

Use the Hartford Aging Index as a benchmark to improve the lives of older people.

Give business incentives to have more flexible employment practices of benefit to both older and younger workers.

Develop care homes that give older people both agency and dignity.

Offer free or cheaper public transport to facilitate getting out.

Fund free or cheaper recreational, educational, sport, and physical activities.

What might communities do?

Make outdoor/recreational areas safe, accessible, and well-lit.

Pilot intergenerational projects and facilities: for example, invite elderly people to the 'Parents and Toddlers' group.

Promote positive ageing role models, for example in the local newsletter or town/village website.

Run an annual event for new retirees in the community to learn about community resources and opportunities.

What might you do?

Have a plan to maintain and build your psychological well-being in old age, as well as a financial plan.

Think about how you might adapt your career and professional skills as you age.

Learn something new, preferably in the company of others.

Take the opportunity to connect with others of all ages as you go about your daily life. It need only take a minute!

Key sources

With special thanks to Vanessa King, who provided helpful suggestions and feedback on this chapter.

Full references and resources are available at our website https://www.creatingtheworldwewanttolivein.org/references/ageing/

1 Brown (1992). *Live your dreams.* Avon Books.
2 https://www.who.int/news-room/fact-sheets/detail/ageing-and-health
3 Gratton & Scott (2016). *The 100 -Year life: Living and working in an age of longevity.* Bloomsbury.
4 Bussolo, Koettl & Sinnott (2015). *Golden aging: Prospects for healthy, active, and prosperous aging in Europe and Central Asia.* The World Bank.
5 Mehrotra & Wagner (2009). *Aging and diversity: An active learning experience.* (2nd Edn, p.88). Routledge.
6 Beard *et al.* (2012). *Global population ageing: peril or promise?* (No. 8912). Program on the Global Demography of Aging. World Economic Forum.
7 Hutchinson & Nimrod (2012). Leisure as a resource for successful aging by older adults with chronic health conditions. *The International Journal of Aging and Human Development, 74*(1), 41–6
8 Clark & Oswald (2006). *The curved relationship between subjective well-being and age.* Paris-Jourdan Sciences Economiques.
9 Charles & Carstensen (2010). Social and emotional ageing. *Annual Review of Psychology, 61*(1), 383–409.
10 Zaninotto & Steptoe. (2019). Association Between Subjective Well-being and Living Longer Without Disability or Illness. *JAMA network open, 2*(7), e196870–e196870.
11 https://www.understandingglasgow.com/indicators/health/comparisons/within_glasgow/males_deprivation
12 Cebulla *et al.* (2019). Work-Life imbalance in extended working lives: Domestic divisions of labour and partners' perceptions of job pressures of non-retiring older workers. *Sozialer Fortschritt, 68*(4), 289–311.
13 Dahlberg, Agahi & Lennartsson (2018). Lonelier than ever? Loneliness of older people over two decades. *Archives of Gerontology and Geriatrics, 75,* 96–103.
14 Holt-Lunstad, Smith & Layton (2010). Social relation-ships and mortality risk: a meta-analytic review. *PLoS Medicine, 7*(7), e1000316.
15 Jackson, Hackett & Steptoe (2019). Associations between age discrimination and health and wellbeing: cross-sectional and prospective analysis of the English longitudinal study of ageing. *The Lancet Public Health, 4*(4), e200–e208.
16 https://www.friendshipbenchzimbabwe.org/lay-health-workers
17 Raposo & Carstensen (2018). Can envisioning your future improve your health? *Innovation in Aging, 2* (Suppl 1), 907.
18 Gualano *et al.* (2018). The impact of intergenerational programs on children and older adults: A review. *International Psychogeriatrics, 30*(4), 451–468

The foundations of everyday flourishing

CHAPTER 5

Relationships

Sue Roffey

> *"Loving people live in a loving world. Hostile people live in a hostile world. Same world". – Wayne Dyer*[1]

Why are positive relationships so important for wellbeing?

At all levels, from families to organisations, communities, and nations, it is the quality of our relationships with each other, and the positivity in those connections, that make the most difference for wellbeing. This includes how we have been cared for in infancy, and childhood, how we perceive and position each other, how we communicate, and ways we might cooperate together for the common good.

Unless we are in basic survival mode – and sometimes even then, as widely demonstrated by experiences of the COVID-19 pandemic – it is our relationships that are the crux of our happiness or misery, from how we interact with those closest to us to how we see, and treat each other in the wider world. Relationships, more than anything else, are what matters in creating a world in which everyone can thrive. As Dyer neatly puts it in the quote above, we either see others primarily as a threat, or as a potential ally, and that makes all the difference.

Whereas physical and financial capital counts the material resources at our disposal, and human capital is the knowledge and skills we have, social capital can be defined as the quality of relationships both between people (bonding social capital) and between groups of people (bridging social capital). High social capital not only enables individuals, and organisations to flourish but also provides reliable alliance and support when times are tough.

For over eighty years, the Harvard study of Adult Development[2] has looked at what makes life worth living, initially just with professional men but then widening the data to include women, and those from less privileged backgrounds. Their findings are unequivocal:

> "*Close relationships, more than money or fame, are what keep people happy throughout their lives. Those ties protect people from life's discontents, help to delay mental and physical decline, and are better predictors of long and happy lives than social class, IQ, or even genes*".[3]

The people in our lives can make the good times better by sharing and celebrating with us, and make the bad times more bearable by listening and supporting. As relationships are critical to well-being, it is surprising that we do not pay more attention to what enables people to get on well together, and how to resolve differences when conflict arises. Our society promotes a range of 'literacies', but needs to be equally, if not more, attuned to the emotional literacy that underpins healthy relationships. Unless young people are fortunate enough to be in a family where positive relationships are modelled and discussed, or in a school where social and emotional learning is a regular part of the curriculum, they may not learn the attitudes and skills that enable them to establish and maintain positive connection. What does this mean for how they feel about themselves and the world around them? We need to develop emotional literacy at all levels of society.

Advertisers give out a continual, if subliminal, message that in order to feel good about ourselves we need certain products and deserve luxuries. The internal dialogue risks becoming "what does this mean for *me?*" rather than "what does this mean for *us?*" This way of thinking can damage any relationship.

This chapter is not just about how we get on with others at home, and in our families, it is also about how well we relate to those in our neighbourhoods, community, work, in our country, and even those we have never met. What happens at one level impacts on how we interact with others, and how we talk and think about other people. If we see the world in terms of 'us and them' we may not appreciate what we have in common, nor our responsibility towards each other. In the COVID-19 pandemic it was notable that in some communities the overall response was to support the mantra to stay at home and save lives, whereas others were more focused on their own freedoms, regardless of the danger to others of spreading the disease. Systems, however, are not static – change over time is not only possible, it is inevitable.

The quality of relationships impacts on our wellbeing in every sphere of life. Companies and institutions that actively build harmonious relationships not only improve the wellbeing of everyone but are often more successful than those where employees are embattled, stressed, and untrusting.[4] Schools where the quality of relationships is part of policy and practice have better outcomes for both staff and students.[5]

Having relationships that give us reliable alliance, acceptance, and genuine affection is not soft or insignificant, it is the foundation for just about everything else.

Reflection:

Thinking about the best relationships you have experienced, what did these make you feel about yourself, and the other people involved?

There is an extensive literature on relationships, so this brief chapter only provides headlines in a highly complex area of study. How we think and feel about ourselves as individuals determines how we think and feel about other people, so this is our starting point.

A positive sense of self

Our sense of self is the primary foundation for relationships with others. It informs what we need in our relationships, and whether we tend to see others as a threat, or an ally. It determines whether we are able to be interested in the lives and welfare of others, or relate to them only in terms of our own needs. This applies to close relationships, interactions with colleagues, and how we position those in the wider community. During the COVID-19 pandemic, people often developed new or stronger relationships in their neigh-bourhoods, and many volunteered to help others. This experience is likely to have changed not only how they perceive and connect with others, but also given them a more positive sense of self.

The two basic interrelated components are how we think about our-selves (self-concept), and how we feel about ourselves (self-esteem). There is also our ideal self – who we would like to become, and self-respect – the part of our self-concept that evaluates the extent to which we see ourselves as a good person. Those with a positive sense of self usually have values that enable them to behave with integrity, not being unduly swayed by what others say nor doing what is simply expedient. They have no need to tell others how wonderful they are.

Although childhood experiences impact significantly on how we think and feel about ourselves, there are things we can do to develop or maintain a healthy sense of self and self-acceptance. The positive psychology principles of awareness and attention, consid-ered choices, and compassion underpin the suggestions below.

- Your inner dialogue determines how you think about yourself and other people. Some of these thoughts will be negative and unhelpful – can you engage with more positive thoughts, ones that are less judgmental, forgiving, and more hopeful?
- Optimistic thinking may mean re-positioning issues, focusing less on problems and more on identifying where you want to go, and the first step in that direction.[6] When you expect things to go well, they are more likely to – and the opposite is also true. Writing down three things you are grateful for every day helps you notice what is going well, and can change your outlook.[7]
- Being kind to yourself includes not blaming yourself for every-thing that goes wrong. Although you might have some respon-sibility, this will invariably be shared with circumstance, chance, and other people. Forgiving yourself is helped by appreciating that everyone makes mistakes, and no one is perfect.
- Mindfulness is being fully in the present moment, aware of feel-ings, thoughts, sensations, and the environment, without judg-ment. This allows you to put aside past and future anxieties, and relieves stress. It is both a natural disposition and a learned skill. There is good evidence for the benefits, especially against anxiety and depression.[8]

- It is easy to use up valuable emotional energy on things that won't matter much tomorrow or even next week. Getting things into perspective where possible enables you to 'not sweat the small stuff'.
- A focus on strengths rather than deficits can make you feel better about yourself, as well as about others – not just strengths that are demonstrable today, but those in development. Beyond academic, sporting, or creative abilities, these include strengths of character, such as patience, determination, warmth, and humour.
- Having meaning in your life is a significant aspect of wellbeing: doing things that inspire and energise you, whether that is supporting a team, being with family, creating art, being an activist, or learning something new. You will like yourself more if you spend time in purposeful activity.
- Do those around you increase or drain your energy? Supportive people are warm, friendly, show interest in what is important to you, listen well and help you be the best of yourself, even if at times this means being a 'critical friend'. When you nurture these relationships with reciprocity, they form the backbone of your wellbeing.
- Regular exercise, good nutrition, enough sleep and time to relax help to provide physical and mental resilience. If you feel well physically you have more resources to draw on. For some this is not easily achievable – see the Health and Society chapters for more information.

People struggling with negative life experiences, and challenging mental health issues may need therapy, or other support to be able to do some of the things suggested above, and many cannot afford this, but some ideas cost nothing, or very little, and are worth a try if they help you to think well of yourself.

Reflections:

When do you feel most contented, calm, or energised? What is happening then?

What enables you to be your best self? When have you been proud of who you are?

Positioning others

How we see others is critical to both self-acceptance and the health of our relationships. If we are always comparing ourselves to others, we are likely to focus on unattainable 'perfection', rather than valuing who we are. We may also experience emotions of envy, injustice, and anger for not having what others have. Anger may be useful when it drives positive action, but at an individual level it can undermine wellbeing. We may also see others primarily as competitors, and aim to get the better of them – perhaps understandable where there are scarce resources, but less so where there is enough for all.

Overall the world is safer than it has ever been, but when the media focus primarily on reporting incidents of crime, fraud or terrorism, people can become frightened and suspicious. That can lead to a default position where others are seen as potentially dangerous – and especially so if they are from a different race, or religion – the Black Lives Matter movement has brought this into sharp focus. The alternatives are understanding, collaboration, and consensus. This involves having an education system that promotes inter-cultural understanding, a media that does not undermine, let alone demonise sections of the community, an economic system that reduces the gap between the haves and have-nots, and political leadership that promotes unity rather than a divide and rule approach. Conversations that place everyone from a similar background into the same basket can enhance negative stereotypes when left unchallenged. When someone says or intimates about a race, or other minority group 'they are all like that', a non-confrontational comment that shows you don't agree may be enough to stop bigotry becoming acceptable.

Learning about relationships

Where do people learn what constitutes a healthy relationship? Children at home model themselves on what they see and hear around them. This gives messages about how to treat others. Children also learn from their peers, especially when they go to school. The conversations young people have as they grow are critical to how they position others, whether this is about individuals in their immediate world, or about people of other cultures and races. Stereotyping whole groups of people can destroy understanding and compassion, and lead to division and discrimination.

Social and emotional learning puts relationships on the curriculum, and this is becoming more accepted as educators realise that, not only does this improve relationships across the school, but it also has a positive impact on engagement and learning.[9] More in the Education chapter.

Relationships are presented in the media in numerous films, soaps, and series and these are often conflictual and negative, because filmmakers often believe that this makes for good stories. Without an aware and critical eye, this can be seen as the norm.

ASPIRE to positive relationships

The ASPIRE acronym was developed from the common strands in the 17 chapters of *Positive Relationships: Evidence-Based Practice Across the World*[10] and used in practice since. It stands for the principles of Agency, Safety, Positivity, Inclusion, Respect, and Equity. Although each principle stands alone, it is evident that they are interrelated. Relationships are more likely to flourish when all six are in place. Using this acronym, we illustrate each principle in practice for relationships at home, at work, and in the wider world. All of them are aligned in one way or another to the positive psychology principles and core competencies in the Introduction.

Agency
Self-determination is a key factor in wellbeing. Being involved in decisions that concern you, having the right to take action and being responsible for those actions, enhances a sense of agency.

Domination (power over) is at one end of a continuum, while agency (power with) is at the other. Where an individual, or group has power over another and takes away their freedom to make choices for themselves, relationships at any level become compromised. In close relationships, this can lead to coercive control, where one person dictates to the other who they see, what they do, what they wear, and how they spend their days. Coercive control is now illegal in the United Kingdom and Ireland and similar laws are in discussion in other countries.

Reflection:

How can we teach young people to recognise the difference between a healthy and unhealthy relationship, and to recognise the early signs of control – even when presented as protection, or loving possession?

A healthy relationship in any context, including for those who are in a position of authority, involves empowering others. In working environments agency is found where people are given tasks to complete, but how they do so is up to them. No-one performs well when being micro-managed. Being given a say in how policies and procedures are made also increases a sense of individual purpose and commitment to an organisation.

The mantra in schools is often 'teacher control'. Although teachers being *in charge* of what is happening in the classroom is important, *controlling* students is neither a positive model for relationships nor does it enable children to develop problem-solving skills. When people are given both choice and a voice, they are more likely to take responsibility for their actions.[11]

Responsibility is the corollary of agency. Sometimes things do not go well, or poor decisions are made. Rather than trying to push blame elsewhere, saying sorry matters for the health of any relationship. While politicians seem to believe that admitting mistakes will do them damage at the polls, the opposite may be true. Without acknowledgement of hurt or error, things cannot move forward.

Saying Sorry

The 'Stolen Generations' are children of Aboriginal and Torres Strait Islander people, who were removed from their families by the Australian federal and state agencies and church missions between 1910 and 1970 in a process of 'assimilation'. It is estimated that this happened to 1 in 3 Aboriginal children, who were often placed in brutal children's homes and were punished if they spoke their own language. This has resulted in inter-generational trauma.[12]

In 2008 the then Australian Prime Minister, Kevin Rudd, made a powerful public apology that was broadcast across the nation. Although there is criticism of the continued lack of action to redress inequalities, many have said that the apology was an important moment that went some way to healing.

Safety

People in a healthy relationship feel safe: physically, emotionally, and psychologically. Safety entails honesty and trust, believing that people have goodwill towards you and will not set out to hurt you. You feel safe when others keep their word and you can rely on them.

The Gottman Institute found that couples who are able to disagree about something safely have more chance of a long and healthy relationship.[13] The four approaches that undermine this are: criticism, contempt, defensiveness, and stonewalling. Here is what they mean, with alternative ways to promote safety.

Criticism is not just a complaint about an incident but an attack on the person. *"You haven't taken the rubbish out"* becomes *"you are just lazy and selfish"*. Safety is maintained by using 'I' statements in conversations: *"I get so frustrated when you don't take the rubbish out"*.

Contempt is toxic to any relationship. This can include sneering, sarcasm, and both verbal and non-verbal put-downs. When this deteriorates into anger there is little chance of a resolution. You see this in on-line trolling. Listening and responding to what someone says by trying to meet them half-way shows consideration of feelings, and a willingness to come to a resolution: *"I know you get upset when I forget to take the rubbish out, I'll try to remember"*.

Defensiveness is self-protection under perceived attack. It usually entails denial, blame, and aggression: *"Well, I don't see you doing much around the house lately"*. Teachers who take student behaviour personally may become defensive. This is never helpful. The alternative is to use a 'go with the flow' response such as: *"I didn't realise this was so upsetting, I wonder how we can sort it out for both of us"*.

Stonewalling is withdrawing altogether, often because the person feels overwhelmed. It is best to stop the discussion for a while and return to it when the person is less stressed. Consistent stonewalling, however, is likely to develop into a pattern of interaction that includes the other negative approaches outlined here. Regular, respectful communication is an essential ingredient of a safe, and healthy relationship.

Reflections:

What happened in the last disagreement you had with someone?

What might you have done differently?

Positivity

Positive communication, together with empathy, compassion, and a sense of fun enhance both personal relationships and social capital in an organisation.

One of Gottman's findings was the importance of how people spoke to each other, not only in conflict situations but in everyday conversation. It is the quality of these micro-moments of interaction that matter. A healthy relationship has a ratio of more than five positive statements to every negative one. This includes acknowledgement, appreciation, and affection. People who tell significant people in their lives what they value about them are filling their 'relational piggy bank', giving them more to draw on if difficult issues arise. Expressing gratitude is powerful, not just for specific behaviours but for who people are – their strengths and qualities. Being open in communication is also valuable as it enhances trust. Honesty combined with kindness is more likely to lead to resolution of problematic issues than blunt honesty which might result in defiance and defensiveness.

Cognitive empathy is being able to see a situation from someone else's point of view, and understand what this might mean for them. Affective empathy is being able to put yourself is someone else's shoes. Compassion is the desire to reduce suffering.

Active constructive responding is an example of empathy in practice:[14] this is where someone shares a cause for celebration and others wholeheartedly join in. Responses that burst your bubble, by their lack of interest, or pointing out the negatives, can be hurtful. An example might be sharing news of a forthcoming wedding. The potential responses are: talking about something else (passive destructive); saying *"oh lovely"*, and going on to talk about something else (passive constructive); saying how much it's going to cost, or showing dislike of a partner (active destructive); or looking delighted and asking for all the details (active constructive). The last of these is much healthier for the life of the relationship!

Reflections:

How did you respond last time a partner, friend or colleague was sharing good news about something in their lives?

What was your experience when you last shared good news with others?

Some have a predisposition for empathy, but it is a skill that can be learnt, along with kindness and positive communication. It is also a critical element of childhood – it is harder to develop empathy if you do not experience being cared for and about.

Acts of kindness are not only for those who might reciprocate but perhaps also for others we will never know personally – like raising money to help with overseas disasters. Not only does giving to others enhance our own wellbeing it is also treating others as we would want them to treat us in similar circumstances. 'Pay it forward' is the idea that recipients of acts of kindness do not necessarily repay the giver in an act of reciprocity but show kindness to others.

Positive feelings in relationships are also about having fun together. A good relationship is where people routinely enjoy each other's company. Oxytocin is the hormone involved in activities related to reproduction. It promotes feelings of warmth and connection. It is also released when people laugh together – promoting social bonding. Even though physical distancing at the height of the pandemic meant that people could no longer hug each other, there was an explosion of humorous videos on the internet, rapidly shared on social media platforms so that we were still often laughing together.

The Charter for Compassion works to establish and sustain cultures of compassion locally, and globally through many vehicles including the arts, business, and education. *"Born of our deep interdependence, compassion is essential to human relationships, and to a fulfilled humanity"*.[15]

Inclusion

Feeling you belong is recognised as a component of wellbeing. But belonging can be either inclusive or exclusive. Exclusive belonging is where only those 'like me' are acceptable, and this can lead to bullying and treating others as inferior. It is at the root of many social ills including racism, homophobia, religious intolerance, and human rights abuses. Exclusive belonging is found when conversations are around 'them and us' and where favours are given to privileged 'insiders'. There may be assumptions about the values, capabilities, and behaviours of those who do not 'belong'. The positives for those who are inside such a group is that it gives powerful sense of alliance, the downside is that in order to maintain your place within the group, you have to abide by group norms, often determined by a powerful few. Gangs are one example of this.

Inclusive belonging is where everyone matters, regardless of who they are, or where they are from. It acknowledges our shared humanity and understands that more connects us than divides us. According to Isaac Prilleltensky, 'mattering' happens when people not only feel valued but are able to add value.[16] Participation may need to be facilitated so people are empowered to make a difference. As Black Lives Matter has highlighted, inclusive belonging needs to be more than lip service or tokenistic, it entails sharing power, and privilege, and may therefore be challenging to those who feel entitled. Equity and justice is in everyone's longer-term interests.

Reflection:

In joining a new group, what do people do and say that helps you feel you belong?

The Foundation for People with Learning Disabilities (part of the Mental Health Foundation) have published a booklet entitled *Thinking About Inclusion: Taking Personal and Corporate Responsibility for Welcoming Everyone*. It is full of ideas and actions, and can be downloaded from their website.[17]

Respect

Respect is not easily defined, even though being treated with respect is what many people say is the basis of a good relationship – and you can certainly tell when respect is not present. It is aligned with being considerate, showing awareness of circumstances, including cultural protocols, treating people as if they mattered, and their concerns as valid. It is often missing where there is a power imbalance – such as when people in positions of authority, feel they have the right to intimidate others to follow their bidding. The #MeToo movement and awareness of institutional abuse has made this more visible, but there is still a long way to go to change how people relate to each other in such circumstances.

In the pandemic respectful communication occurred when policies were agreed in collaboration with relevant bodies, and not simply imposed or first heard from the media.

Respectful communication is the art of being fully present to someone and paying attention to what they are saying. This entails active listening, not making quick judgements about motivation or intention, not interrupting, or intimating they are talking nonsense. If necessary, it means disagreeing without being dismissive. By respecting children and taking their concerns seriously, we model how we expect them to behave towards others.

Basic courtesy is respectful as it is a way of being considerate – e.g. not pushing into the front of a queue, asking rather than demanding. Respect is also shown when efforts are acknowledged and not taken for granted. Expressing genuine thanks can go a long way to maintaining a positive relationship.

Equity

Whereas equality is treating everyone the same, equity is about fairness. One illustration of this is the couple where one person does all of the cooking, but the other cleans up the kitchen. If both are happy that this is a fair arrangement the relationship will thrive. If the expectations are that one of the couple will do paid work and then all the unpaid work at home, this is likely to set up resentment. An equitable relationship is linked strongly with agency – it is making decisions together and coming to a negotiated solution, so that everyone feels comfortable with what has been agreed.

Reciprocity is part of equity. Things are not fair if they are one-sided. But sometimes people need more help than at other times. Relationships at work can be problematic when people are paid differently for the same role, for example, because of their gender. Bigger issues of equity are addressed in the chapter on Society.

Reflections:

How do the ASPIRE principles reflect your understanding and experience of positive relationships?

Can you identify what is missing when a relationship is not working well?

Hope and aspiration

Despite Facebook encouraging us to have many 'friends', it is not having multiple relationships that matters so much as the quality of them. Do the people in our lives support and care about us, and do we support, care and show kindness to others?

The Golden Rule says we should treat each other the way we would want to be treated. A version of this overriding principle is found in all the main religions of the world. Here are just seven of them with quotes from their religious books. This information is worth sharing in education, in the media, and in political life.

The Golden Rule

- Buddhism: *"Hurt not others in ways that you yourself would find hurtful"*.
- Christianity: *"Whatever you wish that others do to you, do so to them"*.
- Hinduism: *"This is the essence of morality, do not do to others that which if done to you would cause you pain"*.
- Islam: *"no one of you is a believer until you desire for your neighbour that which you desire for yourself"*.
- Judaism: *"What is hateful to you do not do to your neighbour, that is the basic law, all the rest is commentary"*.
- Shinto: *"The heart of the person before you is a mirror. See there your own form"*.
- Sikhism: *"Do as you desire goodness for yourself as you cannot expect tasty fruits if you sow thorny trees"*.

In a socio-ecological framework the quality of relationships inter-acts bi-directionally across systems, from the interpersonal level to family, organisational, community, and socio-political. What happens in one part of this ecosystem influences others. If relation-ships at work are healthy and attuned to the ASPIRE principles, for example, then individuals will have more resources to be kind, responsive, and supportive at home. The quality of our relation-ships makes all the difference to wellbeing in all the contexts of our lives. We need to pay attention to what this means so we can build the positive.

Ideas for action

What might governments do?

Engage in respectful political debate that listens to different views without contempt and derision

Treat social problems as a national issue – not laying the blame on specific communities.

What might communities do?

Run activities that enable people to get to know each other and break down stereotypes.

What might schools do?

Model and teach ways of being that enhance positive relationships and how to deal well with differences, and conflicts.

Make all communities feel welcome.

What might families do?

Show respect to each other, and have high expectations of children's social behaviour.

What might individuals do?

Develop an awareness of how we speak with and about others, and the far-reaching consequences of this for both close relationships, and the wider community.

Learn about emotions and how to manage and express these safely.

Key sources

There are more websites, organisations, movements and charities with the aim of building positive relationships than can be counted. Full references and resources are available at our website https://www.creatingtheworldwewanttolivein.org/references/relationships/

1 Dyer (2004). *Staying on the Path*. Hay House Inc.
2 https://www.adultdevelopmentstudy.org
3 The Harvard Gazette (2017). *Good genes are nice, but joy is better*.
4 Baker & Dutton (2007). Enabling positive social capital in organizations. In Dutton & Ragins (Eds.), *Exploring positive relationships at work: Building a theoretical and research foundation* (325–346). Lawrence Erlbaum.
5 Spratt *et al.* (2006). Part of who we are as a school should include responsibility for wellbeing: Links between the school environment, mental health and behaviour. *Pastoral Care, September 2006*, 14–21.

6 Conversano *et al.* (2010). Optimism and its impact on physical and mental well-being. *Clinical Practice and Epidemiology in Mental Health, 6,* 25–29.

7 Dickens (2017). Using gratitude to promote positive change. A series of meta-analyses investigating the effectiveness of gratitude interventions. *Basic and Applied Social Psychology, 4,* 192–208.

8 Shonin, Van Gordon & Griffiths (2015). Does mindfulness work? *British Medical Journal BMJ 2015;351:h6919*

9 Durlak *et al.* (2011). The impact of enhancing students' social and emotional learning: a meta-analysis of school-based universal interventions. *Child Development, 82*(1), 405–432.

10 Roffey (Ed.) (2012). *Positive Relationships: Evidence Based Practice Across the World*. Springer.

11 Anderson & Graham (2016). Improving wellbeing: having say at school. *School Effectiveness and School Improvement, 27*(3), 348–356.

12 Australian Institute of Health and Welfare (2018) *Aboriginal and Torres Strait Islander Stolen Generations and descendants. Numbers, demographic characteristics and selected outcomes*. Australian Government.

13 Gottman & Silver (2007). *The Seven Principles for Making Marriage Work.* Orion. Also search YouTube for the Gottman Institute.

14 Gable *et al.* (2004). What do you do when things go right? The intrapersonal and interpersonal benefits of sharing positive events. *Journal of Personality and Social Psychology, 87*(2), 228–245.

15 charterforcompassion.org/

16 Prilleltensky (2020). Mattering at the Intersection of Psychology, Philosophy and Politics. *American Journal of Community Psychology, 65,* 16–34

17 Foundation for People with Learning Disabilities (2012). *Thinking About Inclusion: Taking Personal and Corporate Responsibility for Welcoming Everyone*. https://www.mentalhealth.org.uk/file/2062/download.

CHAPTER 6

Health

Felicia Huppert, Dóra Guðmundsdóttir,
Marten de Vries

> *"Health is created and lived by people within the settings of their everyday life; where they learn, work, play, and love". – World Health Organization, (1986)[1]*

Towards positive health

From its foundation more than 70 years ago, the World Health Organization (WHO) recognised that health was a positive state, *"not merely the absence of disease or infirmity"*.[2]

Good health plays an important role in human happiness and wellbeing and contributes to our ability to lead a full life. The COVID-19 pandemic has highlighted its importance to us, as most people have been willing to forego aspects of personal and social life to remain healthy. Health extends beyond individuals to society as a whole. Families, organisations, and social institutions all function better when people and populations have good physical and mental health.

Both physical and mental health matter

Every one of us experiences problems with physical health at one time or another, so receiving effective and timely treatment is important for our wellbeing. It is just as important to receive prompt and effective treatment for mental health problems. Around one third of us can expect to have a serious mental health condition during our lifetime. Yet, according to The Lancet Commission on Global Mental Health, the availability and quality of mental health interventions across all countries is poor. In high-income countries, only 1 in 5 people with clinical depression receives minimally adequate treatment, and this plummets to 1 in 27 in low-to middle-income countries. This results in monumental levels of lost human capabilities and avoidable suffering. There is also a strong economic case for major investment in mental health.

The Commission also recognises the pressing need to expand the focus, going beyond mental health conditions, to the improvement of mental health for the whole population. To achieve this, we need to understand and foster the attitudes, behaviours and circumstances that promote good mental health.

The remainder of this chapter explores the factors that determine good health and examines how we can promote health and wellbeing for all. This will require changes in individual behaviour, and a social environment that supports positive change.

Reflections:

How would you describe good health?

Are there things you are already doing to lead a healthy life?

What do you think would be needed to optimise health for all?

The science of population health reveals that when we implement health promotion strategies across the population, we not only increase the number of people with good health, but also substantially decrease the number with health problems, as shown in Figure 4. Health promotion is a win-win strategy.

Health literacy plays an important role in promoting population health, helping individuals and organisations obtain, understand and accurately judge the reliability of information about health.

Teaching health literacy to children

A ground-breaking international health promotion project worked with primary school children to challenge false beliefs about health that are rife in Uganda, such as the myth that herbs are the best treatment for cancer and HIV, or that burns can be healed by applying fresh cow dung. Nine school lessons, based on comic books, activities and songs, taught children how to critically evaluate health claims and make more informed decisions. Almost 11,000 nine-year-olds in 120 schools participated in the randomised controlled trial, half receiving the intervention. All schools were tested on their understanding of how to evaluate claims about health treatments. 69% of children in the intervention schools passed the test compared to just 27% of controls. This shows that by applying critical thinking skills, health literacy can be successfully taught even in primary school.[3]

Reflections:

Where would you go to find information about how to improve your health?

How would you decide if the information is reliable?

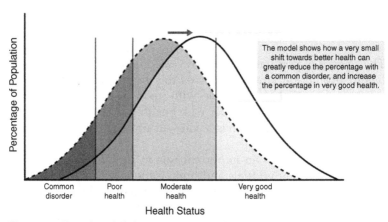

Figure 4: Positive shift in population health

The left-hand bell curve represents the population distribution of any common disorder.

The right-hand bell curve shows the shift after improving population risk and protective factors, or following a positive intervention.

Modified from Huppert, FA (2009). Psychological well-being: Evidence regarding its causes and consequences. *Applied Psychology: Health and Wellbeing, 2009, 1*(2), 137–164.

How much does health depend on our healthcare system?

Although the quality of healthcare systems plays an important role in the treatment and prevention of ill-health, these systems focus on disease and only play a small role in producing and maintaining health. We might expect that the more a country invests in these systems, the better their health. Health spending and positive outcomes, however, bear surprisingly little relationship to each other. More important than the actual amount spent appears to be the equality in health spending across sociodemographic groups, and resulting access to healthcare. Nordic countries regularly top the list, whereas the United States ranks 175th in the world.[4] The prohibitive cost of healthcare has made it unaffordable to millions of low-income, often ethnic-minority households in the United States, which may partly explain the devastating effect of inequality in the COVID-19 pandemic, where vastly disproportionate numbers have died in low-income and non-white populations. The pandemic has highlighted the urgent need for a strong, well-funded health system available to all.

One reason for the lack of relationship between expenditure and good health is that traditional measures have focused on treatment, and to some extent on prevention, rather than the amount actually spent on *supporting* health. This would include what individuals spend (e.g. fitness equipment, gym sessions, stress reduction courses), and the extra cost of healthy eating, particularly in disadvantaged areas.

Can low income families afford to eat well?

A 2019 study by the Food Foundation found that after paying housing costs, the poorest 10% of English households would need to spend 74% of their disposable income on food to meet a healthy eating standard compared to 6% in the richest 10%.

Individual factors that influence health

We focus here on how characteristics and behaviours at the individual level can influence health while recognising that they are influenced by social processes. Research has identified many individual characteristics and behaviours that have health benefits. These include the psychological principles described in the introduction – supportive relationships, a sense of autonomy, feeling competent, positive emotions and attitudes, and a sense of meaning.

It has long been known that the quality of our social relationships has a profound impact on our health. People who receive support lead longer, healthier lives than those who do not. It has now been shown that *providing* support to others has even greater benefits. Researcher Stephanie Brown and colleagues followed a large group of elderly couples over many years, and found that those who provided practical or emotional support to others were much less likely to die during the study period than those who did not.[5] The difference could not be attributed to a host of health, behavioural, and socio-demographic factors. This suggests that substantial health benefits may result from policies and practices that encourage people to support others (for example through volunteering or mentoring).

Autonomy is about having choice, and researchers Richard Ryan & Edward Deci and colleagues have shown improvements in health-related behaviours when people are offered a choice.[6] Children aged 4–6 who could choose what vegetables they ate, consumed many more vegetables than children offered no choice. In adolescents, studies show that when parents support their child's autonomy, they are less likely to engage in high-risk behaviours such as early use of tobacco, alcohol, and marijuana. In adults, randomised trials confirm the benefits of autonomy and autonomy support in smoking cessation, diet improvement; and sustained involvement in physical activity. If people have choice over what exercise they do, how, when and where they exercise, they become more motivated to maintain an exercise regime and have a greater sense of perceived competence. The health benefits of having a sense of autonomy and a feeling of competence can also be seen in clinical settings. When doctors ask patients what outcomes really matter to them, patients feel more motivated and competent, which leads to improvements in health-compromising behaviours and taking prescribed medications.

Happier people tend to have better health and longer, healthier lives. But it is not clear if these health benefits are a direct result of their positive mood, since they also have healthier lifestyles, more friends, and more positive interpersonal experiences. To establish whether positive mood can produce, health benefits researcher Barbara Fredrickson and her colleagues conducted experimental studies.[7] They showed volunteers videos designed to induce positive, negative or neutral mood states, and then exposed them to a stressful task – being given a couple of minutes to prepare a speech. They found that participants in a positive state showed much more rapid cardiovascular recovery from stress than those in a negative or neutral state, and it is known that a rapid recovery from stress is beneficial for health. Other studies have shown that positive emotions and optimism are associated with a healthy pattern of stress hormone secretion compared to negative emotions and pessimism.

How do positive emotions exert their effect on health? A series of studies by Sheldon Cohen and colleagues suggests that effects on the immune system are key.[8] In their studies, a common cold virus was administered via nasal drops to several hundred healthy volunteers who were kept in quarantine. The more positive the participant's emotional style, the lower their risk of developing a cold. Further, the more sociable the participants the less likely they were to develop a cold. Participants with a higher positive emotional style also produce significantly more antibodies to the Hepatitis B vaccine.

Having a sense of meaning has health benefits including physical health and increased life expectancy. The health effects may stem from the association between meaning and reduced stress, more adaptive coping, and greater engagement in health-promoting behaviours.

Body and mind always interact
It is unhelpful to think of body and mind as separate entities, they always work together, and both are responsive to our lifestyle and daily habits such as regular exercise, good nutrition, and adequate sleep. Most people readily accept that physical health can have an

impact on mental states, but the reverse is also true – mental health problems are a major contributor to a wide range of chronic physical conditions. Our mental states can impact our physical health, and this is recognised in the WHO statement, *"there is no health without mental health"*.[9] This section focuses on the management of stress and pain as good examples of the interaction between body and mind, and describes how both mental and physical states can be improved through mindfulness practice.

Managing stress and pain

Mild or moderate stress is part of normal life and can be good for our physical and mental performance. Only when stress is intense or prolonged does it cause problems. Intense stress triggers a cascade of physiological responses in hormones, immune function and the central nervous system which can lead to numerous physical and mental health conditions, including chronic fatigue, metabolic disorders (e.g. diabetes, obesity), depression, and immune disorders.

Research shows that the amount of harm stress causes is influenced not only by the severity of stress but by our attitude towards it.[10] If our heart is pounding from anxiety, we can think of this as a danger signal or we can reframe the experience as our body giving us the energy we need to rise to a challenge, and perhaps learn from it. Viewing stress as a helpful part of life, rather than as harmful, is associated with emotional wellbeing, increased productivity at work, better health and improved physiological responses to stress – even during periods of high stress. Of course, wherever possible, we have to ensure that high levels of stress do not result from unreasonable demands imposed by the systems with which we interact.

How stressful is a maths test?

Prior to undertaking a maths exam, students were randomly assigned to a stress reappraisal intervention or a control group. The intervention group was taught about the adaptive benefits of stress arousal whereas controls were instructed to ignore the stress. Stress reappraisal resulted in less test anxiety and improved test performance. Other studies have shown that the benefits of instilling a 'stress-is-enhancing' mindset may persist for weeks or years.[11]

Like stress, pain is part of normal life, and our attitude towards it can have a profound effect on the experience. When we feel pain, we tend to tense and brace, or tell ourselves stories about how the pain will never go away and our lives will be ruined – which only makes the pain worse. Mindfulness training is one way of changing our attitude to pain by approaching it with interest and curiosity, observing how it ebbs and flows, opening and softening into it, and not over-identifying with it. This in turn reduces the experience of pain and explains why mindfulness training has been adopted in many pain clinics.

Reflections:

Have you noticed times when your physical health impacts your mental functioning or emotional health – either in a positive or negative way?

Have you noticed times when your mental functioning or emotional health impacts your physical health – either in a positive or negative way?

Mindfulness and compassion as foundations of physical and mental health

Mindful awareness is both a characteristic of some people and a skill that can be learned – described in more detail in the Introduction. Mindfulness training programs have been shown to produce widespread benefits across many outcomes in clinical and general population samples. In patients with mental health problems substantial benefits have been shown in depression, anxiety and substance abuse. A study of patients with a history of recurrent depression by Willem Kuyken and colleagues showed that over a 60-week period patients who had received mindfulness training were one third as likely to have a relapse compared to those receiving usual treatment, and one fifth as likely compared to those receiving active treatment (anti-depressant medication or psycho-education).[12] Mindfulness training can rewire the brain by strengthening neural pathways that are conducive to healthy behaviour, whereas medication can only facilitate changes in neural firing. Physiological benefits of mindfulness training include reduced systolic blood pressure, better regulation of the parasympathetic nervous system which has a calming effect, improvements in immune function, and telomerase activity which is a marker of healthy biological aging. The self-compassion that is integral to mindfulness training has been shown to mediate some of the health benefits.

Mindfulness training not only reduces symptoms of mental and physical health problems, but also enhances wellbeing through developing skills and processes that enable us to function at our best, physically, mentally and socially. These include the basic skills of awareness, attention, emotion-regulation, self-compassion, and self-acceptance that enable us to feel more in control of our lives, more able to appreciate positive experiences and manage difficult ones. Mindfulness also enhances interpersonal relationships and prosocial behaviour that play a major role in personal wellbeing, while at the same time contributing to the wellbeing of the wider community.[13]

Mindfulness and compassion in healthcare staff play an important role in effective patient communication, and safe and compassionate care. More mindful clinicians listen more deeply and are rated more highly by patients on communication and their overall experience.[14] A large study found that teams of nurses who had higher levels of mindfulness were less likely than other teams to make patient medication errors.[15] Because mindfulness training has a positive impact on clinicians' wellbeing and treatment outcomes, it is increasingly being offered in healthcare settings, and since 2002 has been part of the core curriculum for medical students at Monash University in Australia.

Social determinants of health

Social determinants encompass things that societies can change, and all of them affect what people do and the circumstances in which they do them. Most research on the social determinants of health has focused on problems. These are briefly summarised before examining implications for the social determinants of good health.

Many well-known risk factors contribute to the prevalence of disease, including smoking, alcohol, poor diet and inactivity. But are these behaviours solely the responsibility of individuals or are there social conditions that predispose people to unhealthy behaviours? International studies show there is a social gradient in health. Most diseases become more common and life expectancy is shorter the lower the social standing. This may be linked to people further down the social ladder having more stressful lives and worse environmental quality, both of which can directly damage health and cognitive functioning. Unhealthy behaviours may be the consequence of disadvantage, rather than, as some believe, ignorance or irresponsibility. According to Richard Wilkinson and Michael Marmot:

> *"Disadvantage has many forms and may be absolute or relative. It can include having few family assets, having a poorer education during adolescence, having insecure employment, becoming stuck in a hazardous or dead-end job, living in poor housing, trying to bring up a family in difficult circumstances and living on an inadequate retirement pension. These disadvantages tend to concentrate among the same people, and their effects on health accumulate during life. The longer people live in stressful economic and social circumstances, the greater the physiological wear and tear they suffer and the less likely they are to enjoy a healthy old age".*[16]

They argue that societies will be healthier if people are free from insecurity, exclusion and deprivation, and can play a full and useful role in their society's economic, social and cultural life.

Among the social determinants of health are the 'commercial determinants' of health, defined as *"strategies and approaches used by the private sector to promote products and choices that are detrimental to health"*.[17] The retailing of tobacco products, alcohol, and foods high in sugar, salt and fat is big business and embedded in an economic system that prioritises wealth creation over health improvement. There have been successful efforts to counter the health-damaging effects of commercial interests. Banning smoking in public places, and litigation against tobacco companies, combined with substantial price increases on cigarettes, as well as advertising bans, and reducing visibility and attractiveness of cigarette packets, has led to a substantial decline in smoking related diseases and deaths in almost all countries.[18]

Do we drink less if alcohol costs more?

The Scottish government recently tackled the alarming rise in alcohol-related health and social harm resulting from cheaper alcohol leading to higher consumption. In a world first, they set a high minimum unit price that resulted in a 25-year low in alcohol consumption – their lowest level of drinking since records began in 1994. Households that usually bought the most alcohol showed the greatest reduction in alcohol purchases. Minimum unit pricing not only reduces total alcohol consumption but shifts consumption towards drinks with lower alcohol content.

Michael Marmot and colleagues' review *Fair Society, Healthy Lives*[19] makes six policy recommendations that are beginning to be implemented by many regional health organisations.

1. Give every child the best start in life.
2. Enable all children, young people and adults to maximise their capabilities and have control over their lives.
3. Create fair employment and good work for all.
4. Ensure a healthy standard of living for all.
5. Create and develop healthy and sustainable places and communities.
6. Strengthen the role and impact of ill-health prevention.

A whole of society approach to health

Since, as we've shown, social processes play a large part in creating health and wellbeing, it is important to strengthen the positive social mechanisms across all sectors of society. The COVID-19 pandemic vividly illustrated that the response was most effective when political parties, scientists, media, communities, business organisations and neighbours worked together to minimise risk and harm.

Another practical approach to creating a social context that supports health is to ensure that healthy choices become the easy and affordable choices. Reducing taxes on foods like fruits and vegetables, and increasing taxes on unhealthy foods is one approach. Providing options that encourage healthy food choices in schools and workplaces, and reducing unhealthy options is another.

A good example of a whole of society approach to health is the intervention to decrease youth drinking in Iceland.

Why youth drinking plummeted in Iceland

Key parts of the strategy involved using taxes to make alcohol more expensive and therefore less accessible for youth, and 1% of the tax revenue from alcohol was reserved for alcohol prevention and health promotion programs. In 1998 the prevalence of youth drinking in Iceland was 42%, the highest in Europe, and after a comprehensive intervention it decreased to 5%, the lowest prevalence in Europe. This change happened because there were actions at all levels; the government, municipalities, schools, youth centres, parents and youth themselves all played their part.

The health challenges of the recent past are likely to be different than those we will face in the near future. New challenges include the increases in loneliness, sleep deprivation, vaping, recreational drugs, anti-vaccination movements, and social media addiction, as well as the widespread rise in unemployment and mental health issues following the COVID-19 pandemic, and the near-certainty of future pandemics. There are also social problems associated with traumatic experiences following forced migration and displacement due to major conflicts, and increasingly to global warming, which can create substantial stress for both the displaced and the receiving communities. Failure to deal effectively with the new challenges that are developing in today's complex and globalised world can have profound negative consequences. Responding to such challenges with compassion and a whole of society approach may be the most effective way to improve population wellbeing.

Co-creating health

Patients have traditionally been considered passive recipients of services provided by hierarchical healthcare systems, but health outcomes and user satisfaction are greater when there is collaboration between members of the public and health systems.

Impressive results from a co-created service

To reduce the high rate of preterm births, a maternity service for Indigenous families in Brisbane, Australia, was co-designed by Aboriginal community health organisations and a maternity hospital. In the study of over 1000 births, preterm births were almost halved over a four-year period, compared to a group receiving standard maternity care. This is expected to have additional downstream effects on the health of Indigenous children and their families.[20]

The Health 2020 strategy of the WHO lists amongst its top priorities: empowering people, strengthening people-centred health systems, and creating resilient communities and supportive environments. The importance of this approach became evident during the Covid-19 pandemic in which the success of the public health measures such as hand washing, social distancing, wearing masks, and contact tracing apps, depended on people, organisations and communities working together. But how can we continue to engage all relevant parties to improve a population's health? A variety of models now incorporates the bottom-up perspective. Individuals can become partners in health improvement, and community support groups can work with health systems to create horizontal, overlapping professional and community networks that embrace collaborations toward positive health. This can lead to optimally designed systems better tailored to the specific needs of individuals or groups. A key insight is that creating health is not ultimately what the health system does but what people do to secure their health. In positive health approaches, every voice counts.

Technological advances have improved grass-root engagement with health promotion in the form of digital health and lifestyle resources, and social media. Apps and other online resources were intensely implemented during the COVID-19 pandemic, to provide support on health-related issues. This included apps promoting healthy eating, which also had the fun spin-off of sharing recipes and perhaps eating together. There were innumerable examples of online exercise and yoga classes, and a huge demand for resources to improve mental wellbeing. For example, downloads of the Headspace app, already used by millions to learn mindfulness, doubled during the pandemic.

Creating health for all

Health is produced by the society and everyday life settings, where people work, live, love and play. The first principle for optimising health for all is to go beyond treatment and prevention to implement the wide-scale promotion of positive mental and physical health for everyone in every context. In a population with overall good health, even the devastating effects of a pandemic such as COVID-19, which differentially affects those with underlying health problems and those from disadvantaged or ethnic minority groups, would be minimised. The second principle is to recognise the key role of the social context in both the occurrence of health problems and the development of optimal health. The refusal to allow healthcare systems to discriminate against disadvantaged groups in the future would go a long way towards optimising health for all. The third principle is including the voice and pro-health activities of members of the public in a more collaborative health system. This would link the formal health system with social networks, moving towards a genuine health alliance poised to meet the health challenges of today and tomorrow. A health system that applies these three principles would be a system that truly maximises health and flourishing across human populations.

Reflections:

If you wanted to improve health for all, what strategies would you prioritise?

What are you currently doing to promote good health in your family or community?

Ideas for action

What might governments do?

Consider health in all policies.

Implement health impact assessments.

Develop laws and regulations that promote healthy living.

Tax unhealthy choices.

Ensure there are no taxes on healthy choices.

Reserve a percentage of taxes from unhealthy products for prevention and health promotion.

Teach health literacy in schools and beyond.

Find ways to include the population's voice (demand-side) in health policy planning.

What might communities and local government do?

Become healthy cities, healthy municipalities.

Implement health impact assessments.

Become a health-promoting workplace and support other workplaces.

Support health-promoting schools.

Form health support groups and destigmatise health problems.

What might the healthcare system do?

Promote health as well as treat and prevent diseases.

Facilitate grassroots health discussions and partnerships to inform planning.

Assist patients in achieving the health outcomes that are important to them.

What might schools do?

Adopt a whole school approach to health promotion.

Teach mindfulness as the basis for social and emotional learning and resilience.

Teach health literacy.

Motivate parents and children to live a healthy life.

What might families do?

Provide adult role models for healthy behaviours.

Motivate, educate and support children to make healthy choices.

Provide healthy choices at home.

What might youth do?

Encourage peers to see the healthy options as the 'cool' options.

Key sources

Full references and resources are available at our website https://www.creatingtheworldwewanttolivein.org/references/health/

1 WHO. (1986). *Ottawa charter for health promotion*. World Health Organization. https://www.who.int/healthpromotion/conferences/previous/ottawa/en/
2 WHO. (1948). *Official records of the World Health Organization* (Vol. 2). World Health Organization.
3 Nsangi *et al.* (2017). Effects of the Informed Health Choices primary school intervention on the ability of children in Uganda to assess the reliability of claims about treatment effects: a cluster-randomised controlled trial. *The Lancet*.
4 Global Health Security Index (2019).
5 Brown *et al.* (2003). Providing social support may be more beneficial than receiving it: Results from a prospective study of mortality. *Psychological Science*.
6 Ryan & Deci (2017). *Self-determination theory: Basic psychological needs in motivation, development, and wellness*. Guilford Publications.
7 Fredrickson (2009). *Positivity*. Harmony.
8 Cohen (2005). The Pittsburgh Common Cold Studies: psychosocial predictors of susceptibility to respiratory infectious illness (Keynote Presentation at the 8th International Congress of Behavioral Medicine). *International Journal Behavioural Medicine*.

9 WHO (2001). *Mental health: a call for action by world health ministers.* World Health Organization.

10 Jamieson *et al.* (2018). Optimizing stress responses with reappraisal and mindset interventions: An integrated model. *Anxiety, Stress, & Coping.*

11 Jamieson *et al.* (2016). Reappraising stress arousal improves performance and reduces evaluation anxiety in classroom exam situations. *Social Psychological and Personality Science.*

12 Kuyken *et al.* (2016). Efficacy of mindfulness-based cognitive therapy in prevention of depressive relapse: an individual patient data meta-analysis from randomized trials. *JAMA psychiatry.*

13 Donald *et al.* (2019). Does your mindfulness benefit others? A systematic review and meta-analysis of the link between mindfulness and prosocial behaviour. *British Journal of Psychology.*

14 Beach *et al.* (2013). A multicenter study of physician mindfulness and health care quality. *The Annals of Family Medicine.*

15 Wang *et al.* (2020). Enhancing Compassion in Healthcare: A Multi-Level Perspective. In Lansbury, Johnson, & van den Broek, *Contemporary Issues in Work and Organisations Actors and Institutions.* Routledge

16 Wilkinson & Marmot (Eds.). (2003). Social determinants of health: the solid facts. World Health Organization, *Anxiety, Stress, & Coping.*

17 Kickbusch, Allen & Franz (2016). *The commercial determinants of health.*

18 Global Burden of Disease Collaborative Network. (2018.) *Global Burden of Disease Study 2017 (GBD 2017) Results.* Institute for Health Metrics and Evaluation (IHME).

19 Marmot *et al.* (2010). *The Marmot review: Fair society, healthy lives. The Strategic Review of Health Inequalities in England Post-2010.*

20 Kildea *et al.* (2019). Reducing preterm birth amongst Aboriginal and Torres Strait Islander babies: a prospective cohort study. *E Clinical Medicine.*

CHAPTER 7
Community

Marten de Vries

"Alone, we can do so little; together, we can do so much" – Helen Keller[1]

What is community?

As Helen Keller put so succinctly, throughout history and throughout the world people have created communities for support, safety and information exchange. We are all born into a community of some kind, both seen and unseen (virtual), and spend our lives in one or many. Having evolved in social groups, our attention is to a large extent structured by what is important to those communities. Although urbanisation and technology are transforming communities, they remain the home ground for our wellbeing: a place we can experience support and belonging and comprehend the context, tempo, limits and possibilities of our lives; a resilient buffer when things go wrong; a positive platform for social action to set things right. Although communities can be repressive or hostile to others outside the in-group, they predominantly empower collective action and counteract the scourge of loneliness. Community is the basis of 'social capital', where individuals can invest in and gain access to physical and psychosocial resources through social roles, functions, narratives and rituals, vital for developing identity and connection across the life span. For most of us, community is a vehicle for addressing the positive psychology principles of connection, positive feelings and meaning. As Zygmunt Bauman remarked, *"Community feels good"*.[2]

Communities once had discrete geographical boundaries, but this is no longer the case. Although a place is still often the basis for shared concerns, community today may best be defined as a group of people who have a common interest, purpose or need, shared either through common values, resources, location and lifestyles. Members can communicate their relationship either face-to-face or by virtual means.

Community interests contrast to those of the individual, family or small group, where maybe only a few have a common interest. Communities as discussed here have some form of 'intactness' either on the ground or 'in the ether' that provides a sense of alliance and possible nurturance.

Why community matters

During the COVID-19 pandemic, communities became animated as the world shrank in lockdown. Away from the daily bustle of work, school and daily tasks, attention shifted to the immediate environment. Concerns became local, reduced to home and neighbourhood, with outings limited to the grocery store and pharmacy. In this smaller world we had more time to notice and appreciate a simpler life, including neighbours who often transformed from strangers to genuine caring, volunteering and interacting individuals. Neighbourhood social media sites became commonplace, and local activities such as clapping for health-workers together, singing and playing music from balconies and even shared 'community viewing' of the same entertainment on the internet, enabled connection, coping and resilience worldwide. Not only was there outreach towards migrants and other special groups but migrant organisations themselves shared information, donated to hospitals, provided free meals and took other forms of social action. One such example is a group of mothers from the Vietnamese community in the Czech Republic, who organised mask-sewing, donating 13,000 reusable masks. Such spontaneous mutual support, and neighbourhood action groups at all levels of society, are an ode to the often-latent coping power of community. This issue now is how we maintain this trend toward collectivity and respect for each other.

To retain the now realised benefits of community, it is vital that we continue to build on these positive relations. To do this we can utilise participation in both existing rituals and customs, such as Carnival, religious holidays, regular celebrations, get-togethers, as well as develop new creative approaches. Both offer natural emotional connection, from joy to concerns and story sharing of group experience. Studies show that in areas where people know and have contact with their neighbours, the sharing of common goals and narratives result in higher social trust and wellbeing.[3] Communities then can provide a stable place to be, to grow through different phases of life and family cycles, offering continuity and support. For millennia this has been the case, but in industrialised societies, communities have more transient populations. This requires an increased and sustained effort to establish new positive ways to be together.

Community building

Community building is an ongoing process that requires social action; the ability to engage constructively together and transform the physical (digital) and social environment. Actions such as helping the needy, responding when things go wrong, and addressing health, economic and political challenges lie at the base of empowering positive relationships and effective communities. Listening to one another and sharing information and know-how is essential. Under severe community stress, informal 'social security' systems[4] are activated that may have lain dormant. During a disaster although individuals may be numbed, groups may burst into collective action, mobilising altruistic social support and providing a buffer to further calamity. One example, described below, comes from community action after the Chernobyl nuclear disaster, with resources for the entire community sustained long after the stress subsided.

Children of Chernobyl

After the Chernobyl nuclear disaster in 1986, during which communication and factual information for the evacuated was sparse for up to two years, women in the adjacent town of Pripyat sprang into action. Concerned about their children's health, and at a time when pregnant women were encouraged to abort, they organised into a Children of Chernobyl group that both lobbied for openness and initiated a global search for information. Eventually, they came to the attention of a New York research group[5] who had previously investigated community exposure in the aftermath of The Three Mile Island 1979 disaster. The mothers' stories and grass roots action ignited a process of interventions, community responses and research. This included a range of issues such as radiation effects, the impact of relocation, traumatic physical and psychological responses as well as endemic mistrust. The mothers not only drew attention to the critical need for health support for their children but brought issues of nuclear safety to global attention.

Community relationships can flourish when spaces and places to talk are readily available, In the EURODEP study,[6] less depression was found in communities where the elderly had access to public places such as parks, coffee houses, taverns and gyms etc. Such places facilitated social networks as daily contact became a natural part of life. At the Kakuma refugee camp in the Kenya desert, created in the 1980's after the turmoil in South Sudan and 40 years later still housing millions, 'places' were established where people could meet, talk and socialise in some semblance of normality. The meeting places helped significantly with the social healing[7] of trauma. Spaces and activities that allow people to participate socially contribute to secure relationships that improve both mental and social health.

Reflections:

What communities are you part of?

How are you supported by these communities?

In what ways do you provide support to these communities?

The vulnerability of communities in today's world

Throughout history communities have been challenged by unpredictable health, social, economic, technological, migration and environmental changes. Today is no exception, as transient lifestyles are beginning to predominate, and people move away from their home localities in pursuit of education or work.[8] Fifty-five per cent of the world's population already reside in urban settings. Globalisation and population movement often leaves little room for developing critical local community relationships. For instance, one sad indicator reported by UNICEF, is that over fifty million children were on the move away from their natal communities at the turn of the century. This not only creates problems for the uprooted but also confronts the hosting population with 'people not like us'. Feelings of being socially disconnected are exacerbated within the context of growing social inequality, and insecurity created by the banal and often racist rhetoric of populist leaders.

As Alvin Toffler (*Future Shock*) and Margaret Mead (*Culture and Commitment*) predicted decades ago, traditional social and family structures have been altered and stable generational hierarchies have gone topsy-turvy, affecting traditional community structure. The fast-moving lifestyles of urban landscapes also fit generations differently: the young are often attracted to the fast pace of city life, while the elderly and young families may have difficulty accommodating the bustle.[5]

Our search for personal recognition also challenges communal thinking. Many studies depict the phenomenon of the co-existence of both feelings of loneliness and a strong, often unfulfilled, craving for belonging. Zygmunt Bauman suggests that individualism, now dominant in western societies, is characterised by the tension between desire for personal freedom and need for community security. His somewhat dark social critique[1] argues that there is an irreconcilable trade-off between security and freedom, between identity and belonging. From this position there may be little to be gained from community constraints and much that might be lost. He suggests this can become a self-perpetuating process. However, self-determination theory suggests that this is not inevitable. The apparently conflicting desires for the security of community and the freedom to do what we want can be placed in a more positive light. Self-determination theory describes the striving for both autonomy and social connection as basic ingredients for meeting our psychosocial needs. Finding the best balance between the self and belonging in the social group remains a goal and a challenge.

> **Reflections:**
>
> *Is there a tension between your needs and community expectations?*
>
> *How does your community deal with such tensions?*

Family and community

Communities may be challenged further by family disruption and generational issues. With high rates of separation and divorce, there are an increasing number of fragmented families, who may struggle to maintain social connections. Although not new, family ties today are often comparatively short lived. After the first two decades of life, grown children move away from their family home and parents move on to a second life. Young people may then meet a wide range of potential challenges such as unemployment, substance abuse, academic stress and poor mental health.[9] Schools, communities and family networks may play a diminishing role in developing attitudes and influencing the behaviours of the young, as peer-to-peer on-line connectivity and information replaces these traditional roles. For family and friends, contact often relies on appointments and regulated quality time. Family excursions away from home may be one of the only means to experience being in a family. In studies of modern daily life, family appears as more an abstract construct, mostly in our minds, with time budget data showing an actual paucity of within family contact. This is particularly true of the busy modern family in the West that has become essentially a sleep/eating unit with work, school day-care and extra-familial activities taking up the bulk of time.[10] On the other hand, the salience of the family ideal demonstrates the power of family and community as a deeply ingrained concept, sustained over time and place, and without the constant rejuvenating social contact to experience it. Perhaps our positive experience with local relations during the pandemic will go some way towards challenging these helter-skelter lifestyles. One benefit of the lockdown in many families has been the increased amount of time that fathers have spent with their children. Perhaps a realisation that this has the potential to strengthen the positive, for both adult and child will help to maintain this change.

The impact of external forces on community cohesion

As our struggle with COVID-19 made clear, even resilient communities are vulnerable. Powerful political, economic and ecological forces, as well as digital malware disruption, can influence our thoughts and perspectives, potentially tearing at our social fabric. This is not new as colonisation by Western powers across the world has undermined and often destroyed strong cultures and communities that have functioned well over millennia. A more recent stark example of the impact of external destructive forces on communities comes from the Digo people of Kenya.

Exploitation and community collapse

The Digo culture of the Kenya coast have, over the last two decades, experienced a series of man-made catastrophic events, propelled by external exploitation from larger economic and institutional sources. These resulted in the loss of many ritual traditions, resource depletion through land and sea-grabs by the economically powerful. Under these pressures the Digo culture's rich semi-subsistence culture has come to significant collapse with demoralisation, health and nutrition decline as well as emigration. Such threats to traditional communities in today's globalised world are not rare. Efforts to maintain global resilient communities need to include a focus on protecting them from risk, but also what we can learn from them.

As in the Digo experience, much of the pressure on community well-being occurs outside the awareness, control and power of citizens and communities. Our awareness of the influences of large powerful economic, biological or digital forces, and the negative dynamic they may create, is essential to actively confront them in order to remain a resilient community. Attention to connecting people, talking and listening (the little things), sharing information and contributing meaningfully to all facets of community life, are vital central values.[11] Developing personal and community communication skills provide tools for reclaiming control in such situations. Creating and using social rituals that include new coping information supports collective action and agency. They can facilitate the necessary social cohesion and feelings of belonging necessary to thwart the drift to dystopia. Through the haze of our busy-ness, can we, personally and communally, retain and take back control of our communities and help us flourish? The response to COVID-19 suggests that we can. The rise of the Black Lives Matter movement shows how powerful that can be.

Building flourishing communities from inside and out

Governments have a major role to play in supporting communities. There is, however, critique of governments' role in community building. George Monbiot wrote in *The Guardian* during the pandemic,

"Governments whose mission was to shrink the state, to cut taxes and borrowing and dismantle public services, are discovering that the market forces they fetishized cannot defend us from this crisis". Beyond the social damage of neo-liberal approaches, governments and social institutions have increasingly recognised that communities are essential for economic and social growth. In several countries a supportive mix of awareness, participation, and communication raising programs has focused on developing local leadership and empowering communities from the inside out.[12] For example, Dutch participation laws for local governments, although not without problems, are a good example of facilitating communities through stimulating volunteering and civic participation.[13] In the United Kingdom, *Community Capital: The Value of Connected Communities* reported interventions which build and strengthen networks of social relationships. The report makes it clear that communities and their connectedness are crucial to achieving wellbeing. People who said that they feel part of a community were the most likely to report high subjective wellbeing. Investing in community capital involves understanding what social patterns, assets and deficits exist within a community. Investments supporting resilience were shown to improve people's health, wellbeing, and quality of life followed by increased employability, more equitable distribution of power and decreasing demand on existing services. Importantly, the impact of better social relationships on wellbeing was found to be stronger than, for example, social status or life circumstances.

As we have seen, national initiatives that are most effective in stimulating resilience are ones that increase local control, and strengthen social relationships and participation. For success, however, it is key to work from the inside out with the members of the community themselves, tying individuals together with collective action. This creates shared narratives which support the maintenance of an on-going a sense of community.

Reflection:

Are you aware of any government programs for supporting community participation?

Community narratives, storytelling, the open discussion of events and situations is an important part of creating a positive shared perspective.[14] This can facilitate addressing challenging issues. Community evaluation of situations, however, can go both ways. Social outcomes may be determined by the direction and tenor of community discussion and leadership, as the experience of Guinean villages during the war in 2000 demonstrates.

Stories of hope or conflict

Abramowitz,[15] explored the reaction in Guinean communities after violent conflict with Liberian and Sierra Leonean forces. His study illustrates the supportive or destructive nature of group appraisal and narratives. While all communities suffered great distress, communities that maintained their social ritual and practices including reciprocity, charity and shared stories of hope that things would return to normal, had improved wellbeing and economic conditions. This compared with those communities that drifted into internal conflict, abandoned ritual cohesive practices and shared morose narratives of being neglected, wronged and at odds with one another.

Positive community appraisal of a situation is linked to maintaining a focus on community assets, strengths, skills and history to mobilise individuals and promote flourishing.[16] Sharing realistic stories can create understanding and offer fresh points of view facilitating social agency. Community leaders play an important role by stimulating participation and modelling desirable roles, as well as being open to a range of perspectives. The immediate feedback of people's participation in community life can open avenues of hope and optimism, spurring the community into positive action.

Reflection:

How can we help to establish storytelling in our own communities?

Community begins at home – and in the neighbourhood

The basis for a competent community is laid down by our experience at home and thereafter in the neighbourhood. The home is the workshop where behaviour is modelled, rewarded (or punished) and the basic principles of belonging can be learned. It is where we experience give and take as well as the security of being cared for. The individual experience of trust in the family home is transformed through practice with multi-households (villages, friendship networks, neighbourhoods). The home is where values and the rules of engagement that bind people together are first understood. The combination of our homes, neighbourhoods and schools constantly negotiate and develop our social identities. The rise of community interdependence, altruism and caring was notable during the pandemic and often reported in the media. In the long run, however, a more balanced *quid pro quo* and reciprocal relationships are required to make community work. The 'give and take' between households is the motor for a prosperous community life. Positive emotions of respect, caring and gratitude that can flourish in such a context, can take us beyond reciprocity to altruistic community function. Our ongoing engagement and nurturance of positive interactions are a hoped-for outcome in the future.

Achieving flourishing communities

Under normal community conditions, accessible social events open to all can connect diverse groups within the community who have shared but not entirely overlapping interests.

Street party

In 1981 the houses in a London street were 100 years old. It was an excuse to have a street party to celebrate. A small group of organisers contacted their neighbours and on Midsummer's Day everyone turned out in the sunshine to dress up, share food, watch children's shows, dance to Irish music and a steel band and have fun together. In the 42 houses in this street were families from the Caribbean, Cyprus, Turkey, Poland, India, Ireland and Scotland as well as white English. From that moment on people recognised each other, and in many instances able to greet each other by name, maybe even have a brief conversation – something had changed. No longer were the residents strangers to each other, but neighbours sharing a street and a city – "*We had become a community*".

Individuals during the pandemic often took part in a larger connected social network using digital platforms.[17] One such example, of a community using diverse digital together with face-to-face approaches is the *Action for Happiness* (AFH) initiative that asked, *"how do you share positive psychology practices at scale and low cost to inspire people and catalyse action in local communities to build both individual and collective well-being"*? AFH used bottom up action with individuals and communities to take more care of their own wellbeing and bring people together. With a digital platform to share knowledge, stories, ideas for action as well as downloadable resources, it developed an engaging framework – '10 Keys to Happier Living' – with the acronym *GREAT DREAM* (Figure 5).

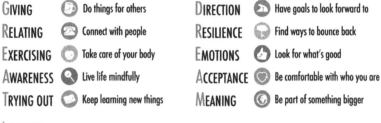

GIVING	Do things for others	DIRECTION	Have goals to look forward to
RELATING	Connect with people	RESILIENCE	Find ways to bounce back
EXERCISING	Take care of your body	EMOTIONS	Look for what's good
AWARENESS	Live life mindfully	ACCEPTANCE	Be comfortable with who you are
TRYING OUT	Keep learning new things	MEANING	Be part of something bigger

ACTION FOR HAPPINESS

Figure 5: Evidence-based 10 keys to happier living
© Vanessa King for Action for Happiness, 2010, 2016

This became a powerful key to building community. Active social media and word of mouth led to creative community actions across the world. For example, a project on Guernsey shared the 10 Keys with every household on the island, and a network of 'Happy Cafés' spaces rose up organically in communities around the world. AFH further developed a community training program that after completion demonstrated, a powerful effect, not only for psychological wellbeing but also on community participation and levels of social trust.[18]

Alternative rites of passage

Communities also thrive even under the most difficult circumstances with inspiring efforts to create them. Young men living on the streets of Kenya, for instance, who had lost their family of origin and tribal connections, thereby

135

their access to rites of passage into adulthood established a self-ritualising process creating an inclusive community that fostered supportive connections, including a street App. This resulted in educational access, legitimate businesses and identity cards for 350 individuals resulting in full citizenship.

Other successful 'grass roots' initiatives, under less extreme circumstances, have been guided by community leaders capable of enlisting others to action. They have created meeting places, drop-in centres for young and old alike, from which a variety of proactive, community run initiatives have evolved.[16] The role of community leadership in modelling altruism, compassion and practical participation can be contagious, as more and more people become involved. Often using only local resources, the communities with positive leadership can achieve a common voice, develop a local identity, initiate rituals (lunches, coffee hour, café's, regular events, discussion groups, community radio, Apps) and create a self-reliant community that can acquire real social and political power.

Black Lives Matter

The power that can be released by the coming together of a disparate community has been evidenced by the extensive global protests following the death of a black man at the hands of the police in the United States. Not only black activists but many young people of all races have demonstrated together in predominantly peaceful marches and gatherings. They had one purpose in common, to raise awareness and change the way black communities were seen and treated by those in authority – specifically the police but also elsewhere.

Strike for climate

Another example of community organisation demanding change is the one led by Greta Thunberg who began as an isolated individual outside the Swedish parliament with the message that humanity is facing an existential crisis through climate change. Her lone protest captured the imagination of many others fearing the same political inaction. She in effect coalesced a community of like minds that has grown exponentially, and is unlikely to disappear while the threat exists and grows.

Other special interest groups have formed communities worldwide[19] addressing not only the political and environmental concerns above but also more day to day issues. These networks can be quite extensive and have been especially helpful in alleviating the burden for individuals and their families experiencing chronic health problems. Ranging across illnesses from depression to bi-polar to cancer to HIV to post-traumatic stress, they have used both face-to-face and web contacts to offer information and support, often more readily than professionals. Such networks may prove of value to counter the expected increase in mental health problems experienced following COVID-19 infection, with its lingering physical and psychological problems. They are experienced as positive both by their members and surrounding communities. Such self-help groups have historically also played an important political role in bringing issues to the attention of the public and pressing for policy change.

For diaspora communities torn and separated by conflict, virtual connection is a lifeline. Despite its problems as a young medium, internet connectivity plays an increasingly important role in the wellbeing of diverse communities and individuals worldwide. We need to work with this powerful force to keep it positive.

Reflections:

In what ways can you contribute to your community?

How have you seen these communities change over time?

Conclusion

Innumerable examples demonstrate the supportive role and power as well as the vulnerability of communities. Although some may complain that our neighbours *"are not there when you need them, but at your doorstep when they are in need"*, communities remain our place to be, grow and share our lives. Communities provide the frame of reference for our social roles and functions. When communities can prioritise positivity, they provide a central frame of reference for understanding ourselves and those around us. Communities may be supported through practical social action and enabled through altruism and compassion. Stimulating communities from the bottom up as well as through positive social policies has been shown to increase wellbeing and health while fuelling collective action. If we can protect the positive functions of community in its various and changing forms, we will assist with improving quality of life for many in our dynamic world.

Reflections:

How can you find out what's happening in your community or what your community needs?

What would enable your local community flourish?

Ideas for action

What might governments do?

Promote community participation.

Encourage and assist community leaders.

Support self-help groups and community projects.

What might communities do?

Create times and places to meet face to face or virtual.

Ritualise regularly occurring social events.

As a community support families and family networks.

Create a community app.

Provide a community platform for the young and elderly.

What might individuals do?

Participate in community life.

Discuss community issues openly, develop a pro-active position.

Develop mutual support groups.

Key sources

Full references and resources are available at our website https://www.creatingtheworldwewanttolivein.org/references/community

1 Lash (1980). *Helen and Teacher: The Story of Helen Keller and Anne Sullivan Macy*. p. 489, Delacorte Press/Seymour Lawrence
2 Bauman (2001). *Community*. Polity Press.
3 Parsfield (Ed.) (2015). *Community Capital: The Value of Connected Communities*. Royal Society for Arts.
4 Janzen (2001). *The Social Fabric of Health: An Introduction to Medical Anthropology*. McGraw-Hill.
5 Bromet *et al.* (2000). Children's Well-being 11 Years After the Chornobyl Catastrophe. *Arch Gen Psychiatry. 2000, 57*(6), 563–571.
6 Copeland *et al.* (2004). Depression among older people in Europe: the EURODEP studies. *World Psychiatry, 3*(1), 45–49.
7 Richter *et al.* (2010). Care as a turning point in sociotherapy. *Medische Anthropologie, 22*(1), 93–108.
8 U.N. (2018). https://www.un.org/development/desa/en/news/population/2018 – revision-of-world-urbanization-prospects.html
9 Kessler *et al.* (2007). Lifetime prevalence and age-of-onset distributions of mental disorders in the World Health Organization's World Mental Health Survey Initiative. *World Psychiatry, 6*, 168–76.
10 Stone & Nicolson (1987). Infrequently occurring activities and contexts in time use data. *Journal of Nervous and Mental Disease, 175*(9), 519–525.
11 Prilleltensky (2012). Wellness and Fairness. *American Journal of Community Psychology, 49*(1–2), 1–21.
12 Kretzmann & McKnight (1993). *Building Communities from the Inside Out: A Path Toward Finding and Mobilizing a Community's Assets*. Institute for Policy Research.

13 During *et al.* (2017). The Dutch Participation Society Needs Open Data, but What is Meant by Open? In Adria, & Mao (Eds.), *Handbook of Research on Citizen Engagement and Public Participation in the Era of New Media* (304–322). IGI Global.

14 Born (2014). *Deepening Community: Finding Joy Together in Chaotic Times.* Berrett-Koehler.

15 Abramowitz (2005). The poor have become rich, and the rich have become poor: Collective trauma in the Guinean Languette. *Social Science & Medicine, 61,* 2106–2118.

16 Norris *et al.* (2008). Community Resilience as a Metaphor, Theory, Set of Capacities, and Strategy for Disaster Readiness. *Am J Community Psychology, 41,* 127–150

17 Martino *et al.* (2017). Community psychology's contributions to happiness and well-being. In Brown, Lomas, & Eiroa-Orosa (Eds.). *The Routledge International Handbook of Critical Positive Psychology* (351–367). Routledge

18 Krekel *et al.* (2020), '*A Local Community Course that Raises Mental Wellbeing and Pro-Sociality'*, Discussion Paper, Centre for Economic Performance, London School of Economics and Political Science, January 2020. ISSN 2042–2695

19 Janzen (1982). Drums Anonymous: Towards an Understanding of Structures of Therapeutic Maintenance. In de Vries, Berg & Lipkin Jr. (Eds.), *The Use and Abuse of Medicine,* (154–66). Praeger.

CHAPTER 8
Leisure

Bridget Grenville-Cleave & Sue Roffey

> *"What is this life if, full of care,*
> *We have no time to stand and stare?"*
> *–W.H. Davies*[1]

Why is leisure important for wellbeing?

On a popular TV quiz show the presenter asks participants what they do for a living and then asks what they like to do when not working, giving each answer equal airtime. Leisure time is not an add-on to the 'real' business of life but integral to it.

Leisure refers to those things we choose to participate in for their own sake, often for fun, entertainment or personal improvement. The average number of minutes spent per day on leisure activities ranges from 386 minutes in Finland to 206 minutes in Mexico, with men spending more time on leisure than women. The global COVID-19 pandemic, with lockdown and social distancing measures implemented in many countries, upended both work and leisure. Working remotely and not participating in team sports, going to the cinema or cafes became the norm. Alternative leisure activities came into their own. Many people found creative ways to continue their hobbies online, or took up one of the many new learning opportunities which emerged. Whether these become long-term changes remains to be seen.

Sociologist Robert Stebbins coined the phrase 'serious leisure' to refer to any amateur, voluntary or hobby activity that might be turned into a career.[2] How we use our 'free' hours, whether casually or seriously, has a significant impact, not only on our wellbeing but also on our sense of identity and sense of meaning. For those who work, whether paid or unpaid, leisure can be a way to detach from work stress, recharge and get things in perspective. It can provide the opportunity to do something less or more challenging, or use different strengths. If we cannot easily build on our interests and strengths or experience positive emotions through work, then our leisure time may be the place to do this. For those who find work mundane or overly controlled, leisure can provide an opportunity for choice and excitement. For those who are not working, leisure activities can be a way of connecting with others, forgetting worries, or doing something meaningful. As such, leisure activities can put positive psychology principles into practice – expressing autonomy, doing something meaningful, improving existing skills, or connecting with others.

Notwithstanding COVID-19 we often feel we have very little time for leisure or less time than we used to, but is this true? And is all leisure equally good for wellbeing? We will explore leisure trends, consider the diverse activities we may engage in, why it matters if we don't have this free time, and what positive psychology can tell us about different types of leisure activity.

Reflections:

How do you typically spend your leisure time?

How do your leisure activities affect your wellbeing?

What positive changes did you make during the pandemic?

Do we have time for leisure?

There was a time when researchers predicted a future where, enabled by technology, we would have more time for leisure because we needed to work less. Although average working hours fell significantly between 1870 and 1980, since then they have barely changed or even increased in many countries, for example the United States, United Kingdom, Australia and Canada.[3] Some people have to do more than one job to make ends meet and for others the boundaries between work and home are getting fuzzier: many find it hard to achieve an acceptable work-life balance. With technology such as smart phones and email, it can be impossible to switch off from work even at home. Countries such as France,

Italy and the Philippines have given employees the right in law to disconnect from work-related electronic communications when not at work. Of course, the increase in remote working caused by the pandemic may continue, and we don't yet know whether or how it will impact leisure time and activities longer term.

On top of a stressful job, people often have to do additional administrative work that can spill over into what should be 'free' time. In many countries, government ideology promotes choice for 'consumers' of public services – such as parents choosing schools for their children or patients choosing which hospital to be treated in. Although having some choice is good for wellbeing, too much can lead to anxiety, which psychologist Barry Schwartz calls the *"paradox of choice"*.[4] Spending more time investigating and weighing up options before making decision eats into our free time. Some people are 'maximisers': they want to make the very best choice. This can lead to never-ending research, examining all possible options in depth. And there is always something better just around the corner. Between 2007 and 2019, for example, there were 24 different iPhone models, each one more sophisticated than the last.

Given the important part that leisure plays in our physical and mental wellbeing, it is perhaps surprising that there is no official recommended daily allowance, as there is for portions of fruit and vegetables in our diet or the number of hours of sleep we get.

Current research indicates that doing recreation activities together is positively related to family satisfaction and stability. The stay-at-home message of the lockdown during the pandemic has meant that some families are spending more time together than ever. How they use that time is likely to prove critical for their wellbeing and future relationships.

Reflections:

How much time do you have every week that you would describe as free time to do what you want?

How has this changed over time, and why?

It is not just having leisure opportunities that matter to a life well-lived, it is also how we perceive our time and how we spend it. 'Busy-ness' can be a badge of honour for some people.[5] There is much in the media and on-line about the over-occupation of children, especially those from privileged backgrounds whose time is completely taken up with worthy pursuits such as music lessons, sports coaching and extra tutoring. What is missing from some children's lives is time to let their imagination roam, to make up stories and games with friends and to deal with their own boredom rather than looking to others for stimulation. No parent wants their children to miss out, but in ferrying them from one activity to another, are we denying our children an important part of their development, the joy of free time?

Is all leisure good for us?

One of the key benefits of participating in activities of our choice is that they make us feel good. Positive psychology research suggests that experiencing frequent positive emotions enhances wellbeing. But not all leisure pursuits that people regard as pleasurable enhance wellbeing, even though this is our initial goal – for example drinking alcohol or taking drugs. We often do these things to change how we feel, to experience the positive emotions of excitement, conviviality or pleasure, or to feel less negative about ourselves and the world – numbing the pain. Sometimes it is to fit in and feel part of the group: a sense of belonging is crucial for our wellbeing. Mood-altering substances are not always damaging, but the addiction that can follow may destroy lives as well as bodies. Other compulsive activities like gambling usually start out as a fun pursuit but, if unchecked, can deteriorate into obsession, debt, panic, depression, criminal behaviour and the breakup of relationships.

How we choose to spend our free time is an issue for wellbeing, even at a young age. For example, in the EU Kids Online study in 19 countries, the average time children spent online per day was 2 hours 47 minutes.[6] The same study found that in most countries, 14 to 16-year-olds spent nearly twice as much time online as nine to ten-year-olds. Not only is this a lot of screen time, it is time spent sitting down indoors. One clear impact of the COVID-19 pandemic is in changing the negative stereotype of online gaming. There is now an appreciation that, as long as gaming does not become an addiction, it not only facilitates creativity but can also enable social connection, a sense of agency, belonging, engagement and a sense of achievement, a boon in a lockdown. Nevertheless, the World Health Organization has published recommendations for children under 5 to reduce sedentary time and increase active play time. Psychologist Peter Gray is an advocate for children and young people's free play, where play is chosen and directed by the participants, especially outdoors. He argues that play is not just about having fun. It has many crucial functions, most notably enabling children and young people to learn how to control their emotions, solve problems, make decisions, exert self-control, follow rules, develop interests and skills and of course make friends and learn how to get along with others. 'Play' might seem trivial to some adults but is a critical enabler of healthy physical, psychological and social development. Gray links the decline of play in the United States and elsewhere with deteriorating mental health in children and young people.[7] Adult play is also robustly linked to different indicators of wellbeing.

Providing affordable recreation for young people

One country which is taking children and young people's leisure seriously is Iceland. It has introduced a Leisure Card, which provides subsidies to encourage youngsters aged 6 to 18 to actively participate in over 100 different recreational activities, including sports, dance, youth clubs and music groups. Studies have shown that when children and young people are involved in organised recreational activities, they are less likely to become involved in antisocial behaviour and/or become socially isolated. By actively participating in a range of self-selected leisure activities, children and young people learn to be more adaptable, make new friends, their self-esteem and self-image improve, and they learn to cope better with everyday life.

A study by Joel Goh and colleagues[8] suggested that a lack of work-life balance contributed to 120,000 excess deaths a year in the United States. The damage to family life, relationships and overall wellbeing is probably incalculable. Unemployed people may have more leisure time but perhaps not the psychological or financial resources to make the most of it. Working parents, especially full-time working mothers, have the lowest levels of leisure time and leisure satisfaction. Something needs to change.

What does positive psychology research say about leisure?

The Greek word for leisure is *schole* – from which we derive our word school. For the ancient Greeks, leisure was more about self-improvement than having fun or just passing time. It was a way to better the human condition and improve the art of living. In current times Joar Vittersø's research indicates that leisure not only gives us positive feelings, it also enables us to recover from the demands of modern life and acts as an arena for personal growth.[9]

David Newman and colleagues identify six ways in which leisure time enhances wellbeing.[10] These are linked to the key positive psychology principles outlined in Chapter 1:

- Detachment – switching off from work.
- Recovery – relaxing.
- Autonomy – having choice.
- Mastery – developing skills.
- Meaning – doing something we feel is worthwhile.
- Affiliation – feeling close to others.

> **Reflection:**
>
> *How does your favourite leisure activity relate to the framework above in enhancing your wellbeing?*

Active and passive leisure: Context matters

Some leisure pursuits are relatively passive, such as watching sport or artistic performances, whilst others are active, such as taking part in sport, drama or creative activities. Some researchers argue that many people have developed a vicious cycle of having to work harder and harder to maintain a chosen lifestyle. This inevitably leads to mental and physical tiredness which, according to Seppo Iso-Ahola,[11] promotes more sedentary leisure. It is a balancing act: after a hectic day at work we may not have the energy for anything too physically demanding and just need downtime. Technological advancements in the home entertainment industry over the past 20–30 years in the developed world also encourage people to stay at home watching an entire series streamed from the internet rather than go out to the cinema or theatre. Although this risks people becoming 'couch potatoes' in normal times, during the pandemic lockdown when all venues were closed, the opportunity to watch a wide variety of visual entertainment was highly valued. In some cases, TV programs encouraged active involvement such as exercise classes or sharing a film night with others online. Perhaps combinations of passive, active, face-to-face and online leisure may become the 'new normal'.

The rest of this chapter explores some of the possibilities for using leisure time and its relationship with psychological wellbeing. There are so many it is impossible to include them all, so what follows are broad categories.

Sport and physical activity

From fly-fishing to football, running to rugby, swimming to sky-diving, sport is an integral part of life and for some people the very cornerstone of their existence. We watch it, play it, read and talk about it. It can be individual or social, organised or informal, competitive or just for fun. Physical activity provides a huge range of wellbeing benefits. For those who engage more actively, sport and other physical activities not only encourage us to value and care for our bodies, they also involve many of the positive psychology principles; increasing competence, experiencing positive emotions, providing a sense of meaning and connecting with others. The most popular physical activities amongst adults across the world are walking, football and running, whereas adolescents also enjoy athletics. Research suggests that doing exercise in a green (outdoors) space boosts self-esteem and mood, whilst the impact of green together with blue exercise (on/in water) is even greater. Relatively short (12 minute) walks can boost mood, even when indoors.[12] Those who engage more passively with sport can feel connected to others who support the same team, experience highs (and sometimes lows) of emotion depending on how well the team performs and become fully absorbed by what happens on the pitch, field or court. Big sporting events, such as the Olympic and Paralympic Games, can bring people and countries together in a spirit of inclusivity, appreciating and recognising sporting achievement and excellence. Knowing that there will be another chance to succeed after a loss is an important aspect in practising a growth mindset, being optimistic and developing resilience. During the COVID-19 lockdown competitive face-to-face sports took a major hit, but personal endeavours continued with more people walking, running, cycling and dancing in their living rooms, gardens and local parks.

Sport for all

The Paralympics has grown from 400 athletes with a disability from 23 countries participating in 8 sports in 1960 to thousands of competitors from over 153 countries in 22 sports in 2016. Disability used to be seen as an individual 'problem' but media coverage of Paralympic games and interviews with Paralympians have changed perceptions. The developing view is that people with disabilities are less restricted by their impairments than by the barriers put on them by society. Paralympians are not only admired role models but also highlight changes needed for others to be able to experience optimal physical and psychological wellbeing.

Reflection:

Are you keen on a particular sport? How does this boost your wellbeing?

Creativity and the arts

This covers a wide range of activities, including painting, gardening and cooking. Making art or artefacts is a way of expressing imagination, experiencing flow and having a sense of achievement. It also provides relaxation, calms difficult emotions and takes the focus away from problems. The wellbeing benefits associated with knitting for example, include distraction from negative emotions or pain, feeling focused, relaxed, in control and more successful.

Crafting has always been popular in the United States and is increasingly so elsewhere. Qualitative research, specifically on quilting, also suggests that such activities can aid the cognitive, emotional and social processes which support wellbeing.

For some the enjoyment of the arts is not active but passive. This includes visiting galleries, which research suggests can lower our stress levels, provide conversational topics and enable us to see life from different perspectives, as well as provide cultural nourishment.

The same may be true of watching films, plays and other performances, which can deepen our empathy and understanding and increase our delight, as well as provide important moments of escapism. During the COVID-19 pandemic galleries and museums across the world created free on-line visits, thereby engaging a new audience.

Music

Music can bring us together, boost our health, bring meaning to our lives and be the source of a wide range of transformative positive emotions from joy and rapture to excitement and fun to calm, serenity and solace. Music is also a means to express identity, make our voices heard and show support and solidarity with others, as we have seen in the surge of new songs aligned with the Black Lives Matter movement.

An orchestra that unites cultures

The West-Eastern Divan Orchestra was founded in 1999 by the conductor Daniel Barenboim and academic Edward Said, and named after an anthology of poems by Goethe. Based in Seville it consists of musicians from Egypt, Iran, Israel, Jordan, Lebanon, Palestine, Syria and Spain. Barenboim says this of the multi-national character of the orchestra, especially the inclusion of Israelis and Palestinians: *"The Divan was conceived as a project against ignorance. A project against the fact that it is absolutely essential for people to get to know the other, to understand what the other thinks and feels, without necessarily agreeing with it".* The orchestra performs around the world, showing that making music together goes beyond the boundaries of place, politics and religion.

The pianist of Yarmouk

For four years, Aeham Ahmad, a refugee in a camp just outside Damascus, wheeled out his piano to play music in the rubble of bombed-out Syrian streets. Surrounded by people coming to escape their everyday horrors, he both lifted their hearts and in videos showed the international community what people were dealing with. Now living in Germany, Ahmad has written his memoir, describing this as 'therapy'.

Music can be both active and passive. Musicians frequently experience a sense of flow, a form of wellbeing which occurs when the skill needed to play a piece of music is broadly in balance with the challenge and complexity of it, resulting in complete absorption. There is a clear link between music and singing, especially in groups such as a choir, and health and wellbeing.[13] A qualitative study of an older people's community choir in Manchester linked singing to the relationships, meaning and accomplishment elements of Martin Seligman's PERMA model of wellbeing. Even during the COVID-19 pandemic, people found innovative ways to continue to play and enjoy music and singing, such as setting up choirs and orchestras online.

The Song Surgery and other arts-based interventions for health and wellbeing

In Ambleside in the United Kingdom a novel idea is taking shape in the form of an experiment that uses the transformative power of poetry and music to improve mental health and wellbeing and overcome conditions ranging from anxiety to insomnia. People are being offered unusual remedies at a 'song surgery', courtesy of the opera singer Bibi Heal. She tailors the songs she prescribes and performs according to the needs of the person seeking help. This is just one of many examples of 'social prescribing', with others being evaluated in a large study at Kings College, London. The project will study three interventions: movement and music sessions for stroke patients, singing for women with postnatal depression, and dance for people with Parkinson's disease.

Being in nature

Colin Capaldi and colleagues[14] report that on average people spend less than 10% of their day outdoors and that participation in outdoor leisure is declining, even though people who feel more connected to nature tend to experience more positive emotion, vitality and life satisfaction compared to those less connected to nature. Numerous studies link the sensory inputs from nature, such as the sound of birdsong or moving water, views and scents with health and wellbeing. This is covered in more detail in the Environment chapter.

Volunteering

Volunteering is something many people do to make a positive contribution to society. The Corporation for National and Community Service in the United States reported that in 2018 over 77 million adults (30%) volunteered 6.9 billion hours through an organisation.[15] If we include those who informally volunteer for friends, family and neighbours, these figures would be much higher. A European Commission study of volunteering across the EU[16] estimated that in 2010 approximately 20% of the total population participated in voluntary work, although the percentages vary from country to country. In Australia the figure is 31%.[17] There is growing evidence that doing something freely to help others is good for our wellbeing. During the COVID-19 pandemic, the media was full of stories of communal effort, where people came together to help those less fortunate. In the United Kingdom, a call for volunteers to support the NHS resulted in over three-quarters of a million signing up, more than could be engaged.

Reflection:

Have you ever helped a neighbour, raised money for a good cause or worked as a volunteer? How did it make you feel?

Do it now!

Michael Frisch, creator of Quality of Life Therapy, says: "*People shouldn't wait for vacations. Rather, they should grab, steal, and enjoy brief pockets of time, be it 5 to 30 minutes, to take a walk, read a book, or call their partner to say 'hi'. Intervals of pure play and relaxation are essential to happiness and contentment. No one can keep up a non-stop frenzied pace day in and day out*".[18] Frisch suggests that people sometimes forget their favourite recreational pursuits, so he proposes that we remind ourselves with a Playlist of those activities which renew and refresh us.

Reflections:

What would you include in a Wellbeing Playlist?

Look at your Playlist. When did you last do any of these? Is it time for a change?

How did your recent experience of Covid-19 lockdown influence your recreational activities?

Ideas for action

What might governments do?

Develop employment legislation that enables everyone to have a work-life balance.

Provide education that values and encourages creativity, physical activity, drama, music and reading for pleasure.

What might communities do?

Provide facilities for a wide variety of leisure activities that people can afford.

Protect open space such as parks, nature trails, walking and cycling paths, waterways and coastal areas.

Establish a shared allotment scheme to grow vegetables.

Support adult education.

What might individuals do?

Get together to share interests: book and film clubs, knitting circles, walking trails. Some of these can be done online too.

Attend and invite others to watch sports matches or events together – especially those who might otherwise not get out.

Key sources

Full references and resources are available at our website https://www.creatingtheworldwewanttolivein.org/references/leisure/

1 Davies (1911). *Songs of Joy and Others.*
2 Stebbins (2006). Serious leisure. In *A handbook of leisure studies* (pp. 448–456). Palgrave Macmillan.
3 Huberman & Minns (2007). The times they are not changin': Days and hours of work in Old and New Worlds, 1870–2000. *Explorations in Economic History, 44(4):*538–567.
4 Schwartz & Ward (2004). Doing better but feeling worse: The paradox of choice. *Positive psychology in practice,* 86–104.
5 Gershuny (2005). Busyness as the badge of honor for the new superordinate working class. *Social Research: An International Quarterly,* 72(2), 287–314.
6 Smahel *et al.* (2020). EU Kids Online 2020: Survey results from 19 countries. London School of Economics and Political Science.
7 Gray (2011). The Decline of Play and the Rise of Psychopathology in Children and Adolescent. *American Journal of Play,* 3(4), 443–463.
8 Goh, Pfeffer & Zenios (2015). The relationship between workplace stressors and mortality and health costs in the United States. *Management Science,* 62(2), 608–628.
9 Vittersø (2011). Recreate or create? Leisure as an arena for recovery and change. In Biswas-Diener (Ed). *Positive psychology as social change* (pp. 293–308). Springer.
10 Newman *et al.* (2014). Leisure and subjective well-being: A model of psychological mechanisms as mediating factors. *Journal of Happiness Studies,* 15, 555–578.
11 Iso-Ahola (1997). A psychological analysis of leisure and health. In J. Haworth (Ed.), *Work, Leisure and Well-Being.* Routledge.
12 Miller & Krizan (2016). Walking facilitates positive affect (even when expecting the opposite). *Emotion,* 16(5), 775.
13 Daykin *et al.* (2018). What works for wellbeing? A systematic review of wellbeing outcomes for music and singing in adults. *Perspectives in public health,* 138(1), 39–46.
14 Capaldi *et al.* (2015). Flourishing in nature: A review of the benefits of connecting with nature and its application as a wellbeing intervention. International Journal of Wellbeing, 5(4), 1–16.
15 https://www.nationalservice.gov/newsroom/press-releases/2018/volunteering-us-hits-record-high-worth-167-billion
16 Mathou (2010). Volunteering in the European Union. Final Report. GHK.
17 Australian Bureau of Statistics (2014). Information needs for volunteering data. https://www.abs.gov.au/research/people/people-and-communities/discussion-paper-information-needs-volunteering-data/information-needs-volunteering-data.
18 Frisch (2006). Quality of life therapy: Applying a life satisfaction approach to positive psychology and cognitive therapy. Wiley.

The world around us

CHAPTER 9
Media

Marten de Vries

"In no area is competition more important than in the marketplace for ideas. A well-informed citizenry is essential for a well-functioning democracy. A media that is controlled by only a few companies, or wealthy individuals will result in their views dominating the national discourse"– Joseph Stiglitz[1]

Why media matters

The Colombian Truth Commission, in the context of a fragile peace after a 50-year civil war, is faced with the challenge of reconciling a society traumatised by violence and community disruption. The Commission grapples daily with convening conflicted groups: government, FARC revolutionaries, paramilitaries, diverse ethnic, rural, and urban communities; with the promise that a peaceful and positive future lay ahead. It struggles to unravel accountability and *"what is truth, whose truth and who will eventually own the truth(s)"*. They strive to engage the public with websites, social media, commercials, and awareness raising debates, but had failed in their eyes to connect with the people. They unexpectedly asked: can media help? and can it help speak to the 'truth'? Indeed, to whom do we turn, or what can we do, if our aim is through positive communication to do less harm and create compassion? Their question is also our question: can media help to create a world we want to live in?

Media-based communication has become the cornerstone of modern life. It has accelerated the reach and speed of information exchange, creating the possibility of influencing behaviour, and stimulating a sense of community. The impact of media has perhaps never before become more evident than during the COVID-19 pandemic. With social distancing measures imposed during the lockdown, everyone turned to media, social media in particular, to maintain valuable connections with family and friends, as well as to inform, entertain, and distract.

Media became a beacon in the often lonely storm of isolation. 80% in the United States and United Kingdom say they are likely to continue their current level of media use. Staying in control of these communications will be important for the future – and, as Joseph Stiglitz notes at the head of this chapter, that control must not be restricted to the hands of a self-selecting few.

Changed media habits during the COVID-19 pandemic

Facebook reported over 37–50% increase in messaging during March 2020. WhatsApp reported the largest increase in usage from 40–76% dependent on country and phase of the pandemic.

As people wanted to see one another, there was a significant increase in the use of Zoom, Teams, and other interactive platforms.

As countries moved deeper in to the pandemic, media consumption increased across all in-home channels: web browsing increased by 70%, followed by (traditional) TV viewing increasing by 63% and social media engagement increasing by 61% over normal usage rates.

China experienced a 58% increase in usage of local social media apps including Wechat and Weibo.

Increased usage across all platforms has been biggest in the 18–34 age group.[2]

Our ability to use media during the pandemic benefited from work over past decades to make communications more responsive to social contexts and values. Socially minded pioneers employed media for the public good and the wellbeing of the world's communities. Anchored in the lived experience of people, and guided by development and human rights approaches, they established a 'many-to-many' communication strategy, linking cultures and diverse perspectives. Incredibly successful, this created the frame for the rapidly growing social media platforms.

The utility, easy access and openness of social media was not only a boon during the pandemic but promised an increase in mutual understanding, constructive dialogue, and the promotion of participation. But social media's openness is both its strength and weakness and allows misuse. Fake news trolls, and the business plans of large social platforms, saw opportunities. One example is the rampant misinformation campaigns during the pandemic that muddled COVID-19 factual public health information. Now that COVID-19 has opened the media landscape like never before, can we use it to also stem these impending problems and retain the positive perspectives and momentum for wellbeing set out by media pioneers? Safe and reliable communications are essential in building the world we want to live in.

> **Reflection:**
>
> *In what ways has media contributed to positive connections in your life, and compassion in your communities'?*

Within the complex global landscape, we propose a media aligned with positive psychology principles in inviting us to be open and accepting of others; support who we want to be; facilitate feelings of belonging in enabling communities, and provide the security that traditional face-to-face relationships once did. Media with the power to inform but also inspire hope and wonder, not thriving on social division and hatred. As active citizens, we need to stay in control of the media we have, so compassion and secure connections can provide opportunities for action on the things we care about.

Eyes wide open

During the pandemic in 2020 the world was glued to their mobile phones and Apps for information, while social turmoil, inequality, racial injustice, climate change, and population migrations continued around them. Too much information can lead to overload and uncertainty about what is real. Mental health problems were already an issue of global concern and health agencies have warned that they have been exacerbated by COVID-19, driven by human and economic loss, fear of contagion, isolation, family disruption, and social distancing.

Positive psychology principles offer guidance in how to remain human and empathetic in a context of ever-increasing social change and control, and the manipulation by media platforms. Mindful awareness is critical. The competition for our attention has resulted in a race to reduce individuals to profiles, with the goal of controlling our behaviour for financial and political gain. Many social media platforms are based on such industrial practices, not, as is often claimed, for fostering open communication, and positive connections. Media companies, political organisations and others have become supremely skilled at this, using the latest findings in psychology and neuroscience to capture, hold, buy and sell our data. Only displaying information that caters to our interests' limits our knowledge base, and reduces exposure to alternative views that may challenge deeply held assumptions. Especially during a crisis, public health communications have to be seen as credible, transparent, and trustworthy, but the sheer volume of COVID-19 uncritical misinformation and disinformation online was often 'crowding out' accurate public health guidance.[3]

Reflections:

Are you aware of social media platforms using knowledge of your interests and lifestyle, to promote specifically targeted products?

What do you feel about that?

The misuse of social media technology for profit and political gain is 'hiding in plain sight' and accelerating. This fuels uncertainty about what is 'real', and what is manipulation. Several recent studies have demonstrated the impact of media on our mindset by comparing reactions to reading, seeing and hearing positive and negative news. One study found both lower social trust and less helping behaviour after reading negative news, or even just negative headlines.[4] Social media platforms use the same techniques as gambling organisations to create psychological dependence. These methods have been shown to have effects on the brain similar to drug use.[5] Even the presence of your smart phone in the same room significantly reduces available cognitive capacity.[6] And perpetual online mindset influences how we think and feel. We are vulnerable.

The trust in state-owned media as the best protection for citizens has faded, as media censorship, propaganda TV, and the cynical use of social media in elections by major world powers have become the norm. Years ago, media philosopher Marshall McLuhan warned – as Tim Berners-Lee, the founder of the web, does today – the web is not the global village we hoped for. Instead, a retreat into narrow groups of mutual 'likes' has encouraged tribalism, populism, and the misuse of power. In his effort to save the internet, Berners-Lee calls for a new 'internet contract' signed by governments, institutions and business. This aims to stem misuse through developing best practices, and taking direct action – such as forbidding political commercials – before the net becomes a 'digital dystopia'.

Trustworthy information

Traditional nationwide news channels (broadcast and newspaper) are the most trusted sources of information with 52% of people identifying them as a 'trustworthy' source. Government agency websites are regarded as trustworthy by only 48% of people, suggesting that government measures are not providing citizens around the world with assurances and security. Reflecting the loss of trust from recent election cycles, social media platforms are regarded by only 11% of people as a source of trustworthy information.[3]

The misuse of public trust is not a new phenomenon. Broadcast platforms have fuelled hysteria with inflammatory reporting, been responsible for flagrant war mongering, and used subliminal 'hidden persuaders' – such as sex, money, food, and violence for a variety of nefarious purposes. Traditional media, although under pressure today as a trustworthy social resource, has served the public well with in-depth, well-informed and fact-checked reporting. It has also brought people together through covering social and sporting events and by producing uplifting entertainment for a large public. We need to keep it that way.

Reclaiming the media we want and need

The question then is not so much what can media do to increase well-being, but what can we do to use or re-create media for wellbeing?

All media platforms work well when we interact with them, steer them with scientific and experiential fact, and intervene when caution is appropriate (child porn, abuse, calls to violence, etc.). Our communities, broader society, and democracy itself, all require our involvement to maintain an independent exchange of accurate and uncensored information.

The COVID-19 surge in media use shows that we have more control than ever before with the burgeoning of creative ways to socially engage and inform. Work, school, and learning have all continued on-line. Platforms such as Zoom, Microsoft Teams, neighbourhood Apps, alongside 'community viewing' of productions or games, connected people and decreased the impact of isolation. As a result, people became more interested in their immediate environment. Offices and schools moved into homes, creating a profound increase in on online activity that is likely to persist. More participatory media and evolving interactive platforms will become available, providing the means to reach millions almost instantaneously. Such platforms are likely to play a major social and political role in the future.

A number of journalistic initiatives are leading the way to keep us informed and optimistic. 'Constructive journalism', coined in 2015, challenges traditional negative news biases, drawing on positive psychology concepts of sharing solutions toward positive action. These initiatives have shown that positive news stories can enhance engagement, and positively influence attitudes.[7] Broadcast initiatives such as *World's Best News* and *Bright Vibes* provide positive information and stories often left untold in other media. These media initiatives invite viewers to participate in a kinder world.

Citizen journalists reporting on the Coronavirus outbreak in Wuhan and elsewhere, and open source investigations such as Bellingcat, are essentially transparent non-institutional fact-checkers that have made useful contributions in uncovering actual facts from reports in the mainstream media. This includes, for example, the downing of flight MH17 above the Ukrainian conflict; Iraqi weapons misinformation;

and the beginnings of the health crisis in China. Such transparent journalistic approaches are carried out by people in their free time from private homes, often taking considerable risks in combating fake news. Media watchers call their work 'a war for democracy'. They serve as an inspiration for us all to use media for the common good.

As these examples during the pandemic show, media is no longer just in the hands of big platforms and producers: media is now also us, the audience. As the singer Jello Biafra said: "*Don't hate the media; become the media*"; many are following that call.

Although often exploited unknowingly, we are also primed with a growing media sophistication. Over the last decades we have developed new communication tools and habits. Although differing from country to country, the use of social media by the young is legendary. Youth are often more tech-savvy, and can provide advice for older citizens increasing cross-generational connection. Media has become a powerful ally to actively facilitate 'boundary crossing', reaching out between generations, citizens, professionals, and governments, with the potential to empower populations.[8] This has been evident in the Black Lives Matter and #MeToo campaigns, bringing together people from across divides for a common purpose. Media productions can be coupled to practical social interventions, achieving proven positive impact on mental, physical, and social health such as the Triple P Program in Australia and the multi-media @teacher5aday platform supporting teachers in the United Kingdom.

A successful multi-media social intervention

The Triple P program in Australia[9] is a mixed-media, multilevel intervention for communities and families aimed at addressing a range of mental health related behaviours. It uses innovative community media-based preventive approaches linked to traditional specifically family-targeted interventions. In over 40 controlled trials across different cultures, positive outcomes were sustained for over 1 year. Improvements were realised in dysfunctional parenting strategies (e.g. being coercive), stress and anger, depression, alongside improving parental relationship quality, with a positive effect on children's conduct problems and the reduction of verified cases of child abuse in communities.

One of the first platforms was YouTube, with a global reach of billions, particularly in the 18–34 age group. Beside entertainment, their editorial aim is to *"connect and empower people for positive change".* YouTube is used by individuals and groups including high social value organisations such as Doctors Without Borders, American Civil Liberties Union, the Rainforest Alliance network, TED talks, and many others.

Social media is still relatively new and in the early stages of development. We have a lot to learn in how to use these tools positively. Giuseppe Riva and his colleagues[10] propose a 'positive technology' to improve the connectedness between individuals, groups, and organisations. The quality of experience is their guiding principle.

The openness of social media not only risks exposure to misinformation and bullying, but also has the potential to confront unprepared youngsters with new choices from gambling to predatory sex. Families, schools, and communities need to engage the young in early and open communication about their social media use. Much can be done to manage the downside. Controlling screen time for children, and parents co-regulating their use of media with them, can create a safer experience for children and a more open family environment. Critical internet literacy skills taught in school can help students learn to interpret messages and gain trust in the digital landscape. Educational games, like the fake news game, invite kids to create their own fake news, helping them to identify what is, and is not true, and reducing their susceptibility to the persuasiveness of misleading news articles. Such approaches provide an accessible and enjoyable tool to achieve awareness for both children and adults.[11] At the social level, we might consider regulating Vloggers, YouTubers, TikTok-ers and Facebook-like platforms with similar criteria by which TV and films are monitored. Regulation is complex and requires citizen involvement to monitor both freedom of speech and abuse potential.

Reflection:

How is the way we use social and traditional media linked to our own wellbeing, and that of our communities? What do you think you might change?

Aspiration and action

When broadcast media is co-produced with local populations, it empowers communities in sharing ways of dealing with human problems.[9] This requires partnerships across social disciplines with national and local broadcasters, tech platforms, journalists, and the performing arts. Media personnel are often eager to use experienced stories and scientific concepts to guide programming. The examples below demonstrate the engaging and dramatic effects that can be achieved when this relationship is activated.

Examples of informative dramas and their impact

In the 1970s 'telenovelas' (TV soap operas) successfully modelled adaptive behaviour in the slums of Rio. Since then, many dramatic educational messages focused on local issues have had a similar positive impact. For instance, in the San Francisco Mood study, a collaboration between science and media resulted in a prime-time program on depression. This increased attention to mood in the entire population of San Francisco, as well as decreased symptoms in depressed people.

The MTV *Shuga* soap series in South Africa and Nigeria (soon in India) informed and opened the discussion about HIV prevention for and together with the young.

The Dutch series *Bianca in the Neighbourhood* depicted personal and community problems. This was co-produced with low SES neighbourhoods in an often humorous manner and when followed by small group viewings facilitated open discussion of difficult topics.

The Team soap series in Kenya was a response to post-election violence that scarred the country. It dramatically depicted ethnic issues within a multi-cultural, mixed-gender football team. Broadcasts were followed by a talk show. The re-airing with community mobile units reached 70% of the Kenyan population. The Team opened a national discourse on violence and ethnic relations, not only decreasing tensions' but also resulting in sustainable social initiatives at the grassroots level. Most importantly there was less violence during the next election.[12]

> **Reflection:**
>
> *What programs have you seen or heard that have shifted your understanding or beliefs about an issue, positively or negatively?*

Community radio is used world-wide to provide information and create a local voice, ranging from urban and rural western communities to African societies, slums and refugee camps to traditional indigenous communities in Latin America. Although radio has also incited harm, as in Rwanda and elsewhere, it has overwhelmingly been a medium of connection and positive development especially when linked to actual community realities. Today anyone can set up a local 'radio station' using web broadcasting. Communities need to ensure that any such initiative builds the benefit of all citizens.

Power of community radio

Radio Santa Maria, in the Dominican Republic, is a model for international community radio producing material with the local population, schools, workers, and community groups etc. Communities are stakeholders and co-producers of content, design, and dissemination. Broad multi-media productions from print (comics) to interactive TV programming are offered, along with practical agrarian information on crop maintenance, market prices, and the weather.

The initiatives above are just a few examples illustrating media's power to grab our attention, help us identify with, and positively engage with challenging issues. Part of the trick in media story-telling is the inclusion of symbols that create identification, and become emblematic for the aim of the productions. Iconic and symbolic referents have worked well, for instance, in the *Bianca in the Neighbourhood* series, in which the character Bianca, who runs a Fitness Centre, consistently models empathic action in attempting to solve her client's problems only to encounter a tangle of complexity in often funny situations. People were soon overheard saying with a wink, *"I'm doing a Bianca"*, to help overcome the stress of complex social contexts. Other examples include the 'frog' logo of the Rainforest Alliance that helped consolidate climate activities globally, and the multi-ethnic football *Team* in Kenya that became a symbol for ethnic tolerance. Identification with such symbols can become emblematic, influencing social behaviours. One area where this is important is in combating racial prejudice. Over the last years, major broadcasters and social media platforms, have become sensitive to their role in contributing to racial and ethnic stereotyping, but the Black Lives Matter movement reminds us that more needs to be done. Media can and should play a crucial role in influencing behaviour by including persons and characters that depict black lives, and that of other minorities in realistic, positive ways helping create models for the ongoing struggle for ethnic and racial equality. This also applies in other areas, such as the portrayal of ageing.

Psychologist Alfred Bandura asserts that mass media not only creates personal attributes but can also alter existing ones.[13] Individuals learn behaviours by imitation, watching others, whether in person or in the media. The imitation and empathy with positive models increase an individual's sense of self-worth and efficacy, potentially resulting in behaviour change. On the other hand, media can also support negative behaviours with deleterious consequences.

Reflections:

Have you ever found yourself identifying with a fictional character?

In what way positively, or negatively, did this influence your actions?

What is needed for successful community media?

At the basis of a community media intervention is shared storytelling. Telling stories can create a common language that bridges the gap between people, set boundaries of what is acceptable or not, and create shared meaning. The French philosopher Pierre Rosanvallon proposes[14] a 'narrative democracy', where storytelling the lived experiences of people informs policy, not just population statistics and polls. Interactive media can play a constructive role in supporting a democratic process by airing constructive stories alongside accurate reporting, thereby helping to counteract the negative impact of undemocratic, or disruptive events.

The most important ingredient for successful community media is an assessment of grassroots readiness and interest. Engaging the target audience in all phases of research, production, dissemination, and especially post-production community embedding is important. Actual events, stories, concerns, and experiences form the basis of scripts for video, radio, or print rendering the target group co-owner of the production. This can be seen in what used to be called docudramas and now called fact-based dramas. These give the human perspective on events and public policies, building understanding and empathy for those involved. When presented in public formats an open discussion of the relevant issues can support community connectivity, and lead to positive social action. Sustaining social activities thereafter requires only limited resources; 'coffee money' and providing a place to meet. The implementation of this social process will have to be evaluated and creatively transformed in the 'new Normal' social distancing of the post COVID-19 period.

Going forward: being media

During the pandemic a quantum jump in media use took place as we turned our attention to seeking connection, and information. Our attention is a precious resource; developing the skills to choose where to direct it can help us maintain or regain control of media tools and services. We can do this by:

- Increasing awareness of how the internet and media can influence the way we think, what we choose to do.
- Checking that our use of the media is in accordance with our values.
- Taking charge of the media we have in constructive ways.

Scrutinising communications and sustaining participation in new and traditional media by both citizens and professionals is essential to our wellbeing in our post-pandemic future. For example, we needed to guard against the sheer volume of COVID-19 misinformation online in early 2020, which crowded out accurate public health guidance. Similarly, those denying climate change were over-represented in the media by 49%, swamping reports based on scientific evidence on which some 95% of scientists agree.[15] Journalists and editors should be called upon to adjust such disproportionate attention. Our susceptibility to misinformation and manipulation remains a serious problem until we learn to manage and participate actively in the public discourse with our new media tools.

One way to take action is to work closely with sources that already have the attention of the wider public or the means to achieve it. Developing links with media personnel, and inviting journalists to participate in social interventions, research protocols, and policy development, can open avenues of influence. This is particularly important when broadcasters risk harming wide sections of the community. Social media as well as direct personal responses have been very effective in such corrections and potentially altered the nature of broadcasting. This has recently been expanded at the entertainment level, with opportunities to influence scripts, including characters and outcomes. Fan websites such as fanfiction.net and AO3 Wattpad have a huge following – 1.5 million authors have placed 5.5 million stories with 80 million readers – who encourage people to place their own stories, choose their own endings and provide tips for better scripts. This interactivity increased during the pandemic and created on-line communities with their own language norms.

Retaining a larger presence on the internet and social media is one way to counteract hearsay and bias. Interacting with, or changing internet providers can enable individuals to assume personal control of the internet space, but collective action is needed to exert greater influence on providers. There are enough alternative platforms today to allow such shifts. Our personal initiative and group influence can hold the internet to a value system in line with the common good. Elinor Ostrom, Nobel Prize winner for Economics, has suggested that there are several alternative models for participation by whole communities.[16] These include using open source technologies such as 'wikis', that allow people to collaborate as well as modify data, for practical and social ends. The community itself has responsibility for the environment we live in, including the virtual one. We have choices!

Reflections:

How can you engage and collaborate with media sources to help shape the medium for the common good?

How might local knowledge combine to produce recognisable characters to model positive values and behaviour?

How can you engage and collaborate with media sources to help shape the medium for the common good?

The citizen's arsenal for proactive media has expanded – on-line petitions, blogs and e-mail letter campaigns, websites, Twitter, YouTube, and Instagram, Apps – don't forget the telephone – all have the potential to draw attention to important but often unreported issues. We need only to think of the #MeToo campaign to grasp the impact of Twitter, and the open source influence of Bellingcat initiatives.

Neighbourhood Apps are simple to implement, have been extensively used, and have a significant cohesive effect improving safety and focusing on day-to-day concerns, even providing a voice to street children, and the homeless. Consumer-to-consumer networks (TripAdvisor, TrustPilot, etc.) are seen as trustworthy means of information exchange.

Media communication does not occur in a vacuum. We all have a part to play. One essential role is countering the 'echo chamber' of polarising groups, where 'likes find likes', through the inclusion of a collective presence with many viewpoints and cultural differences on all forms of media. Sharing stories focused on strengths and compassion can provide support across social boundaries, increasing understanding, and fostering a stronger sense of community. Media provides the possibility that such positive efforts can be read, seen, or heard by millions, as seen during COVID-19.

Our answer, then, to the Colombian Truth Commission's question cited at the beginning of the chapter, is that media *can* contribute to the search for the 'truths' we find important, by focusing attention on an open public discourse of different views. To achieve this, as 'owners' of today's multi-media tools, we are responsible for maintaining positive attention in the media we use and want. This requires vigilance and sustained effort in using psychological science and media resources in support of a global conversation of hope.

Ideas for action

What might governments do?

Develop legislation to curtail abuse on the internet and social media.

Ban political commercials from the internet.

Open discussion on the costs and benefits of government monitoring of the web.

What might media do?

Focus on maintaining their reputation as a trusted resource.

Become aware of the powerful impact of negative news.

Use the quality of the experience of the audience as the guiding principle for programming.

Fact check fake news and provide room for citizen journalism initiatives.

What might communities and citizens do?

Become aware of how the internet and media can influence the way we think.

Check that our use of the media is in accordance with our values.

Develop media skills (Blogs, vlogs, You Tube. Apps etc.) and engage with media providers to prevent harm and influence positive programming.

Discuss social media use within the family.

Develop Apps that positively connect people, community radio, etc.

Key sources

Full references and resources are available at our website https://www.creatingtheworldwewanttolivein.org/references/media/

1 Stiglitz (2019). *People, Power and Profits: Progressive capitalism for an age of discontent*. p. 75. W.W. Norton.
2 CUBE (2020). https://consumerunderstanding.be/whatsapp-sees-40-surge-wake-COVID-19-pandemic/
3 Worrall & Pazzanese (2020). Battling the Pandemic of Misinformation. *The Harvard Gazette*. May 2020
4 Han *et al.* (2019). The effect of negative energy news on social trust and helping behavior. *Computers in Human Behavior 92*, 128–138.
5 He, Turel & Bechara (2017). Brain anatomy alterations associated with Social Networking Site (SNS) addiction. *Sci Rep 7*, 45064.
6 Ward *et al.* (2017). Brain Drain: The mere presence of one's own smart phone reduces available cognitive capacity. *Journal of the Association of Consumer Research, 2*(2).
7 McIntyre & Gyldensted (2017). Constructive Journalism: An Introduction and Practical Guide for Applying Positive Psychology Techniques to News Production. *The Journal of Media Innovations, 4*(2), 20–34.
8 Knibbe, de Vries & Horstman (2017). Engaging cultural resources to promote mental health in Dutch LSES neighbourhoods: Study of a community-based participatory media project. *Health Promotion International, 32*, 567–576.
9 Sanders, Montgomery & Brechman-Toussaint (2000). The mass media and the prevention of child behaviour problems: the evaluation of a television series to promote positive outcomes for parents and their children. *Journal of Child Psychology and Psychiatry and Allied Disciplines, 41*, 939–48.
10 Riva *et al.* (2012). Positive technology: using interactive technologies to promote positive functioning. *Cyberpsychology, Behavior, and Social Networking, 15*, 69–77.
11 Roozenbeek & van der Linden (2019). The fake news game: actively inoculating against the risk of misinformation. *Journal of Risk Research, 22*(5), 570–580.
12 de Vries (2014). Mental Health, Mass Communication and Media. In Okpaku (Ed.) *Essentials of Global Mental Health*. Cambridge University Press.
13 Bandura (2001). Social cognitive theory of mass communication. *Media Psychology, 3*, 265–98.
14 Rosanvallon (2008). *Counter-Democracy: Politics in an Age of Distrust*. Cambridge University Press.
15 Petersen, Vincent & Westerling (2019). Discrepancy in scientific authority and media visibility of climate change scientists and contrarians. *Nat Commun 10*, 3502.
16 Ostrom & Ostrom (2014). *Choices, Rules and Collective Action*. ECPR Press.

CHAPTER 10
Society

Sue Roffey & Felicia Huppert

> *"It is in your hands to create a better world for all who live in it". – Nelson Mandela*[1]

What makes for a good society?

Imagine a society where kindness is the default mode of interaction, and people are not hungry, homeless, or rejected because of their race, religion, gender, disability, sexuality, or social position – a future in which everyone is flourishing and valued equally. What difference might it make if promoting the common good was a central principle in policymaking, and not just an empty electioneering promise? This utopian vision is almost laughable, except that there are efforts at making this happen, and despite many negative news stories, things are slowly moving in a more positive direction. As Mandela suggests in the quote above, it is up to all of us.

It has long been known that what is happening in a society affects the mental health and wellbeing of the population. According to the Centre for Society and Mental Health at Kings College London: *"the factors that promote mental health or lead to mental health problems lie in our societies, schools, workplaces, and communities, as well as in the way we live our contemporary social lives".*

> ### View from the grass roots
>
> According to the New Statesman report, *Rethinking Poverty:*
>
> *"... when asked which qualities are most important for a good society, 10,112 respondents ranked social qualities such as fairness, freedom, security, and tolerance above economic concerns.*

Having well-paid work and the absence of poverty are impor-
tant chiefly because they help people to live fuller lives ... For
most people, the good life is not about having a lot of money;
it is about having enough to pay for the basics – food, shelter,
transport, etc. – as well as occasionally enjoying a few luxu-
ries ... When a focus group of low-paid people was asked about
what constituted a good society, they focused upon opportu-
nity, agreeing that people should have the chance 'to do well in
life and realise their ambitions'. A good society should 'provide
opportunities for work and ensure that everyone has a stake in
society'."

The Report accordingly proposes the following principles for
a good society:

- Everyone having a decent basic standard of living so
  people are secure and free to choose how to lead their
  lives;
- Being able to develop potential and flourish both materi-
  ally and emotionally;
- Treating everyone with care and respect;
- Enabling all citizens to participate and contribute to building a fair and sustainable future for the next generation.

A good society may be defined as one that is organised to ensure that
most citizens flourish in their lives. Individual wellbeing is largely
dependent on environmental factors – the family and social context
in which individuals live and work. Margaret Thatcher's 1987 statement *"there is no such thing as society"*[2] suited her political stance, but
wellbeing within a society depends on 'us' not just on 'me'. In the
COVID-19 pandemic most countries required citizens to stay indoors,
not only for their own safety but also to stop the virus spreading out
of control. Most citizens did as they were asked, thereby reducing the
spike in new cases that could overwhelm health services, but in some
places there was a vocal cohort who resented having their freedoms
curtailed – as far as they were concerned, each person should be able
to do what they like, regardless of the impact on their fellow citizens.

Sociologist Amitai Etzioni sees a good society as *"one that nourishes*
both social virtues and individual rights"[3] – one that balances order

and autonomy, shared values and individual values, communal and personal needs, and social responsibilities and individual freedoms. All freedoms need to be considered in the light of what works for everyone. Etzioni further advocates that people adopt 'the Golden Rule', choosing to treat each other as they themselves would want to be treated.

These approaches are supported by evidence. Although there are cultural differences, the *World Happiness Report 2017* found that, across 155 countries, freedom to make life choices and social support are the two largest predictors of positive emotion and positive life evaluation. The top six countries on both these measures are Nordic or Northern European, which typically have the lowest levels of inequality, good access to education and healthcare, high levels of press freedom, and a system of social welfare for those in need. High levels of wellbeing have societal benefits, as individuals who are thriving are more likely to be productive at work, kind towards others, and behave in more pro-social ways.

What gets in the way of a society where everyone can flourish?

One of the main obstacles to universal wellbeing is the tendency of governments to prioritise economic growth at the expense of what we know leads to good lives for people and the planet.

In a flourishing society every citizen's basic needs would be met. One in nine of the world's population are living with the severe deprivation. Dirty water and inadequate sanitation are a primary cause of around 3.4 million deaths every year. UNICEF estimates children under five years old living in situations of crisis or conflict are 20 times more likely to die from diseases linked to unsafe water and sanitation than from direct violence. Habitat for Humanity has estimated that up to 150 million people across the world are homeless, and another one and a half billion have inadequate shelter. While 820 million people in the world today go hungry, it is estimated that a third of the food produced for human consumption is thrown away. It is not so much food resources that are the problem, but their distribution.

In 2015, the United Nations adopted the 2030 Agenda for Sustainable Development. Building on the principle of *"leaving no one behind"*. The new Agenda emphasises a holistic approach to achieving sustainable development for all. This includes 17 Sustainable Development Goals (SDGs). The alleviation of poverty worldwide is SDG 1. Universal provision of clean water and sanitation is SDG 6.

Reflections:

What do you feel about people going hungry and homeless in societies where some individuals are very wealthy?

Whose responsibility is it to ensure that basic human needs are met?

What influences your views on this?

If we seek to improve lives, we need to understand what underlies the widespread failure to meet basic human needs. One contributing factor is that many of the poorest nations in the world are characterised by totalitarian regimes, political turmoil, weak financial institutions, inadequate infrastructure, and corruption. But perhaps the major factor is discrimination – the belief that some people are less worthy than others. In many countries, negative attitudes towards minority groups, or those who do not conform to social norms such as sexual orientation, denies these groups their basic human rights and prevents them from living their lives fully and without fear. This impairs the wellbeing of those who discriminate, as well as those discriminated against. A study of 108 countries finds that higher tolerance towards diversity is associated with higher levels of societal wellbeing.[4]

Reflections:

How would you feel if people were saying things about your gender, race, religion, or other aspects of your identity that were untrue or just nasty?

Should we restrict the use of language that demonises others? If so, how might we do this?

Even in countries where people have lived together for centuries, differences in belief, or appearance, may inhibit recognition of our shared humanity and the application of basic human rights. More than 150 years after the 13th Amendment abolished slavery in the United States, most US adults say the legacy of slavery continues to have an impact on the position of black people in American society today.[5] This came dramatically to the fore in the global civil unrest following the death of an unarmed black man, George Floyd, in Minneapolis in May 2020, just one of a tragically long line of African-Americans killed at the hands of the police.

According to social psychologist Martha Augoustinos: *"Racism is a pernicious, pervasive, and persistent social problem".*[6] Racism occurs where individual prejudices are supported by broader social and institutional norms, and practices that systematically disadvantage particular groups. Examples of this are the disconcerting rates of incarceration of Black Americans, who represent 12% of the US population but 33% of those in prison,[7] and the even higher rate among Indigenous Australians who represent 3% of the population but 28.6% of those in prison.[8] Although in many liberal Western societies overt white supremacist beliefs are no longer acceptable, unconscious biases, and covert and subtle behaviours may keep discriminatory practices hard-wired. Racism that has been kept alive under the surface can be ignited by powerful figures who give it credibility.

What can positive psychology offer?

Major social changes have occurred throughout history, but we seem to be in a period of accelerated upheaval. With escalating migration, change in traditional work patterns, and in many places the dissolution of extended family networks, societies are more fluid than ever before, with people of different faiths, languages, ethnicity, and cultural norms living in proximity. Especially in the light of the ways different countries have reacted to the threat of the COVID-19 pandemic, and the rise of the Black Lives Matter movement, now more than ever is the time to be asking again and with urgent purpose: what makes for a good society and the good governance of that society?

Positive psychology has given us a fresh lens through which to see ourselves and the lives we lead. This change of perspective is enabling individuals across the world to have a more meaningful, and satisfying existence. Although we acknowledge the complexity of social change, could what we know from evidence on individual wellbeing also transform societies? A number of positive psychologists have begun to explore these issues, but the science is still in its infancy.

Other chapters in this book address many of the domains of life integral to a good society, so here we cover some of the issues not addressed elsewhere

Social connection

That a sense of belonging promotes psychological wellbeing is now well established,[9] but this is often defined as belonging to a specific group, and finding security in being with people 'like me'. Exclusive belonging is 'me and my gang/family/class, community, or country', and although it can have a positive impact on individual resilience, it can easily slip into dehumanising others who are 'outside' the group. Inclusive belonging values all. Making discriminatory behaviours illegal may be necessary to protect human rights across institutions, but it takes more than this to build positive connections between groups. Megan Phelps-Roper came to renounce the strong prejudices with which she had grown up and outlines principles of positive communication in her 2017 TED talk.[10] This is summarised as follows:

- Don't assume bad intent – there are reasons people have developed the attitudes that they hold.
- Ask questions – it helps both sides understand where the other is coming from.
- Stay calm – anger and rudeness bring conversations to an end.
- Make the argument – if we want change, we have to make the case for it.

Positive youth development is about forging connections with prosocial adults in the community. Extensive research shows that the availability of trusted adults who can be protectors, advisors, role models, and skill-builders have a beneficial influence at all stages of a young person's development.

Trust is a key component of connecting with others. Numerous studies of nations and communities show that the higher the trust, the greater the wellbeing. The relationship is bi-directional – when we feel we can trust people, our wellbeing is higher, and when our wellbeing is high, we are more likely to trust people.

Can we trust strangers?

A Toronto newspaper addressed this question in two ways. First, a survey asked readers to express their opinion about the chance of a wallet being returned by neighbours, strangers, and police officers. Second, they placed cash-filled wallets around the city and waited to see if they were returned. They found that strangers were in fact far more trustworthy than people commonly believed.[11]

Mistrusting strangers is one sign of the unease we commonly feel about people we don't know or those we perceive as being different. If people are more trustworthy than we believe, perhaps we could learn to be more trusting, which has benefits for individual and social wellbeing.

Self-determination

Self-determination is one of the cornerstones of positive psychology. This includes choices over aspects of our life such as appearance, work, marriage, sexual orientation, and how we spend our time and money. Freedom to choose bestows dignity. In a good society, however, personal freedom comes with responsibility. A European initiative aims to improve the lives of refugees by providing them with some choice and responsibility, building their confidence and competence to play a full role in their new country.

Transforming life in a refugee camp

The charity Refugee Support recognised that refugees needed more than food and shelter – they needed dignity and some degree of control over their lives. It began in a camp for Syrian refugees in Greece, where volunteers set up a shop in which refugees could exchange tokens for food, and a 'clothes boutique' including changing rooms, creating a little autonomy and normality in a precarious existence. Refugees and volunteers work together in a community kitchen, preparing hundreds of meals a day and there is a language school for almost 200 students. Three cafeterias, two playgrounds, and an artificial football pitch have been built. The model has been extended to other camps in Greece, Cyprus, Bangladesh, and Mexico, with specific programs designed to meet local needs.

Building on what's working

One way that positive psychology can tackle social problems is to focus on what's working well and build on this knowledge to find solutions. Both positive emotions and strengths-based approaches can be harnessed for social good.

Contrary to the belief that positive emotions can lead to complacency, a recent study found that happy people are more likely to take action to improve social problems.[12] Positive psychology does not deny the importance of difficult emotions such as grief or anger, but rather seeks ways to manage or harness them. Although anger can be energising and drive positive social change, it is not helpful when it comes to developing solutions, because it narrows perception, impairs communication, and inhibits innovative thinking.[13] Finding constructive solutions to shared problems is more often seen when people experience positive emotions that lead to cooperative strategies that benefit all parties. Appreciative Inquiry is an approach that explores the art of the possible in a structured conversation. It has been used to create positive social change across diverse contexts, from interfaith action in global peacebuilding, renewing public education in Chicago, and an immunisation program for children in Nepal.

Building better societies

Fairness: equality versus equity

Addressing gross inequalities is essential for societies to thrive. Whereas equality focuses on treating everyone the same, equity goes a step further in offering varying levels of support to achieve greater fairness of outcomes: this involves altering environmental conditions to promote access to opportunities, removing barriers for those who start with disadvantage. This view is expanded with extensive research findings by Richard Wilkinson and Kate Pickett in their book *The Spirit Level*.

Ingrained in some societies is an historical class system that works to keep people 'in their place', whether that is of privilege or disadvantage. Moving between social classes – social mobility – is not just about being rich, but about how you are positioned within this hierarchy. Following the end of the second world war in Europe, there were efforts to address equity issues in the United Kingdom by establishing free health care and free education for all, including higher education, and a welfare state that supported those who fell on hard times. This facilitated a powerful social mobility that has now stalled. The Social Mobility Commission's *State of the Nation* report, published in 2019, said that being born privileged in Britain means that you are likely to remain privileged, while being born disadvantaged means having to overcome a series of barriers to ensure that the next generation are not stuck in similar circumstances. Their recommendations aim to give those from poorer backgrounds a better chance to succeed. School and university leaders, politicians, and employers are all responsible for initiating change to build a more equitable society.

Addressing discrimination?

A critique of positive psychology is that it views discrimination through the lens of individual beliefs, actions and feelings rather than a societal one.[14] Much of the published research emanates from societies with an individualist approach to wellbeing, rather than collectivist. If positive psychology is going to have the impact we hope for, intercultural study is an area for development.

Mistrust, prejudice, and stereotyping leads to discrimination and violence around the world. Breaking this down means developing positive connections with others not like us, and recognising that whereas homogeneity is limiting, diversity benefits society.

Quick and often negative judgements about 'the other' can be transformed through the attitudinal change that comes through positive connections. Many studies support the idea that contact diminishes intergroup prejudice.[15] A campaign #ShareTheMicNow provided an unusual form of online connection by amplifying black voices beyond their usual social media reach. It involved around 50 high-profile white celebrities handing over their Instagram accounts and audiences to black women, in the hope of providing a deeper understanding of the international Black Lives Matter movement.

Reducing racism means acknowledging the pervasiveness of white privilege and working to redress this. Fixed ideas about difference, however, start young, so educational programs are particularly important to prevent prejudice and discrimination from becoming deep-rooted. One such program in Australia, entitled Together for Humanity, works in schools to promote inter-cultural understanding and help students learn to deal with differences. Initiated by Rabbi Zalman Kastel, it involves Jewish, Christian, and Muslim educators working together. Another initiative is outlined below.

Changing children's attitudes towards an 'outgroup'.

In a series of studies, psychologist Rony Berger and colleagues have been training hundreds of primary school children in Israel to think differently about the Arab children with whom they come into contact. Using techniques of mindfulness and compassion, the studies have found substantial reductions in stereotyping and discriminatory tendencies toward the other group, and increases in positive feelings and readiness for social contact. Impressively, the program retained its significant effect 15 months after its completion, despite serious clashes between Israel and the Palestinians during this period.[16]

Diversity also applies to those who do not conform to the 'norm' of sexuality. A positive psychology perspective challenges pathologising of alternative preferences. A 'good' society does not accept that all citizens must be shoe-horned into the same mould. Although some countries still persecute those with a different sexual orientation there have been significant developments in many others, giving same-sex couples equal rights, enabling them to live their lives fully and without fear.

Feeling safe

The Law and Order Index, compiled by Gallup, is a composite score based on people's reported confidence in their local police, their feelings of personal safety such as walking around their local community, whether they had experienced theft or been assaulted/mugged in the past year. In 2018, 148,000 people in 142 countries were asked about their perception of crime on the four measures above. Their answers were then correlated with income distribution. This showed that the more equality of income in a country, the less criminal behaviour. The most significant of the four measures was how safe someone felt walking home alone. In Venezuela, for instance, the 19th most unequal country, four out of five people were anxious about mugging, kidnapping, or extortion. By comparison in Norway, the 12th most equal country, 95% of people said they felt safe walking home alone.

Can reforming police culture increase safety?

Camden County, New Jersey, was one of the most dangerous places in the United States. With a population of 77,000 and over 90% from ethnic minorities, 40% lived below the poverty line, and rates of murder, violent crime, and police brutality led to the police force being dissolved in 2012. Following consultation with residents and community leaders, and with support from both political parties, a new County Police Force was established. The crucial transition was from a value system supporting police rights to practice law enforcement, to Hippocratic Policing – *"minimise harm, and try to save lives"*.[17] The role of police officers was redefined as being facilitators, integrating into the fabric of the community, and helping solve community problems. Training focuses on the need to earn respect and trust, techniques for conflict de-escalation, and the use of force only when absolutely necessary. Whenever force is used, there is an immediate enquiry, and the officer is either offered further training or removed from the force. Over half the officers are from ethnic minorities who have regular, positive contact with residents, hosting block parties, and connecting with schoolchildren. Murder and violent crimes have plummeted, and the relationship between citizens and police has improved dramatically. Camden police officers even joined the protestors in the Black Lives Matter demonstration of May/June 2020.[18]

Positive criminology

When people have been hurt, they usually want justice. Legal systems set out to provide this and at the same time inhibit further lawlessness.

Depriving criminals of their liberty, signals to the electorate that the people in power are 'tough on crime'. Decades of research, however, have shown that imprisonment is likely to deepen criminal behaviour by 'socialisation'.[19] Criminals learn how to be better at crime by association with others. In terms of improving citizen safety, prison doesn't work, except by the temporary removal of some dangerous individuals from the community.

Positive criminology takes a different approach, both to the prevention of crime, and to the response to it. It explores the positive forces and influences in the lives of criminals, which distance them from further crime. It focuses on rehabilitation and restorative approaches that have the potential for different outcomes.[20]

When rehabilitation is the goal

Norway's criminal justice system is an exemplar of positive practice. It separates violent offenders from those committing less serious crimes and where possible gives shorter sentences in conditions that dignify human rights such as one prisoner to a cell. All prisoners have access to education, drug treatments, mental health, and training programs. They are given privileges, but also responsibilities. After release offenders are helped to reintegrate into society, with programs that support them finding a job, and access to social support services such as housing and welfare.[21]

Although the capital costs of this approach are higher than others, the benefits overall make it value for money. There is a low recidivism rate and reduced crime overall in the country. Whereas many offenders were not in employment prior to imprisonment, nearly half are in work five years after release, paying taxes and not drawing on benefits.

Prisons as schools for life, not schools for crime

In 1998 the Singapore Prison Service began converting its prisons into schools for life.[22] Rehabilitation programs were established to involve inmates in prison operations, including peer support. This helped the workload of prison officers, improved inmate and staff morale and relationships, and increased mutual trust, along with improved interactions with the local community. It also produced a one-third drop in reoffending. The program exemplified key lessons from wellbeing science.

Reflection:
How can we ensure the law applies equally to all citizens whatever their status, culture, or ethnicity?

Empowerment of women

Although none of the 193 countries in the UN have met targets towards the 2030 sustainable development goals on gender equality, progress has been made. It is often women themselves who have exemplified the positive psychology principles of agency, optimism and connection in moving the agenda forward. There is evidence of this across the world: promoting girls' education, challenging unequal pay, having stronger political representation, legislating for women's rights to choose, protecting women from violence, and girls from both prostitution and child marriage. The empowerment of women is also good for business. A global survey of 21,980 firms across 91 countries found that having more women at the executive level increased profitability by 15%.[23]

So how can positive psychology principles promote wellbeing for women? This is what appears to have been the strengths of the activists leading these powerful initiatives above:

- Awareness of how inequalities impact on the lives of women and girls;
- Having compassion for those who have no voice;
- Identifying and building on strengths – what good practice already exists and how can this be extended and disseminated;

185

- Empowering women to have autonomy and connecting them with support systems;
- Raising awareness of toxic masculinity, valuing men who speak out against this, and incorporating positive gender education into the curriculum.

Increasing employment prospects

Unemployment has a major effect on both physical and mental wellbeing. It disrupts a sense of competence, meaning and autonomy, interpersonal relationships, and the community connection often provided by having a secure job. Across the world, when national unemployment levels are high, average national wellbeing is lower, negatively affecting everyone, even those still employed. These effects are mitigated where governments provide a social safety net for people who fall on hard times. Supporting the unemployed back to work does more for their wellbeing than providing welfare. Australian researcher Darren Coppin has developed a successful programs for doing this.

Helping jobseekers return to work

A diverse sample of almost 23,000 jobseekers who were receiving welfare took part in Coppin's study. In five three-hour workshops, participants received 31 evidence-based exercises designed to build positive psychological states such as self-efficacy, resilience, and wellbeing. Compared to jobseekers on a government-funded re-employment program, there was a 20.4% increase in job placements, and this rose to 41.9% when a one-to-one component (comprising four forty-minute sessions) was added to the original group workshop. Job placement rates were improved regardless of gender, age, ethnicity, and stage of job seeking readiness.[24]

This has been rolled out successfully using online material to many thousands of job seekers in Australia and the United Kingdom.

This program worked well because there were jobs available. The COVID-19 pandemic, however, has resulted in millions of newly unemployed people, which could have serious and long-lasting effects on wellbeing. Fortunately there is some evidence that when unemployment is widespread, the negative impact of job loss is reduced, reflecting less self-blame and decreased stigma.[25]

Aspiration and hope

It is clear that some societies are doing better than others in ensuring the wellbeing of their citizens. Monitoring the subjective wellbeing of a nation and of specific groups is helpful in pinpointing which are flourishing, and which are floundering, and in assessing progress over time or following an intervention. More countries are including measures of subjective wellbeing in policy design, and New Zealand has gone a step further, including subjective wellbeing as a key indicator when identifying budget priorities (see the Economics chapter).

Another country held up by many as a prototype for societal wellbeing is Denmark. According to the OECD Better Life Index, Denmark ranks above average in housing, work-life balance, social connections, environmental quality, civic engagement, education and skills, jobs and earnings, health status, subjective well-being, and personal security. Only about 2% work very long hours compared to the OECD average of 11%. They appear to spend time nurturing relationships. Danes also have stable government and low levels of public corruption. Voter turnout, a measure of citizens' participation in the political process, was 86% during recent elections; considerably higher than the OECD average of 68%, with a much smaller gap between those in the upper and lower echelons of society than the OECD average, which suggests there is broad social inclusion in Denmark's democratic institutions.

Everyday heroes

The Heroic Imagination Project (HIP) was founded by Philip Zimbardo to inspire positive social change.[26] His mission is to enable ordinary people to become Everyday Heroes. *"Heroes are in all of us. Anyone can be a hero anytime an opportunity arises to stand up for what is right and just, and to speak out against injustice, corruption, and other evils"*. The program has so far involved 35,000 people of all ages and backgrounds to be courageous in small everyday acts that contribute to the social good. This includes:

- Recognising and challenging prejudice, and discrimination by understanding and reversing bias.
- Resisting the bystander effect.
- Genuine, empathic listening.
- Recognising the power of conformity and situational forces to avoid submission to unjust authority.

Ideas for action

What might governments do?

Utilise national accounts of wellbeing not just Gross National Product.

Policies that promote the common good rather than privilege sections of society, developed on the basis of research evidence.

A stronger focus on the prevention of crime and addressing the causes of criminal behaviour alongside rehabilitation programs.

Promote democratic freedoms so everyone is encouraged to vote, and remove barriers to doing so.

Speak truth to the people, forfeiting positions of power if behaviour is dishonest, or otherwise unethical.

What might communities do?

Develop activities that welcome everyone and help break down divisions and stereotypes.

Expose and speak out against injustice.

Provide and promote locally accessible mindfulness courses.

Provide opportunities for people such as refugees to tell their stories.

What might citizens do?

Be aware of what brings meaning and purpose in life.

Vote for representatives that reflect the values of respect, inclusion, compassion, and the Common Good, and have a track record of promoting these in practice.

Engage with grassroots advocacy (see Politics chapter).

What might families do?

Encourage children to interact with others outside their usual social groups.

Show children that they can make a difference with small acts of kindness and compassion.

Talk positively about others.

Challenge bullying behaviours wherever they occur as unacceptable in a civilised society.

Key sources

Full references and resources are available at our website https://www.creatingtheworldwewanttolivein.org/references/society/

1 https://www.nelsonmandela.org/news/entry/nelson-mandelas-speeches-in-2008
2 Woman's Own (1987). *Interview, 23 September 1987.* https://www.margaretthatcher.org/document/106689
3 Etzioni (1996). *New golden rule.* HarperCollins.
4 Alnaji, Askari & Refae (2016). Can tolerance of diverse groups improve the wellbeing of societies? *International Journal of Economics and Business Research, 11*(1), 48–57.
5 Horowitz, Brown & Cox (2019). *Race in America 2019.* Pew Research Centre.
6 Augoustinos (2013). Psychological perspectives on racism. *InPsych, 35*(4).
7 Gramlich (2019). *The gap between the number of blacks and whites in prison is shrinking.* Pew Research Centre.
8 The Guardian (9 June 2020). "Aboriginal deaths in custody: Black Lives Matter protests referred to our count of 432 deaths. It's now 437." https://www.theguardian.com/australia-news/2020/jun/09/black-lives-matter-protesters-referred-to-our-count-of-432-aboriginal-deaths-in-custody-its-now-437

9 Mellor *et al.* (2008). Need for belonging, relationship satisfaction, loneliness and life satisfaction. *Personality and Individual Differences, 45,* 213–218.

10 Phelps-Roper (2017). https://www.ted.com/talks/megan_phelps_roper_i_grew_up_in_the_westboro_baptist_church_here_s_why_i_left

11 Helliwell, Huang & Wang (2016). *New evidence on trust and well-being.* National Bureau of Economic Research. (No. w22450)

12 Kushlev *et al.* (2019). Do happy people care about society's problems? *The Journal of Positive Psychology.*

13 Fredrickson (2001). The role of positive emotions in positive psychology: The broaden-and-build theory of positive emotions. *American psychologist.*

14 Yakusho (2018). Don't worry, be happy: Erasing racism, sexism, and poverty in positive psychology. *Psychotherapy and Politics International, 6(1)*

15 Pettigrew & Tropp (2008). How does intergroup contact reduce prejudice? Meta-analytic tests of three mediators. *European journal of social psychology.*

16 Berger *et al.* (2016). Reducing prejudice and promoting positive intergroup attitudes among elementary-school children in the context of the Israeli–Palestinian conflict. *Journal of school psychology.*

17 Sherman (In Press). Targeting American Policing, Rogue Cops or Rogue Cultures? *Cambridge Journal of Evidence-Based Policing.*

18 Landergan (2020). The City that Really Did Abolish the Police. *Politico.*

19 Cullen, Jonson & Nagin (2011). Prisons do not reduce recidivism: The high cost of ignoring science. *The Prison Journal 91*(3), 48S–68S.

20 Ronel & Segev (2015). *Positive Criminology.* Routledge.

21 World Economics Forum (2019). weforum.org/agenda/2019/03/incarceration-can-be-rehabilitative.

22 Leong (2010). Story of the Singapore prison service: From custodians of prisoners to captains of life. *NS6 International Roundtable.*

23 Noland, Moran & Kotschwar (2016). *Is gender diversity profitable? Evidence from a global survey.* Peterson Institute for International Economics Working Paper.

24 Coppin *et al.* (2020). *Evaluation of The Treatment Utility of a Jobseeker Segmentation and Intervention Program.* OSF Preprints, 2 Jan. 2020.

25 Brand (2015). The far-reaching impact of job loss and unemployment. *Annual Review of Sociology.*

26 Zimbardo, Seppälä & Franco (2017). Heroism: Social Transformation Through Compassion in Action. In Seppälä et al. (Eds.), *The Oxford Handbook of Compassion Science.*

CHAPTER 11

Economics

David Roffey

"To achieve the change we seek, we will need fundamental reform of the way the economy is governed and policy made". – IPPR Commission on Economic Justice (2018) Prosperity & Justice, p3[1]

Economics and wellbeing

All the issues for *the world we want to live in* discussed in preceding chapters exist within the wider system of the economy and the governments that try to manage it. Many of the potential changes raised there imply the need to rethink current ways of working, and economic policies. Fortunately, many thinkers – such as the IPPR Commission on Economic Justice quoted above – have been working on the answers to this problem.

For most of its existence, economics has assumed that individual economic decisions aim to maximise personal benefit. Becoming wealthy regardless of what this means for others has become the mantra of rational economics. This restricted view was compounded when economists decided that prices and consumption – how much things cost, and what people bought ('revealed preferences') – were the only available proxy measures for how well people were doing. There was no way to measure any broader concept of what personal benefits might include. This way of thinking fundamentally conflicts with many of the principles for wellbeing set out in the Introduction: connection with others, kindness, compassion, considered choices, and wise actions.

Many modern economies have been essentially unmanaged, with the setting of interest rates by independent central banks as the only recognised management tool. This has been almost completely ineffective in the post-financial-crisis and COVID-19 world of sustained very low or even negative interest rates. Something this chapter seeks to address is whether we need more engagement of governments in the management of investment, and other economic activities. This question has been thrown into stark relief by the sudden and rapid switch of economic policies seen in many countries following the onset of the COVID-19 pandemic. This has shown that what has often been deemed impossible to do, is in fact perfectly possible when circumstances demand, and with political will.

The more recent growth of 'behavioural economics', for example in Richard Thaler's 'Nudge' theories, has only modified these underlying assumptions by assuming that each of us has limited information and *"the tendency to not behave completely rationally"*, to quote from Thaler's Nobel Prize citation.[2] These theories still treat caring about others, fairness and reasonableness, as irrational aberrations from the benefit-maximising norm. But lack of fairness is the central problem of the modern global economy. The changes sought in the rest of this volume will count for little if this cannot be addressed.

Finally, as discussed in the Environment chapter, looking after the future of the planet requires that we can no longer rely on endless economic growth, driven by profligate use of energy, to produce the resources we need. If we are to survive at all, something has to change.

Wealth and wellbeing

There is no doubt that people are happier when they have enough money to make ends meet. People in developed countries, however, are constantly told that wealth equates to happiness. Being exhilarated by a windfall would be expected. But does this positive feeling last?

China is the most successful example of poverty reduction in modern times, with GDP per capita increasing fourfold between 1990 and 2005, and life expectancy increasing from 67 to 73.5 years. But China's success also comes at a cost. During this period, life satisfaction fell dramatically, and the suicide rate became one of the highest in the world, particularly among white-collar workers, who suffer from long working hours, sleep deprivation, and the lack of replenishment that normally comes from leisure pursuits, and spending time with family.

Positive psychology researchers have been interested in whether greater wealth leads to greater wellbeing. The answer to this, unsurprisingly, is that 'it depends'. But there is clear evidence that spending on others is associated with greater happiness.[3] Wellbeing is undermined if acquisition becomes more important than relationships, sense of purpose, or simply enjoying the simple things of life.

Positive psychology research suggests that we can boost wellbeing by tuning into what we are grateful for, which also appears to reduce materialism.[4] The addition of more luxuries may bring temporary pleasure, but this satisfaction wears off pretty quickly. It does not help us feel better about ourselves except perhaps in having more than others. Would an expensive piece of jewellery, or a flash new car have the same impact on your wellbeing if there was no-one to show it off to?

In their book *The Spirit Level*,[5] Richard Wilkinson & Kate Pickett amass considerable evidence to show that even winning the selfish competition game isn't good for you if it results in a more unequal society, where outcomes are worse on various scales – e.g. health, education, violence – for almost *everyone*, including the 'winning' people near the top (with the possible exception of the super-rich top 1%, who are protected by gates, chauffeur driven cars and private services). The reduction of inequality is SDG 10.

What can be done to promote change?

> "The gross national product does not allow for the health of our children, the quality of their education, or the joy of their play. It does not include the beauty of our poetry, or the strength of our marriages, the intelligence of our public debate, or the integrity of our public officials. It measures neither our wit nor our courage, neither our wisdom nor our learning, neither our compassion nor our devotion to our country, it measures everything in short, except that which makes life worthwhile". – Bobby Kennedy (1968)[6]

A new kind of economy is needed; one that is fairer, more inclusive, less exploitative, and less destructive of society and the planet. But how do we produce this economy? The long-standing theories of Marx and Keynes are rooted in economic structures that have essentially vanished, where governments could manage economies outside the pressures of globalisation and international capital. One of the long-standing problems, as noted in Bobby Kennedy's 1968 speech above, is that we measure, and target the wrong things.

The good news is that there are many economists working on 21st-Century alternatives. These can be found in policy institutes and universities, with others working independently. In the United Kingdom, the All Party Parliamentary Group on Wellbeing Economics involves MPs from all parties. Based in the United States, the Institute for New Economic Thinking brings together more than 450 Nobel laureates, scholars, policy minds, and business leaders who are helping to shape economic thinking worldwide. In 2018, Scotland, Iceland, and New Zealand established the network of Wellbeing Economy Governments' to challenge the acceptance of Gross Domestic Product (GDP) as the ultimate measure of a country's success'.[7]

Since the changes being developed are primarily at the societal level, the main way to support change has to be through support for political and other organisations that are in favour of (at least some of) these changes. But there are other actions we can take, as citizens, campaigners, volunteers, and through our choices as consumers, investors, and influencers of the people around us.

New Zealand Budget Priorities 2019[8]

"… to begin to tackle the challenges identified in the Wellbeing Outlook, the Government has identified five Budget Priorities for Budget 2019:

- Creating opportunities for productive businesses, regions, iwi, and others to transition to a sustainable and low-emissions economy.
- Supporting a thriving nation in the digital age through innovation, social, and economic opportunities.
- Lifting Māori and Pacific incomes, skills, and opportunities.
- Reducing child poverty and improving child wellbeing, including addressing family violence.
- Supporting mental wellbeing for all New Zealanders, with a special focus on under 24-year-olds".

Almost all economic debate is centred along a single dimension: how much should governments intervene to control markets. Apart from extreme liberalisers and hard-core anarchists, no-one thinks that should be no regulation at all – at the very least, it is wise to have some legal backing to enforce a contract or compensate for a failure to deliver what has been promised. The 20th-century Communist experiments that controlled all aspects of markets may have failed, or been radically altered, as in China, but there is considerable variation in degrees of regulation between countries whose regimes fall under the umbrella title of capitalism, from the deregulated entrepreneurialism of the United States, through to the much more managed economies of northern Europe and Asia.

There is considerable evidence that unfettered individualist entrepreneurialism leads to increased inequalities, and adverse effects on the wellbeing of the majority of people. So, what sort of controls on the workings of market economies would help to promote wellbeing? Could we build a system that brings out the best in people, not the worst?

Some aspects of such a system are clear, and common to the proposals of many analysts:

- Recognition that the economy needs to support wider society and public good.
- Recognition of the social and environmental costs of economic actions.
- Community involvement in shaping local economies.
- Regulation and intervention to redress imbalances in power, information, and opportunities.
- More emphasis on 'real' activities rather than finance transactions.
- Support for those who need help to change – at every level from the individual to nations.

Reflections:

What economic changes would you most like to see?

If you, and your friends and colleagues discuss these issues, do you know how to defend your ideas?

Paying for change

"There are no iron laws of economics keeping us from building a more humane world, but there are many people whose blind faith, self-interest, or simple lack of understanding of economics makes them claim this is the case". – Banerjee & Duflo[9]

As Abhijit Banerjee and Esther Duflo have set out, some people resist paying taxes, taking the view that the State is 'stealing' hard-earned money from deserving workers and they have no responsibility towards anyone else. The belief that everyone has the same opportunities and through their own efforts can be successful is the basis of the American Dream. It implies that if you are not successful it is your own fault. This is the reason for tolerating inequality and blaming the poor for their circumstances. But this theory – known as the Belief in a Just World[10] – does not account for being born with privileges or having unexpected disasters befall you. People do not start life with a level playing field, and accidents happen.

A different point of view is that we pay taxes in order for all of us to live in a well-functioning society. According to the World Happiness Report,[11] happiness is closely linked to social equality and community spirit. Denmark does well on both. It has a high level of equality and a strong sense of common responsibility for a strong social fabric. None of the nine major political parties in Denmark seriously supports dismantling the Danish welfare state. Most Danes believe that it is everyone's responsibility to work if they can, and pay taxes to support the common good. If everyone pays their fair share, a social safety net can remain in place to support the young, the old, the sick, and those who find themselves unemployed.

Reflections:

Have you ever experienced real hardship, or do you know someone who has?

What circumstances contributed to this situation, and what helped to alleviate it?

As with the costs of dealing with climate change, opponents of such changes often stress that it is too hard, will take too long, would cost a trillion dollars, could not gain public support without much prior preparation. These arguments tended to hold sway, but have been shown to be illusory by the events of early 2020, when economic responses to the COVID-19 pandemic costing trillions of dollars could be enacted in a matter of weeks, given the political will.

How do we get there?

"Dynamic economies are always in transition, and markets don't manage these transitions well on their own". – Joseph Stiglitz[12]

There are many writers, researchers and policymakers proposing changes in the direction we set out above.

While the US-based Institute for New Economic Thinking's Commission on Global Economic Transformation has published some technical papers and videos, it has yet to produce specific proposals for change. However, the Commission's co-chair, Joseph Stiglitz, has published his own prescriptions in his book *People, Power, and Profits: Progressive Capitalism for an Age of Discontent*, quoted above. These include curbing the influence of wealth in our democracies, and having more government investment in infrastructure, health, research, and education.

In the United Kingdom, the Institute for Public Policy Research brought together a number of leading advocates for change in their Commission on Economic Justice. Its final report[1] gives considerable detail on a 10-point plan, with multiple individual recommendations for action within each point. Although its prescriptions are written for the United Kingdom, most of them would apply equally in other countries. The core of many of the IPPR's 10 points is the need for government to *act*: to intervene in labour markets with laws on good working conditions; to invest directly in improvements in environmental and social projects; to intervene in takeovers and the digital economy when proposals and actions harm the common good; to require directors and managers of companies to look to the longer term, not short-term financial gains. A core principle is openness and accountability – and public consultation on the policy proposals, both at country and local levels. The IPPR in the United Kingdom has also published a briefing paper entitled *Just Tax: Reforming the Taxation of Income from Wealth and Work*,[13] which explores economic justice and presents two sets of proposals about how this might be done:

1. Income from wealth being taxed the same as income from work.
2. A fundamental reform of the tax system, taxing all sources of income equally, together with a gradually rising tax rate as income increases.

Similar conclusions are set out in the New Economics Foundation's November 2019 proposal,[14] *Change the Rules: New Rules for the Economy*: have a living wage; make work secure, including for the self-employed; provide universal welfare and basic services; implement a Green New Deal for investment in environmental policies; establish regional investment authorities, devolved and people-led decision-making.

Reflection:

What impact might the above changes have in your community?

These are proposals for action at government/national level. Clearly it would be a major long-term undertaking to bring all of these changes to fruition, but while they add to a coherent whole, it is possible to move forward piecemeal on many. In particular, some moves on local action, employee involvement in decision-making, and ethical and environmentally sustainable investment can be at least partly be actioned by all of us. The last section of this chapter discusses some examples of these.

Good practice and hope

A wide variety of organisations have been working successfully with some of these principles – some of them for many years: employee-owned business, ethical banks, local and micro-finance ventures.

Employee-owned businesses

Examples of employee owned businesses have been around for many years. These range from Triumph Motorcycles to Goldman Sachs. It is interesting that the John Lewis Partnership (JLP, established in 1929) has recently chosen to rebrand with a strong emphasis on the 'Partners' title and its status as the largest of the 370 employee-owned businesses in the United Kingdom. Its website includes a guide for others on how to create an employee-owned business.

The Mondragon Corporation, in the Basque country of northern Spain, was established as a worker's cooperative in 1956, and has grown to be one of the largest companies in Spain, with turnover of €12BN and more than 67,000 employees, organised in 98 separate cooperatives. It is just one example of the members of the International Cooperative Alliance (founded in 1895) that together employ more than 280 million people – 10% of the world's employed population.

Reflection:

Do you know anyone who works in an employee-owned business – how do they feel about their workplace?

Ethical banking and social investment

Ethical banking also has a long history.

For example, Reliance Bank Ltd was formed (as The Salvation Army Bank) in 1890 by William Booth, when he needed to raise mortgage finance for Salvation Army properties. It is still wholly owned by the Salvation Army Trustee Companies and provides The Salvation Army's banking services. It also provides financial services to many private customers, other churches, charities, and businesses, as well as to The Salvation Army itself. Although it operates as a purely commercial bank, with assets under management of around £180 million,

it also looks to prioritise lending to projects that deliver positive social impact. For example, it underwrites mortgages for
housing long-term disabled people, who have no employment
income, reasonably regarding their entitlement to long-term
disability benefits as being at least as secure as wages for future
repayments – possibly more secure in the current economy.

While many longstanding general investment businesses such as
pension funds have ethical investment policies that restrict their
involvement in some industries, e.g. armaments, tobacco or (lately)
fossil fuels, a new generation of banks are arising that only invest
in projects and companies that add cultural value, and benefit both
people and the environment.

Dutch bank Triodos Bank NV is unusual in that it only lends to
businesses and charities judged to be of social or ecological benefit, including companies in the fields of solar energy, organic
farming, or culture. This 'positive screening' extends its policies
beyond those of ethical banks, which solely avoid investing in
companies judged to be doing harm ('negative screening').

The Bendigo Bank began in Victoria, Australia, in 1858 as a
building society, and converted to a bank in 1993. In 1998 it began
a 'Community Bank' program in which the local community owns
and operates a Bendigo Bank branch (which is separately incorporated) and Bendigo Bank provides all the banking infrastructure
and support. The community company, after paying its branch running costs, shares any remaining profit with the Bendigo Bank. The
program was a response to the massive closure of bank branches in
rural areas. Bendigo Bank has since extended the program to areas
with existing bank services.

Microfinance provides financial services, e.g. small loans and insur-
ance, to poor and disadvantaged clients. Again, some examples, such
as credit unions, have been around since the 19th-century. Examples
range from the giant Grameen Bank – which has more than 9 million
members across more than 80,000 villages in Bangladesh, and since
1983 has loaned more than 28 billion US dollars to its members – to local

village savings, and loan associations that simply work peer-to-peer to manage the finances of perhaps a hundred or more local farmers.

> Kiva.org, based in San Francisco, allows people around the world to lend money (interest free) via the internet to local entrepreneurs – nearly 2 million of them so far – in 78 countries, with individual lenders being able to choose the recipient of their loan funds, and relend once the loan is repaid – as 96% of loans have been since its foundation in 2005. As with Grameen Bank, Kiva emphasises supporting women, with more than 80% of loans so far going to female entrepreneurs.

Taking action

The collection of good practice examples in the previous section show that the proposals in the 'Ideas for action' can work, even in the long term: they have managed to survive and flourish in a world where economic priorities have been dominated by neo-classical, individualistic, market-led policies; imagine what could be achieved if government policies actively encouraged these ventures.

Ideas for action

What might governments do?

Re-position taxation as contributing to a national infrastructure and safety net that is in everyone's interests.

Invest more in these, particularly in renewable energy, and environmental projects.

Invest in education, including for reskilling workers, who are losing their jobs to automation or disinvestment in fossil fuels.

Intervene to stop the creation of near-monopolies, particularly in the digital economy: consider requiring the break-up of existing firms.

Strengthen employee rights for good working conditions.

Consult widely before major changes in policy or reorganisation of public service bodies: consider trials of the new system before national implementation.

What might enterprises and employers do?

Find ways to include your workers in decisions about their and your company's future direction.

What might citizens do?

Get involved: think about what you want, and who could make that happen, then talk to those people – fellow workers, unions, politicians – about these ideas.

For governments to be actively promoting these policies, we probably also need to change the way politics works – so on we go to our next chapter!

Key sources

Full references and resources are available at our website https://www.creatingtheworldwewanttolivein.org/references/economics/

1 IPPR Commission on Economic Justice (2018). *Prosperity & Justice: A Plan for the New Economy.* ippr.org/research/publications/prosperity-and-justice
2 www.nobelprize.org/prizes/economic-sciences/2017/thaler/facts/
3 Dunn, Aknin, & Norton (2008). Spending money on others promotes happiness. *Science, 319,* 1687–1688.
4 Froh *et al.* (2010) Gratitude and the reduced costs of materialism in adolescents. *Journal of Happiness Studies, 12,* 289–302.
5 Wilkinson & Pickett (2009). *The Spirit Level: Why Equality is Better for Everyone.* Allen Lane / Penguin.
6 www.jfklibrary.org/learn/about-jfk/the-kennedy-family/robert-f-kennedy/robert-fkennedy-speeches/remarks-at-the-university-of-kansas-march-18-1968
7 Sturgeon (2019). *Why governments should prioritise wellbeing.* TED talk: https://hls.ted.com/talks/46582.m3u8
8 New Zealand Government (2019). *New Zealand Budget Policy Statement.*

9 Banerjee & Duflo (2019). *Good Economics for Hard Times: Better Answers to Our Biggest Problems.* p.255. Perseus Books.
10 Lerner (1980). *The Belief in a Just World: A Fundamental Delusion.* Springer.
11 Helliwell, Layard & Sachs (2019). *World Happiness Report 2019.* Sustainable Development Solutions Network.
12 Stiglitz (2019). *People, Power, and Profits: Progressive Capitalism for an Age of Discontent.* p.141. W.W. Norton.
13 IPPR (2019). *Just Tax: Reforming the Taxation of Income from Wealth and Work.* ippr.org/research/publications/just-tax
14 New Economics Foundation. (2019). *Change the Rules: New Rules for the Economy.* neweconomics.org/uploads/files/newrules2019a.pdf

CHAPTER 12

Politics

Bridget Grenville-Cleave, Felicia Huppert &
David Roffey

> *"Do we participate in a politics of cynicism or a politics of hope?"* –
> Barack Obama[1]

Why is politics important for wellbeing?

Regardless of where we live in the world, political organisations, including governments, and other institutions engaged in social and public policy, wield enormous influence over all aspects of our lives. Politics can be global and local, and both have far reaching effects on economic and tax systems, education, employment, health and welfare, crime, defence, and our environment. The choices to be made are complex and political decisions have wide-ranging consequences – both intentional and unintentional. This is strikingly seen in the way the world has been dealing with both the COVID-19 pandemic and the Black Lives Matter movement.

In light of the critical importance of these political decisions, we need them to be made in an environment which lends itself to positive human values, nuanced thinking, mature debate, and new ideas, in which different parties work collaboratively. This is not the norm in many political systems. Agreeing on whether issues like poverty, crime, or security need to be tackled is one thing, but different political stances mean that there is often no agreement on what action to take. Whilst healthy disagreement can lead to better solutions, the open hostility that politicians and their supporters show when they demonise others from different parties does not benefit citizens, or the quality of debate. Many of the big issues we face – such as pandemics, climate change, migration, and limited global resources – are complex and unlikely to be solved by one party, or even one country acting alone. As suggested by Barack Obama in the opening quotation, we do have a choice over how we engage with and drive the political process. We stand a much better chance of reaching sustainable solutions if we work on problems together.

It is hardly surprising that politicians' behaviour means that they have been amongst the least trusted occupations. While nurses and doctors are trusted to tell the truth by 95% and 93% of the UK population respectively, this plummets to 17% for government ministers, and 14% for politicians generally. Politicians in other countries have been rated just as poorly.[2] This picture shifted in the early months of the COVID-19 pandemic: in a study that compared levels of trust across institutions in 11 countries, average trust in government rose from 49% in 2017 to 61% in May 2020, making it the most trusted institution for the first time. The study also shows that in the United States, Japan, and France, local government was far more trusted than federal government,[3] though as time went on, trust levels in some countries began to subside towards the longer-term norm.[4]

A global crisis like COVID-19 shows that cooperation is both essential and possible. Although some political organisations generally favour more state involvement in citizens' lives while others favour 'small government', most countries recognise that the private sector could not solve every problem, that substantial state involvement was necessary, and that different political parties needed to work together.

Reflections:

In what ways might cooperation improve the way politicians go about their business?

Do you think that a new form of politics is now needed to address the national and global issues we face?

Positive psychology scholar Tim Lomas defines positive politics as *"the study of the impact of political policies and processes upon wellbeing"*. We propose that positive politics can also provide insight into the way in which wellbeing might impact the political landscape. An example of this is provided in *The World Happiness Report 2019*[5] which shows that the more unhappy people are, the less likely they are to see themselves as global citizens, and the more likely they are to support populist or nationalist parties. The rise in populism has also been fuelled by the general mistrust of politicians, leading to an anti-establishment worldview based on the belief that the political system is run by a corrupt elite with no concern for the ordinary citizen.

Wellbeing research gives us the opportunity to change politics for the better, for example, tackling the widespread public mistrust of politicians, helping us understand each other's political views better, and working together to reach more effective decisions. The rest of this chapter looks at how focussing on wellbeing might achieve these aims.

Some political systems are more conducive to flourishing

What are the characteristics of countries which have higher levels of wellbeing? Large cross-national surveys indicate that they also have political freedom, low corruption, greater income equality, affordable healthcare and a good welfare system. These are more commonly seen in countries with democratic political systems, so there is an alignment between wellbeing and democracy. *The World Happiness Report 2019*[5] has also shown that happier people are more likely to engage in politics. For example, voter turnout during recent elections in Denmark, which has consistently high well-being, was 86% on average, considerably higher than the OECD average of 68%. This suggests that there is broad social inclusion in Denmark's democratic institutions. The Report also shows that happier people are more likely to vote for the current government, whereas unhappier people are more likely to vote for change, or to be disengaged from politics altogether – this effect is independent of age, marital status, education and income – and that while happier people prefer democracy, unhappy people prefer more authoritarian leaders. This suggests that it is in the interest of more authoritarian leaders to keep voters unhappy by fuelling anger, fear, or intolerance, whereas it is in the interest of more democratic leaders to promote wellbeing, and the positive attitudes that entails. So, over and above creating a robust economy, there appears to be a strong incentive for politicians already in office to improve wellbeing. Governments around the globe including in Wales, Costa Rica, and New Zealand have already begun to focus on wellbeing policy.

How can politics promote wellbeing?

If those involved in politics took account of the scientific foundations and principles of wellbeing outlined in the Introduction, the way politics is conducted would change. Although it is a tall order, if those in public life were more self-aware, able to acknowledge, understand, and challenge their own biases, and also develop the skills of constructive communication, then politics could change radically. Studies suggest that voters respond positively to civility, and negatively to its absence. An observational study of the U.S. Congress over a 20-year period shows that civility declined steeply around 2007, and has been low ever since.[6] The study also found that incivility was strongly associated with public disapproval. Further support for this relationship comes from a study using a daily online poll of 2,000 U.S. voters' opinion of former President Trump during his first year in office. Approval ratings were tracked against the civility of his tweets. Perhaps the most surprising finding was that even 'die-hard' supporters evaluated the then president more favourably when he responded to a personal attack with civility, and tended to evaluate him less favourably when he made insulting tweets.

There is evidence that political adverts which attack opponents have the effect of depressing national mood and increasing distrust in government.[7] On the other hand, research indicates that high levels of trust are seen when politicians own up to mistakes, spend public money wisely and set good examples in their private lives – although this last is rated as less important than the others.

A politics that focuses on increasing the nation's wellbeing could lead to a more tolerant, cohesive and resilient society in which people with different political stances are more prepared to work together to solve problems, rather than blame each other for societies' ills.

How can wellbeing promote better politics?

Positive psychology is the scientific study of what works to optimise human flourishing. One of the most powerful is relationships, the love and support we *receive* from others increase our wellbeing, but benefits are even greater when we *give* love and support to others.[8] We all have the capacity for altruism and reciprocity. Although these may have been stifled by years of acting competitively and individually, we haven't lost them - they often emerge in times of crisis. The COVID-19 pandemic has given rise to a wealth of positive stories across the globe demonstrating compassion and generosity towards others: individual fund-raising efforts, hundreds of local mutual aid groups helping the vulnerable in their community, and communal actions spreading joy, such as the singing, dancing, and playing music.

Finding ways to remain positive, even in the midst of difficulty, makes all the difference. When we are in a positive mental state, we see more opportunities, are more creative, more likely to act with kindness and compassion towards others and more connected to, and protective of, the natural environment.

What would positive politics look like?

Using positive psychology principles, political systems could be improved by recognising the fundamental importance of connections – finding ways to bring people together rather than dividing them, fostering constructive discussions to promote greater understanding of the problems we face, putting aside political spin, propaganda, and self-interest. Building consensus for policies means giving consideration to differing viewpoints. The aim would be to develop a politics of collaboration and caring to replace the current politics of divisiveness and fear.

Positive politicians would also consult the public, providing honest, unbiased information that helps them make considered choices. Such an approach has been alarmingly absent from many political systems across the world.

To be able to make informed political choices, people need to be provided with full and accurate information, the opportunity to participate in the political process by minimising barriers to voter registration, and routinely taught citizenship and politics in schools.

Positive psychology is manifested in aspects of various political ideologies, encompassing both progressive and traditional values. Positive politics is not necessarily about parties and politicians agreeing on a policy goal, or even on an action to achieve something. A given policy objective may be accomplished in a variety of ways, which is why we need quantitative and qualitative evidence, and healthy debate to consider all perspectives. This would need to include the inevitable trade-offs and consideration of unintended consequences that follow from different choices. As positive psychologist Ed Diener and colleagues make clear,[9] by adopting a data-driven approach to policies that increase universal wellbeing, the science can reduce the influence of political bias.

A positive psychology approach would actively look for and learn lessons from what is already working well, and politicians would model listening, openness, trust, and pro-social actions. Competition would be balanced with collaboration. The quality of governance and the effectiveness of politicians would be measured, not by reactions to soundbites or even electoral success, but through how those in power actively and respectfully engage with citizens and other parties.

In the United Kingdom, Change.org has created the 'People-Power Index', which they describe as *"a health check of how Parliament is working and how our MPs are listening to, and engaging with, us – their voters"*.

Ultimately politicians would refer to the evidence on what increases individual and collective well-being as the basis for policy decisions, recognising that sustainable wellbeing is at the heart of an effective, well-functioning society. For example, if literacy among 7-year-olds is the chosen outcome, then evidence about how to deliver this in ways that develop skills, alongside maintaining motivation for all pupils, would be helpful. Where evidence is not yet available, positive politicians would be prepared to support the trialling of policies in small areas to see if and how they work, and whether there are unintended consequences before extending them to a whole region, or country.

Crucially, positive politicians would accept that some ideas don't work, and some don't work for everyone. Such 'failure' would be regarded as a learning opportunity on which more effective forms of delivery could be built.

Positive political communication

One approach to creating a climate of openness and respect among politicians is the Global Mindfulness initiative,[10] which has been teaching mindfulness to politicians and legislators across more than 45 countries, using a standard 8-week mindfulness-based stress reduction (MBSR) program. While there has been no formal research conducted, anecdotal evidence is that politicians who have participated report lower levels of stress, say they are less likely to verbally attack people from other political parties and more likely to treat them considerately and seek co-operation. Another movement, Compassion in Politics, is dedicated to changing the political debate from one based on ideas of competition and winning at all costs to one built on compassion and cooperation.

Do people care about compassion in politics?

Public opinion surveys[11] of representative samples of UK adults undertaken in 2019 reported:

- 66% think Britain has become less compassionate.
- 61% would be more likely to engage in politics if politicians were more compassionate.
- 63% agree with the idea of introducing compassion training to parliament.

A public opinion poll in the United States[12] reported:

- On average Republicans and Democrats are equally compassionate.
- Uncompassionate Republicans were much more supportive of ex-President Trump than compassionate Republicans.

A positive and thriving political system is one in which citizens are continuously engaged. In addition to exercising our right to vote, wellbeing benefits accrue from regular participation in the political process. These include feelings of connectedness, purpose, and agency.

Respectful listening is a cornerstone of positive psychology and needs to be a core objective for positive politics. Instead of constantly pushing the party line or arguing political points with the intention of putting others down or changing minds, developing the ability to see things from another's perspective, and seeking common ground, could lead to a less polarised, more gracious and potentially more constructive political landscape. If people know their views have been taken seriously, policies are likely to have more public buy-in. The quality of conversations that might follow from this approach would not only benefit the political process but increase the public's wellbeing through deeper connection and understanding.

A starting point for positive political communication is becoming aware of where our opinions come from and to what extent these have been shaped by our own experience and by outside influences.

Reflections:

How would you describe your political views?

What experiences and values have shaped your thinking?

What might have shaped other people's thinking, particularly those you disagree with politically?

Modern technology, and specifically social media, has made it easier than ever to connect with likeminded people, to share our stories, seek help, and to galvanise support for our ideas. This can be valuable but can also lead to an echo chamber effect where pre-existing beliefs are reinforced and people are not exposed to alternative views. Equally, it can be used to influence and even manipulate voters which only serves to increase polarisation and mistrust – see the Media chapter for more discussion. By being more mindful, we can step back and refocus on our core values and how these might guide us.

Reflections:

If you have ever received social media messages from a political party, how helpful did you find the information you were sent?

In what way, if at all, did the information change how you thought or felt about the issue?

Grassroots politics

No-one can fix politics singlehandedly but we can all be part of groups that exert political pressure for the common good. The rise of social media makes community level and grassroots movements more accessible to a wider number of people. Although this can lead to both individual empowerment and group belonging, we need to be wary of the echo chamber effect. There are many forms of activism: methods range from conversations, blogs and other types of gentle persuasion to petitions, marches, class actions and even protests. A study of revolutions over the past two centuries found that the most effective and enduring method of making lasting positive change was well organised and committed non-violent protest. We can also use everyday choices to make political statements such as supporting companies that have ethical, social and environmental values and boycotting those which don't (see more in the Economics chapter).

Community action is powerful

Grassroots movement

Abahlali baseMjondolo (strapline: 'land housing dignity'), which began in 2005, is the largest grassroots movement to have emerged in post-apartheid South Africa. Translated as 'the Shack-dwellers Movement', it campaigns for land, housing, health, and education for the poor and against forced removals, providing a strong and sustained voice within the political system to protect those in need.

Non-violent protest

The Climate Strike campaign spearheaded by Swedish student Greta Thunberg (also covered in the Environment chapter) sparked global protests by young people against climate change. It is perhaps the world's best-known current example of non-violent protest.

Politically motivated boycotting

Companies have sometimes been made to change their products by the behaviour of consumers. This century many luxury fashion brands including Burberry, Prada and Michael Kors have stopped using animal fur after a sustained backlash from consumers. In an earlier example, the Swiss food giant Nestlé was accused of unethically and aggressively marketing and selling infant formula to new mothers in developing countries. The formula milk was often made up using contaminated water, or so diluted to save money that it didn't provide the necessary nutrients, resulting in many thousands of babies dying of disease or malnutrition. The subsequent media coverage resulted in a worldwide boycott of Nestlé, and eventually the company agreed to adhere to World Health Organization regulations which limited the marketing and promotion of breast milk substitutes.

Making change happen

Changing the voting system

Voting systems impact on political behaviour: the adversarial tone of political debate is amplified when politicians don't have to appeal to all voters, because they can win office simply by getting one more vote than their opponents. This is the 'first-past-the-post' voting system. In proportional representation (PR) voting systems representatives are elected depending on how many votes they get, so these systems result in a greater diversity of views being expressed. Because PR systems usually involve forming coalitions, some people believe that this voting system leads to weak governments or deadlock. But there are many forms of PR, and the most stable countries in the world, such as Sweden, Switzerland, and Norway, all use PR systems.

Involving citizens in policy and decision-making

A citizens' assembly is a group of people convened to discuss important legal, social or political issues and agree on what action should be taken. Citizens' assemblies are part of a wider movement for deliberative democracy, which encourages citizen participation and informed decision-making to complement existing political systems. People taking part in a citizens' assembly are randomly selected and representative of the wider population, for example in terms of gender, ethnicity and social class. An assembly of 100 citizens was established in Ireland (2016–2018) to consider important issues facing the country including the laws on abortion and climate change and how best to respond to the challenges and opportunities of an ageing population.

What happens when citizens are well informed?

Research into the 'Deliberative Polling' process created by Professor Jim Fishkin of Stanford University's Center for Deliberative Democracy, shows that ordinary people (non-experts) are able to discuss complex issues in an informed and balanced way and reach better decisions.[13] In 2019 in one of the most significant political experiments called 'America in One room', a representative sample of over 500 participants from 47 states gathered for a weekend in Grapevine, Texas to deliberate and ultimately compromise. Participants spent four days discussing the merits of five issues at the heart of American politics: healthcare, immigration, the economy, foreign policy and the environment. They answered questions about these issues before and after the deliberation. Overall 95% agreed that by participating, they had learned a lot about people very different from themselves. Furthermore, those who felt that American democracy is working well rose from 30% to 60%, and the percentage who thought people who disagree strongly with their policy views have 'good reasons' for their positions rose from 37% to 54%, while the percentage who thought their political opposites were 'not thinking clearly' dropped from 51% to 33%. Deliberative Polling has been used successfully in many countries, including Brazil, China, Northern Ireland, Poland and South Korea.

According to Professor Fishkin, a democracy that incorporates more public deliberation, providing citizens with the opportunity to discuss important topics in depth, will achieve greater legitimacy.

People-powered change

Across the world there are a number of grassroots organisations set up to harness the power of ordinary citizens to make social change.

MoveOn (USA) is an organisation promoting social justice and political progress, which covers all 50 states of the USA. Established in 1998 by tech entrepreneurs Joan Blades and Wes Boyd, MoveOn is about mobilising American citizens to create a better future for everyone.

In the United Kingdom, 38 Degrees is a similar community of ordinary citizens, currently numbering around two million, which campaigns on a variety of issues including health, politics and the environment. It operates both online and offline, for example, petitioning, emailing and visiting MPs, raising awareness in both new and traditional media, as well as holding public meetings and fundraising for legal action. 38 Degrees has been successful in a wide range of campaigns, both national (such as preventing the privatisation of the national forests) and individual (such as campaigning for the rights of asylum seekers).

GetUp! is the Australian people-powered movement whose strapline is "fighting for a fair, flourishing, and just Australia". It encourages citizens from all political persuasions and all walks of life to take action on the issues they care about, including environmental justice, human rights and democratic integrity. From a population of around 25 million, GetUp has over 1 million supporters, which far exceeds the total number of members of all the political parties combined. It has contributed to some significant changes, including 2017 legislation ensuring marriage equality.

Established in 2007, Avaaz is a global online movement with a simple aim: to galvanise citizens of all nations to create the world that most people want. Avaaz ensures that people are well-informed by countering disinformation and 'fake news' e.g. about the COVID-19 pandemic, political elections and climate change. Like the other movements mentioned above, Avaaz is about empowering people everywhere to take action on important issues which affect people everywhere, including conflict, climate change and corruption.

Crises such as the global COVID-19 pandemic have a way of focussing attention on what really matters. We all want to lead happy and fulfilling lives, and politics *can* facilitate this. As the above examples show, we can change things for the better when we work together. Writer and activist George Monbiot sums this up neatly: *"Community is the place from which a new politics begins to grow … By replacing the politics of alienation with the politics of belonging, we rekindle our imagination and discover our power to act"*.[14]

Ideas for action

What might governments and other organisations do to improve politics?

Ensure politicians of all parties are trained in how to collaborate and communicate effectively with each other.

Fund citizens' assemblies.

Introduce regular public consultation and deliberative polling.

Ensure policies are based on wellbeing evidence.

What might individuals do?

Develop the skill of being open to another's perspective and seek common ground.

Take action on something you care about.

Keep up to date with independent commentaries on government policy and news from different media outlets to get a balanced view.

Key sources

Full references and resources are on our website at https://www.creatingtheworldwewanttolivein.org/references/politics/

1 Barack Obama (2004). Keynote address at the Democratic National Convention, recorded by the New York Times, on 27th July 2004: https://www.nytimes.com/2004/07/27/politics/campaign/barack-obamas-remarks-to-the-democratic-national.html

2 Ipsos (2019). https://www.ipsos.com/sites/default/files/ct/news/documents/2019--11/trust-in-professions-veracity-index-2019-slides.pdf

3 2020 Edelman Trust Barometer Spring Update: Trust and the Covid-19 Pandemic

4 https://www.opinium.co.uk/resource-center/public-opinion-on-coronavirus-13th-may/

5 Helliwell, Layard, & Sachs (2019). *World Happiness Report 2019.* Sustainable Development Solutions Network.

6 Frimer & Skitka (2018). The Montagu Principle: Incivility decreases politicians' public approval, even with their political base. *Journal of personality and social psychology.*

7 Lau, Sigelman & Rovner (2007). The effects of negative political campaigns: A meta-analytic reassessment. *The Journal of Politics, 69,* 1176–1209.

8 Thomas (2009). Is it better to give or to receive? Social support and the well-being of older adults. *Journals of Gerontology Series B: Psychological Sciences and Social Sciences, 65*(3), 351–357.

9 Diener, *et al.* (2017). Findings all psychologists should know from the new science on subjective well-being. *Canadian Psychology/psychologie canadienne, 58*(2), 87.

10 Global Mindfulness Initiative: https://www.themindfulnessinitiative.org/global-political-network.

11 Compassion in Politics. (2019) *Polling to date, June 2019.* https://static.wixstatic.com/ugd/455da7_f0226ae1398c49d097c06de33d2c4dd2.pdf

12 Long (2016). *Compassion in Red and Blue: The Politics of who Cares about Whom.* https://etd.library.vanderbilt.edu/available/etd-07132016-155021/unrestricted/Long.pdf

13 Fishkin (2009). *When the people speak: Deliberative democracy and public consultation.* OUP.

14 Monbiot (2017). *Out of the wreckage: A new politics for an age of crisis.* Verso Books.

CHAPTER 13
Environment

Felicia Huppert

> *"Like music and art, love of nature is a common language that can transcend political, or social boundaries". – Jimmy Carter*[1]

Why is the environment important for wellbeing?

Our physical environment affects all aspects of our lives. We can think of it as a series of widening circles, beginning with our immediate surroundings such as our homes and neighbourhoods, extending to our towns and cities and related infrastructure, to food, water, and energy resources, and to the terrestrial and marine ecosystems of our planet. In each of these circles, there are very real problems that confront us, as well as wonderful examples of what works well. We begin by identifying which aspects of the physical environment can enhance individual and collective wellbeing, and how we can use this knowledge to optimise flourishing. We then examine how the science of wellbeing can be harnessed to protect our ecosystems, and the long-term health of our planet.

How physical surroundings affect our wellbeing

The natural, built, and global environment influence our psychological and physical health, how well we learn, how effectively we function, our creativity, and all aspects of our social interactions.

The natural environment
As noted in Jimmy Carter`s quote above, love of nature applies to people everywhere. Spending time in nature has been shown to

decrease stress, anxiety, and depression, and have positive effects on wellbeing.[2] Studies demonstrate the benefits of both green spaces and blue spaces – large bodies of water such as seas, lakes, and rivers. Even just seeing pictures of green spaces has a calming effect on our physiology.[3]

However, not all natural spaces are equal. A recent study demonstrated that the positive emotions associated with natural environments relate in large part to their aesthetic qualities. Natural environments that are not rated as aesthetic, such as featureless or desolate spaces, do not produce wellbeing benefits.[4]

An often-cited benefit of spending time in natural environments is an increase in physical activity, which in turn benefits physical and mental health – see the chapter on Leisure. This effect is probably due largely to spending time outdoors, but are the benefits of physical activity equal across different types of outdoor spaces? A well-designed study compared the benefits of a 30-minute walk in three pleasant outdoor locations; urban, green, and a combined green/blue space. Mood and physiological stress levels showed comparable improvement in all environments, but green and blue environments were associated with greater mental restoration, and better performance on a cognitive test.[5]

Does a nature view promote healing?

A much-cited study showed that patients healed faster in a hospital ward if they had a view of trees from their window compared to a brick wall. This is often interpreted as evidence for the healing effect of nature. However, there are other differences between these views that may underlie the difference in patient outcomes. One view was pleasant, colourful, complex, and changing; the other was unattractive, undifferentiated, and unchanging, and as the author admits, a lively urban view may be as therapeutic as some nature views. It may well be that nature views can speed recovery, but this remains to be scientifically demonstrated.[6]

Numerous studies report that people who spend more time in nature gain many benefits, such as higher levels of physical activity, creativity, cognitive function, and social belonging. However, caution is needed in interpreting these findings. These studies compare groups that happen to spend different amounts of time in nature. But people who spend more time in nature tend to come from socioeconomically advantaged groups who may have easier access to green and blue spaces. So, the reported benefits of spending time in nature may largely reflect socioeconomic differences. If natural environments really do enhance many aspects of how we feel and function, it is all the more important that such places be made more accessible so everyone can benefit. During the COVID-19 pandemic, unequal access to gardens, nearby parks, coastal areas and other natural places, deprived many low-income groups of the restorative effects of attractive natural spaces, even when local outdoor exercise was permitted.

Benefits of green surroundings for low-income groups

In two large public housing projects in Chicago, buildings differed in whether surrounding trees and grass had been retained, or concreted over. Local authority policies resulted in *de facto* random assignment of residents to apartment buildings. Residents living in greener surroundings reported lower levels of fear, fewer incivilities, and less aggressive and violent behaviour, while police statistics revealed fewer property and violent crimes. Not only were problems reduced, but wellbeing was increased. Tree and grass cover were systematically linked to stronger ties among neighbours, greater sense of safety, more use of common spaces, and healthier patterns of children's play.[7]

The built environment

Most people on earth live in cities or urban areas. According to the UN this figure is around 55%, set to rise to 68% in coming decades. So the quality of our housing and urban areas is of profound importance to those who live, work, or spend time in urban areas. Much about urban life is good, but some features challenge our wellbeing. These include noise, overcrowding, stressful commuting, overheating, and water shortages, while the growing problem of air pollution is linked to both physical illness, and impaired learning and memory.

As with natural environments, some built environments are better for us than others. A recent study shows substantial wellbeing benefits when urban environments are rated as aesthetically pleasing.[4]

It is estimated that urban dwellers spend up to 90% of their time indoors, and there has been substantial research on the qualities of the indoor environment that foster wellbeing, usually defined in terms of comfort. Key features are air quality including natural ventilation, acoustic comfort including protection from noise, thermal comfort such as temperature and humidity, and visual comfort incorporating lighting conditions and views. Offices with these design features generally have higher productivity and employee satisfaction, and less sickness absence. Introducing green plants or green walls has positive effects on stress reduction, positive emotions, and attention restoration, and increases comfort through improved air quality, humidity, reduced sound levels, and attractiveness.[8]

In outdoor urban settings, trees and other plants benefit health, and wellbeing even further. Shading from trees can reduce surface temperatures by up to 19°C, and air temperatures by up to 7°C. The increasing popularity of community gardens also offers opportunities for engagement with nature, creativity, the satisfaction that comes from food production, and social connection.

Open space is a scarce resource in cities with high population densities. Typically, one fifth of space in a city is dedicated to transport, over half of this to cars. Transport policy can help combat pollution and sedentary lifestyles by increasing safe infrastructure for walking and cycling. Reduced road traffic, and increased use of electric vehicles are better for the environment, but all cars insulate people from each other. Well-planned urban environments that separate cyclists and pedestrians from car traffic would increase the safety, enjoyment, and social benefits of cycling and walking. Following the COVID-19 lockdown, cities including Milan, Bogota, and Paris have reallocated lengthy sections of road space exclusively as walking and cycling routes.

The global environment

Improving local environments is crucial for many aspects of well-being, yet local changes take place in the context of global forces. These include the depletion of many natural resources, and the greenhouse effect produced by the accumulation of gases in the atmosphere that trap heat radiating from the earth.

Planet Earth is the ultimate finite resource. We have only one planet, and we need to share and nurture it. Nations may consider that they can do whatever they like in their sovereign territory, but the earth is a single system that does not respect national boundaries. Actions that are taken in one part of the globe can have dramatic effects elsewhere. It is now widely recognised that whole-sale destruction of rainforests in the Amazon basin contributes to the melting of glaciers at the north and south poles, which in turn produces sea level rises in the tropics. The felled trees that once absorbed vast amounts of carbon dioxide now release it into the atmosphere, contributing to the greenhouse effect. Just as alarming is the loss of coastal ecosystems such as mangroves and sea grasses that suck CO_2 out of the atmosphere, and store it in the ground forty times more efficiently than native forests. Planet-wide reductions in these natural sources of carbon storage exacerbates global warming with consequent droughts, famines, forced migration, and catastrophic bushfires. While global warming has produced some short-term benefits – such as improved crop yields and wine production in high latitude regions – with resulting wellbeing benefits for local communities, its effects are overwhelmingly negative for the majority of the world's population

So acute is the distress that many people now feel about the future of our global environment, the term 'ecoanxiety' has been adopted by the American Psychological Association to describe "*a chronic fear of environmental doom*".[9] Watching the slow and seemingly inevitable impacts of climate change unfold, and worrying about the future for ourselves, our families, and future generations, is causing fear, anger, and a sense of powerlessness. A Yale survey in 2018 showed that 51% of Americans felt helpless about the issue of global warming.

How positive psychology can contribute to a flourishing environment

The previous section focussed on the impact of environmental changes on individual and collective wellbeing. We focus now on the way wellbeing influences our response to environmental issues. Feeling empowered by taking positive action to protect our environment increases wellbeing through some of the psychological principles described in the Introduction, including a sense of agency, competence, meaning, and connectedness. Feeling disempowered may induce distressing emotions such as shame, which results from perceived moral failure. Shame can motivate us to act to reduce the sense of failure, but frequently it engenders the passive response of choosing the easiest course of action. Shame is often contrasted with pride, another moral emotion. Pride is experienced in response to achievements associated with social or moral value, and encourages people to persevere despite obstacles. An illustration of the contrasting effects of shame and pride is provided in a study of chocolate cake.

Shame, pride and chocolate cake

Three groups of students were given a rich chocolate cake and instructed to eat as much or as little as they desired. One group was asked to anticipate how much shame they would feel about eating the chocolate cake, another was asked to anticipate how much pride they would feel about not eating the cake, and a control group was given no further instructions.

Which group ate the least cake? The group who anticipated pride ate the least and the group who anticipated shame ate the most.

> This finding has been interpreted as the positive emotion of pride helping people to exert self-control, whereas the negative emotion of shame led this group to take the path of least resistance.[10]

Extrapolating the above finding to other behaviours such as acting pro-environmentally, feeling shame, and thereby taking the path of least resistance, may result in choosing the easier, less eco-friendly option such as continuing to accept single-use plastic bags, or failing to consider ways to conserve energy. If more people can be encouraged to feel positive emotions such as pride, they may be more willing to undertake environmentally responsible behaviours even though these may take more effort, are less convenient, and require greater commitment.

Reflections:

How might we increase the feelings of empowerment and pride, so we can contribute to solving global environmental problems?

How can people work together locally to adapt, or mitigate the effect of environmental challenges?

Shame, guilt and fear are powerful negative emotions that we typically deal with by ignoring the issues that produce them, taking the easy course of action, or justifying our actions. In contrast, positive emotions such as pride, curiosity, compassion, and a sense of agency, encourage change without inviting defensiveness. For this reason, it is now widely recognised that if our goal is to produce behaviour change, positive messaging has a more powerful effect than negative messaging.

Another positive emotion that can uplift and empower us is hope. Hope can be passive or active. The difference between these two forms of hope has been elaborated by Joanna Macy and Chris Johnstone in a seminal book. When a person has passive hope, they can be discouraged from taking action if the chance of a desired outcome is not rated as high. Active hope is based on intention and can lead to action regardless of how high the chances are of success. With active hope we focus on what we want to see in the world, and direct our actions in line with that intention. Our emotions influence those around us, and when even one person has hope, it can be contagious. Like other positive emotions, hope can lead to an upward spiral of increased wellbeing leading to more hope and further action.

In addition to the pro-environmental actions that can arise from positive emotions, the other psychological principles described in the Introduction can also promote behaviours beneficial for the environment. These include feeling connected to nature, and all living things, having a sense of meaning – regarding ourselves as part of something bigger, and the sense of competence and autonomy that come from knowing our actions can make a positive difference.

The Introduction also identified three foundational processes, described as core capabilities that can impact our capacity to take pro-environmental action. Mindful awareness helps us pay attention to the everyday choices we make about energy use, transport, food, clothing, and waste, rather than habitually bowing to commercial pressures by taking the easy or cheap option. Being able to resist the pressure to consume more than we need is an important step towards sustainability. By becoming more aware of our mental states, mindfulness can create a gap between a new desire popping up and making an impulse purchase. Seeing desires as thoughts rather than needs that must be fulfilled, more mindful individuals often find that desires dissipate rather than turn into irresistible consumption. This need not be perceived as denying ourselves – there are many examples that show it is entirely possible to consume less and live both well and sustainably.

Cultivating the core capability of compassion makes us more likely to care about and care for our environment, more likely to conserve and nurture natural habitats, cherish diversity, and preserve heritage buildings and human dwellings, such as ancient rock shelters. Compassion may also help reduce the strain on social and community relationships that results from the polarisation of views on the impacts of climate change. It makes us better able to have respectful conversations with those unconcerned about environmental problems, as we try to gently shift their perspective.

Another core capability, informed appraisal, allows us to carefully evaluate environmental information. For instance, it may help us to recognise that the 97–98% of climate scientists who agree that humans play a major role in climate change have far greater expertise than the handful who disagree. Together with the other core capabilities, this may equip us to make wise choices about our own behaviour, and collective actions to ensure the health of our physical environment in the short and longer term.

Reflections:

What everyday choices do you make that have environmental impacts?

What concerns, if any, do you have about the future of your local environment, or the planet as a whole?

Financial case for sustainability

Concern is often expressed, particularly by those with a vested interest, that high levels of unemployment may result from reducing our dependence on fossil fuels. Unemployment, as we have seen in other chapters (Work, Society), can have negative impacts on wellbeing, but most studies conclude that at least as many jobs will be created as lost. As well as benefiting workers, their families and communities, these jobs will be good for our planet and our future. According to the Director-General of the International Labour Organisation, "*(by) taking action in the energy sector to limit global warming to 2°C, around 24 million jobs will be created, effectively offsetting any job losses*".[11] This requires that appropriate policies be put in place to support workers transitioning to new jobs in sustainable industries. There is also a strong business case for investing in sustainable industries. An influential body of business leaders from 20 countries has estimated that the benefits of investing in climate adaptation could be up to $10 for every $1 invested.[12] As Mary Robinson, former UN Special Envoy on Climate Change, states "*…investing now to limit climate change and to prepare for its effects would cost a fraction of the measures needed if we wait until these adverse impacts make themselves known*".[13]

There has never been a better time to heed this advice. Not only will the capital required to build sustainable infrastructure benefit from historically low interest rates, but forecasts of continuing mass

unemployment following COVID-19 mean that such labour-inten-
sive projects would benefit a high percentage of the population in
the short term, and produce long-lasting benefit for all. This would
be congruent with the UN *2030 Agenda for Sustainable Development*,
which in its preamble puts forward a plan of action for people,
planet, and prosperity. The agenda succinctly states that we can
work towards a world where *"all human beings can enjoy prosperous
and fulfilling lives and that economic, social and technological progress
occurs in harmony with nature"*.

Reasons to be hopeful

There are many reasons to be hopeful. Inspiring and scalable projects are already underway that benefit both people and planet;
there is increasing public pressure on government to take urgent
action on climate change; we learnt during the COVID-19 pandemic
to listen to the scientists; and we have seen that governments can
radically shift social and economic priorities when they need to.

Successful and scalable sustainability projects

We often hear about the destruction of the natural habitat occurring
world-wide, but less about some of the constructive activities taking place to counter these, and protect the planet. As compellingly
demonstrated through international case studies in the documen-
tary film *2040,* most solutions already exist – we just need the will
to implement them. Human innovation and collective goodwill
have the potential to generate even more solutions. We can create a
human-centred future – we can determine how we want the world
to be. Here are some inspiring examples.

Projects are underway to re-green cities and reforest areas in many
parts of the world. As well as providing valuable shade, and reducing excess ambient temperatures, other benefits include decreasing
flood risk, providing habitat for a diversity of animal species, and
capturing carbon, but only if a mix of native trees is used. Most
projects are funded by governments and NGOs, but the largest
project in Africa has been achieved by small-scale farmers. Over
the past three decades, southern Niger has been transformed by
the planting of more than 200 million new trees. This has had the

dual benefit of reducing CO_2 emissions and doubling crop yields. In addition to re-greening, other actions can make cities both liveable and eco-friendly, as the Sustainable Cities Index reveals. Below are two distinctive visions of how this has been achieved in urban settings.

Eco-friendly cities

Copenhagen introduced efficient heating and cooling systems that connect to almost every household, and save around 70% of previous energy costs. Green roofing is widespread, and 45% of Copenhagen's residents commute by bicycle every day.

Singapore has been transformed into an urban oasis with around 47% green cover, and 80% of the population living within a 10-minute walk of a park. By limiting car ownership and building effective public transport systems, pollution and traffic jams have been reduced.

Learnings from COVID-19

Around the world, people marvelled at the reductions in air and water pollution during lockdown, and the resulting benefits for human and other life. Although it is not feasible to fully maintain this recovered state, the experience provided glimpses into what may be possible. Many have expressed the hope that this experience could encourage us to consume less, commute and travel less, reduce household waste, rely more on local supply chains, and above all, maintain the kindness and neighbourliness that shone through the crisis. It has been pointed out that the changes needed to protect the environment, often having been described as too big or challenging to attempt, are no bigger than the changes made over very short periods in response to the pandemic. Taking the decisive, collective and rapid action that characterised the response to COVID-19, is every bit as urgently needed in relation to the climate crisis. The willingness of governments to prioritise population health over economics demonstrated that society is capable of acting for the common good in the face of grave danger. The climate crisis is at least as dangerous to life on earth, and deserves as much decisive, urgent, and collective action. Vast resources were expended on 'flattening the COVID curve'. The same effort needs to be applied to 'flattening the CO_2 curve' before it destroys even more lives and livelihoods.

Reflections:

What do you think is the most important thing to do to improve, or protect the environment?

What environmental actions are you currently taking in your home or community?

Can indigenous thinking save the world?

While urbanisation and globalisation have many socio-economic benefits, they have led to a serious disconnect between people and nature. We have a lot to learn from indigenous people about conservation, sustainable use of resources, and taking care of nature. According to The UN Development Programme, *"there is a growing understanding that indigenous lands and waters represent 80% of the world's biodiversity, that indigenous peoples are effective stewards of these areas, and that these ecologically intact areas of the earth are a vital strategy for tackling climate change"*.[14] The traditions and belief systems of indigenous peoples often mean that they regard nature with deep respect, and have a strong sense of place and belonging. Rather than regarding humans as having dominance over nature, many indigenous cultures regard humans and nature as equal, and interdependent. For over 60,000 years, Australia's indigenous communities cared for their country by using land management that worked with the environment. This includes traditional burning techniques to reduce undergrowth by means of cool, slow burning fires, thereby removing the fuel for larger high intensity fires. It has been proposed that adopting these indigenous techniques could prevent the catastrophic bushfires that are an ever-increasing threat to rural and urban life. When non-indigenous populations and governments show respect for traditional cultural values, we empower these groups to play a vital role in ensuring the survival of future generations of humans and wildlife.

Young people are the future

As the impact of climate change intensifies, it is the children and young people of today who will face the worst effects – and young people are stepping up to the mark. Environmental education in many schools and colleges is preparing young people to lead the way towards sustainable development. An extensive review by the North American Association for Environmental Education and Stanford University found that among children from kindergarten to Year 12, environmental education produced a wide variety of benefits. 83% of students reported enhanced environment related behaviours such as reducing water use, increasing recycling, and participating in community clean-ups. Because children are often naturally interested in learning about the environment, environmental education was found to be an effective tool to teach topics such as mathematics, chemistry, biology, and ecology, and the 'fun' factor increased motivation to learn. The benefits of environmental education go beyond imparting knowledge. Other positive impacts included improving academic performance, enhancing critical thinking skills, and developing personal skills, such as confidence, autonomy, and leadership. Educating the citizens of the future is essential for meeting the UN Sustainable Development Goals by 2030.

Youth-led protests are also having a global impact. One of the best-known examples is FridaysForFuture (FFF), the brainchild of Swedish schoolgirl Greta Thunberg. FFF is an international movement of school students who take time off from class to participate in demonstrations, demanding action to prevent further global warming, and climate change. Millions of school children around the world have taken part in the strikes, often supported by teachers, parents, and the general public. The power of non-violent civil disobedience arises from engaging broad support across the population.

To quote Jane Goodall, "*Fortunately, nature is amazingly resilient: places we have destroyed, given time and help, can once again support life, and endangered species can be given a second chance. And there is a growing number of people, especially young people, who are aware of these problems and are fighting for the survival of our only home, Planet Earth*".[15]

When sustainable action is fuelled by positive motivations of care, compassion, pride, and love it can be an inspiration to others. From this perspective, sustainability is no longer perceived primarily as a threat to humanity, but rather the ultimate opportunity to express our humanity.

Ideas for action

What might governments do?

Build the foundations for a clean energy economy through regulations and tax incentives.

Be proactive in meeting the UN Sustainable Development Goals, including healthy cities, sustainable consumption and production, pollution management, and waste disposal.

Invest in conservation, restoration, and enhancement of terrestrial and marine environments.

What might communities do?

Create and maintain sustainable playgrounds, parks, and natural terrains, and improve access for disadvantaged groups.

Provide environmental education for children and local groups, including opportunities to engage in planting and nurturing local wildlife.

Develop local infrastructure to manage access to sensitive natural habitats, promote safe walking and cycling, and make public transport an attractive and sustainable option.

Where appropriate provide training in sustainable agriculture and farming, or in regeneration of forests, waterways, and coastal habitats.

Use positive messaging as a communication strategy to encourage behavioural change.

Celebrate successes, helping people feel collective pride in their environment and achievements.

What might organisations do?

Encourage collective conversations, and pool knowledge and skills to solve problems, and produce innovative solutions.

Implement pro-environmental policies within the organisation.

Ensure other organisations with which they interact have environmentally responsible policies.

Speak out publicly, join global corporate leadership initiatives to advocate for the changes that need to occur in government policy and procedures.

What might individuals do?

Become aware of our routines and their environmental effects so we can make more deliberate choices, such as adopting ethical, and eco-friendly consumption habits.

Draw on our compassionate and altruistic nature to increase prosocial behaviours such as adopting lower-carbon lifestyles.

Have conversations, listen to how others grapple with environmental concerns, and share pro-environmental stories.

Support organisations that champion conservation, biodiversity, and renewable energy.

Personally lobby political representatives.

Put pressure on businesses to improve environmental practices.

Spend time in nature to replenish your body, mind, and heart so you are equipped to take pro-environmental action, and inspire others over the long term.

Key sources

With special thanks to David Roffey for providing support and helpful editorial feedback on this chapter, particularly on climate change aspects.

Full references and resources are available at our website https://www.creatingtheworldwewanttolivein.org/references/environment/

1 Carter (1994). *An outdoor journal: Adventures and reflections.* p.10. University of Arkansas Press.
2 Ryan *et al.* (2014). Biophilic design patterns: emerging nature-based parameters for health and well-being in the built environment. *ArchNet-IJAR: International Journal of Architectural Research*

3 Gladwell *et al.* (2012). The effects of views of nature on autonomic control. *European Journal of Applied Physiology.*

4 Seresinhe *et al.* (2019). Happiness is greater in more scenic locations. *Scientific reports.*

5 Gidlow *et al.* (2016). Where to put your best foot forward: Psycho-physiological responses to walking in natural and urban environments. *Journal of Environmental Psychology.*

6 Ulrich (1984). View through a window may influence recovery. *Science.*

7 Kuo (2003). Social aspects of urban forestry: The role of arboriculture in a healthy social ecology. *Journal of Arboriculture.*

8 Hall & Knuth (2019). An Update of the Literature Supporting the Well-Being Benefits of Plants: A Review of the Emotional and Mental Health Benefits of Plants. *Journal of Environmental Horticulture.*

9 Clayton *et al.* (2017). Mental health and our changing climate: Impacts, implications, and guidance. *American Psychological Association and ecoAmerica.*

10 Patrick *et al.* (2009). Affective forecasting and self-control: Why anticipating pride wins over anticipating shame in a self-regulation context. *Journal of Consumer Psychology.*

11 International Labour Organisation (ILO) (2018). *Greening with Jobs: World Employment Social Outlook 2018.*

12 Global Commission on Adaptation (GCA). (2109). *Adapt Now: A Global Call for Leadership on Climate Resilience.*

13 Robinson (2018). *Climate justice: Hope, resilience, and the fight for a sustainable future.* Bloomsbury Publishing USA.

14 Gurria (2017). *Celebrating indigenous peoples as nature's stewards.* United Nations Development Programme.

15 Goodall (2019). *Dr Jane Goodall speaks about threats to biodiversity following U.N. report.* The Jane Goodall Institute.

PART E

Conclusion

Making choices for a brighter future

Felicia Huppert & Vanessa King

The world today is very different to our world when we began writing this book. The principles of positive psychology and the underlying capabilities we set out in the introduction are more important now than they have ever been.

The widespread and devastating effects of the COVID-19 pandemic on health and economies showed how interconnected we all are, wherever we are. Its aftermath, together with the rampant social injustice brought to the fore by the Black Lives Matter movement, have underscored the harm caused by inequality. Both highlight the need to work together to co-create a more positive, resilient, healthy, and sustainable future for us all.

As we have seen throughout the book, there is a strong relationship between societal conditions and individual flourishing, and this relationship goes both ways. Society influences people, and people influence society. People flourish in societies that prioritise the fulfilment of human needs, and flounder in societies where their needs are not met.

Facing the future together

Across the major domains of life addressed in these chapters we have identified the key challenges to personal, collective, and global flourishing, and have taken a solution-focused approach, providing scientific evidence and stories as examples of what works to meet some of these challenges. Our intention has been to instil realistic hope about possibilities for a better future, by describing ways in which positive change has been and might be achieved. We have invited readers to identify their own challenges and concerns and to explore solutions drawing on personal knowledge and experience, as well as the ideas offered here.

A theme common to many of the challenges across domains is inequality, particularly unequal access to the conditions and societal resources that help to make life go well. These include: love and nurturing in the early years; the availability of a good education; adequate financial resources; secure, meaningful work; the availability of good quality, affordable healthcare; suitable housing; and access to nature. The society-wide damage caused by inequity, compellingly described by Richard Wilkinson and Kate Pickett,[1] and by Michael Marmot[2] has been with us for decades, yet there was a lack of social and political will to address these issues.

The consequence of failing to address these inequities was tragically seen during the COVID-19 pandemic. Although everyone was affected, the virus wrought its greatest devastation on those who were already the most vulnerable in our society — the old, the sick, the poor, and those living in crowded conditions — disproportionately impacting ethnic minorities. Unless we take serious steps to improve the lives of these groups, it is likely that inequities will continue to be further exacerbated as result of any future health, economic, or environmental challenges.

Actions taken by some governments during the pandemic showed that it is possible to prioritise human health and welfare over other considerations, when there is both the need and the will. The rapid and urgent actions in response to the virus demonstrate that society is more than capable of acting collectively in the face of grave danger. We should bear this in mind, and hold governments accountable, when other dangers confront us.

The Black Lives Matter movement has confronted everyone with the injustice experienced by minority groups for multiple generations. This is the outcome of entrenched systemic bias leading to both major acts of discrimination alongside micro-inequities sometimes by those unaware of the impact of their actions and inaction.

You do not have to be overtly racist to unwittingly tolerate or even promote discrimination. The global Black Lives Matter movement may finally have opened the eyes, hearts, and minds of many to say enough is enough.

Taking action to achieve shared goals can be more effective when we act together rather than alone. A fair society will only be achieved through collective and co-operative action. Other complex, systemic problems such as climate change can only be solved if we work together, and hold our politicians to account. Although climate change may be seen by many as a less immediate crisis, it will be even more devastating for life as we know it unless it too provokes urgent and collective action. As psychologist Tara Brach puts it: *"Join with others – it's wiser, healthier and more fun. Working alone deprives us of the energy, hope and vitality that comes when we belong together in our caring"*.

Hope from silver linings

Difficult times can inspire growth and innovation, and a focus on what really matters to people. Although we hear a lot about post-traumatic stress, post traumatic growth is a common response, and often undervalued.[3]

Despite the devastating loss of lives and livelihoods, and enforced isolation for whole populations, COVID-19 had many positive effects. The pandemic has led to a rediscovery of the importance of neighbours, communities, investing in our close relationships, and the wellbeing effects of offering and receiving support. Many have felt benefits from home working, reduced commuting, and, for some, less busyness. We've seen the value of technology for staying connected to those we care about; for work and learning; for health and leisure; and for social good. We've experienced the pleasure of cleaner air, the benefits of quieter roads, and felt the restorative power of being outdoors, or in nature. Millions, perhaps billions of people have focused on what is most important, and glimpsed possibilities of a way of life that is better than before, and this brings with it hope and the momentum for change.

From Me to We and What we share

The way we think, feel and act has a profound effect on our personal wellbeing and also creates a ripple effect on those around us, and the world we live in. If we want to change the world for the better, we need to be willing to take an honest look at ourselves, how we relate to others and to the world around us, and to take steps to change where change is needed. We have seen how the foundational capabilities of mindful awareness, compassion, and informed appraisal make it possible to recognise what needs to be changed, and practising these skills builds the inner resources that enable us to make change happen.

We always have choice over how to act. We can prioritise what is good for me now, or what is good for us in the longer term. As MIT scholar Otto Scharmer puts it, we need to move *"from ego-system to eco-system"*.[4] In other words, to create less short-term, self-serving responses and more joined up, collective, and systemic responses to the longer-term social and ecological challenges we face.

We can think of our lives as a series of widening circles, beginning with ourselves (me); extending out to our close relationships and our communities (we); and out to societal institutions, and to the living planet we all inhabit (what we share).

We may stand unique as individuals, but all other circles we share. Within each circle, every one of us can have an influence. The choice is up to us. We can accept the way things are, or work to improve conditions. In turn, improved conditions will feed back into producing greater collective and individual wellbeing. This will ultimately create a better future for all.

Robert Sapolsky, a renowned biologist and neuroscientist, has said *"What we need to thrive in the future, is a better understanding of the contextual and personal conditions that bring out the best in us"*.[5] The diverse chapters in this book examine such conditions, and explore what we might do across different domains of life.

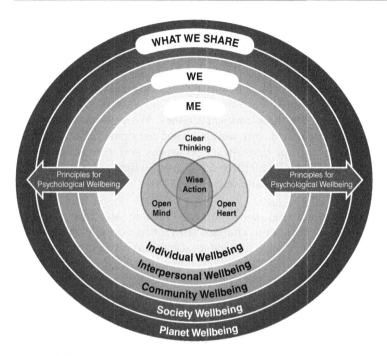

Figure 6: Taking wise action - From Me to We and What we share

Choosing wise action

We have more choice over how to act than we may imagine. Although our perceptions, beliefs and behaviours are conditioned by the world we live in, we may come to recognise and break free from prevailing ideologies, or unhelpful narratives including the idea that we should pursue self-interest and short-term benefit.

The overwhelming volume of information in the digital world can create choice overload. The challenge is how to evaluate information to make wise choices. Wisdom involves understanding the complexity of a situation and choosing to do what yields the greatest long-term benefit.[6] Sociobiologist E.O. Wilson pointed out: *"We are drowning in information, while starving for wisdom. The world henceforth will be run by synthesizers, people able to put together the right information at the right time, think critically about it, and make important choices wisely".*[7]

Acting wisely involves balancing our individual and collective wellbeing needs, both now and for the future. Wise action is supported by the three core capabilities. We need clear thinking (informed appraisal), but we also need an open mind (mindful awareness), and an open heart (kindness and compassion). An action which includes all three capabilities is likely to be wiser than an action that neglects any one of them.

Change is never easy, but change is possible, and this is a great time to begin. Systemic change, which can occur at every level of the widening circles illustrated above, involves three overlapping dynamic phases. The first is ending – letting go of what came before. The second is the void – not knowing what will emerge. The third is a new beginning – renewal and reintegration. When individuals or societies are in a void, as perhaps we are now, it can feel like a wilderness, an unsettling place to be. But it is also a place of freedom to be most creative, enabling us to envision, and design a new future.[8]

The science, stories, and suggestions we have shared in this book will have achieved their aim if they inspire and help empower you to make wise choices, and take action for positive change. Your knowledge, experience and insights are unique, and enable you to make a unique contribution to the community around you and beyond. Your choices and actions, no matter how small, make a difference. Together we can create a brighter world for us all now and for future generations.

Key sources

Full references and resources are available at our website https://www.creatingtheworldwewanttolivein.org/references/conclusion/

1 Wilkinson & Pickett (2011). *The spirit level: Why greater equality makes societies stronger.* Bloomsbury Publishing.
2 Marmot (2004). Status syndrome. *Significance, 1*(4), 150–154.

3 Linley & Joseph (2004). Positive change processes following trauma and adversity: A review of the empirical literature. *Journal of Traumatic Stress, 17*(1), 11–21.

4 Scharmer & Kaufer (2013). *Leading from the emerging future: From ego-system to eco-system economies.* Berrett-Koehler Publishers.

5 Sapolsky (2017). *Behave: The biology of humans at our best and worst.* Penguin.

6 Germer & Neff (2018). The Near Enemies of Fierce Compassion. Center for Mindful Self-Compassion.

7 Wilson, E. O. (1998). *Consilience: The Unity of Knowledge.* p.294. Vintage Books.

8 Bridges (2009). *Managing transitions: Making the most of change.* Da Capo Press.

Index

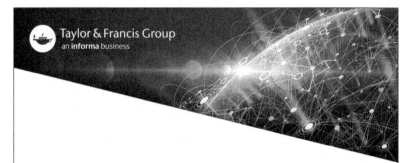

Printed in the United States
by Baker & Taylor Publisher Services